Love's Body

LOVE'S BODY

By

Norman O. Brown

VINTAGE BOOKS
A DIVISION OF RANDOM HOUSE
New York

Manufactured in the United States of America
Vintage Books are published by Alfred A. Knopf, Inc. and Random House, Inc.

Over the years in which I have been not writing and writing this book (1958–1965), two universities have given me sabbatical leaves: Wesleyan University and the University of Rochester. Two foundations have matched these leaves with equal grants: The Guggenheim Foundation and the Center for Advanced Study in the Behaviorial Sciences. One foundation gave me a refuge in a summer of distress: The Yaddo Foundation. I must acknowledge that money has been given to me generously, and freely; without conditions, and without suggestions; with laissez-faire. And, more than money: the many hands and heads at my service in offices and libraries, that remain anonymous. *Alienis pedibus ambulamus.*

Thanks to the publishers, a page has been designed which, by including the references in the body of the text, is a perpetual acknowledgement of my indebtedness to a very great company, both living and dead: my authorities, my authors.

Contents

At least in the life of the mind, ventures should be carried through to the end. This book is a continuation of a voyage begun with *Life Against Death;* a continuation faintly foreshadowed in the last chapter of that book, "The Resurrection of the Body." But as is said over and over again at the end of Euripides' plays, the demonic is polymorphous; the gods decree many surprises; expectations were not realized; God found an opening for the unexpected; that was the way this business turned out. The continuity is fractured, and one item from the record is missing here, a Phi Beta Kappa Oration delivered to the Columbia University Chapter in May 1960 and published in *Harper's* Magazine in May 1961 under the title, "Apocalypse: The Place of Mystery in the Life of the Mind." It records a shaking of the foundations; and faintly foreshadows, like false dawn, the end.

N. O. Brown

Love's Body

I

Liberty

Freud's myth of the rebellion of the sons against the father in the primal, prehistoric horde is not a historical explanation of origins, but a supra-historical archetype; eternally recurrent; a myth; an old, old story.

Freud seems to project into prehistoric times the constitutional crisis of seventeenth-century England. The primal father is *absolute monarch* of the horde; the females are his *property*. The sons form a *conspiracy* to *overthrow* the despot, and in the end substitute a *social contract* with *equal rights* for all. This anachronistic history directs us to look for the recurrence of the archetype in the seventeenth century.

Cf. Freud, *Moses and Monotheism*, 130–133, 188.

In the *First Treatise of Civil Government,* Locke attacks Sir Robert Filmer's defense of absolute monarchy, entitled *Patriarcha.* Sir Robert Filmer, like Freud, identifies patriarchy and monarchy, political and paternal power. Filmer, like Freud, derives constitutional structure from a primal or prehistoric mythical family, from the paternal powers of our father Adam. Like Freud, Filmer attributes to the primal father unlimited power over his sons, including the power and propensity to castrate them.

Locke contradicts Filmer's primal fatherhood—a "strange kind of domineering phantom, called 'the fatherhood'" he says, a "gigantic form"—with the postulate of all men in the primal state of nature free and equal. To vindicate liberty is to vindicate the children, *liberi,* the sons, against paternal despotism. Locke kills Filmer's fatherhood, lays that phantom. The battle of books reënacts Freud's primal crime.

Locke, *Two Treatises of Civil Government,* 6, 7.

Liberty means equality among the brothers (sons). Locke rejects Filmer's rule of primogeniture, which transmits the full power of father Adam to one of his sons, and makes one brother the father of his brethren. How can a man get power not only over his own children, but over his brethren, asks Locke. "Brother," he says, "is the name of friendship and equality, and not of jurisdiction and authority." Against Filmer's fatherhood Locke champions liberty, equality, fraternity. Locke has father Adam's property divided equally among all his sons. Liberty, equality: it is all a dispute over the inheritance of the paternal estate.

Locke, *Two Treatises of Civil Government,* 92.

But the equality of brotherhood is a leveling in the presence of a father; it is a way of dividing what belongs to a father—"the father's equal love." Locke's equality in the state of nature belongs to men as sons of God. Liberty means sonship. To make all men free and equal in the state of nature, Locke allows no man the status of father, and makes all men sons of the Heavenly Father. The phantom of fatherhood is banished from the earth, and elevated to the skies. "The state of Nature has a law to govern it, and reason, which is that law, teaches all mankind who will but consult it, that being equal and independent, no one ought to harm another in his life, health, liberty or possessions; for men being all the workmanship of one omnipotent and infinitely wise Maker, all the servants of one sovereign Master, sent into the world by His order and about His business; they are His property." Procreative power itself is transferred from the earthly to the heavenly father. The parents are only guardians of the children they had begotten, "not as their own workmanship, but the workmanship of their own Maker, the Almighty." God is the "author and giver of life." Parents are only the guardians of their children: fathers are not even fathers of their children. Filmer's sons were subject to castration; Locke castrates the earthly fathers. Thus the defense of sonship turns into the discovery of another father, the "real" father; and the real question in politics is Jesus' question, Who is my father?

Locke, *Two Treatises of Civil Government,* 119–120, 143, 37; cf. 147. Cf. Freud, *Group Psychology,* 89, 95.

Here is the inner contradiction in liberty, equality, and fraternity. Sonship and brotherhood are espoused against fatherhood: but without a father there can be no sons or brothers. Locke's sons, like Freud's, cannot free themselves from father psychology, and are crucified by the contradictory commands issuing from the Freudian super-ego, which says both "thou shalt be like the father," and "thou shalt not be like the father," that is, many things are his prerogative. Fraternal organization in the body politic corresponds to ego-organization in the body physical. As fraternal organization covertly assumes a father, ego-organization covertly assumes a super-ego.

Cf. Freud, *The Ego and the Id,* 44.

The dispute between fathers and sons is over property. In Filmer's patriarchal system paternal power is a property which is inherited and which consists in having property in one's own children. To be the subject of a king is the same as to be the son of a father; and to be a son is the same as to be a slave. But *libertas* is what distinguishes the sons (*liberi*) in the family from the slaves. Locke vindicates the rights of the sons, giving to each one the fundamental right of property in his own person, i.e., the right not to be a slave. At the root, liberty and personal property are identical, and identical also with sonship. But at the same time—the same inner contradiction—property essentially belongs to a father. It finally turns out that the property holders Locke undertook to defend own nothing: it all belongs to the Heavenly Father. "However in respect of one another men may be allowed to have property in their distinct portions of the creatures, yet in respect of God, the maker of heaven and earth, who is the sole lord and proprietor of the whole world, man's propriety in the creatures is nothing but that 'liberty to use them' which God has permitted." It is God's ownership of us—who are therefore his slaves—which excludes slavery as a relation between men.

Locke, *Two Treatises of Civil Government,* 28.

Sonship, or brotherhood, freed from its secret bondage to the father principle—sons after the order of Melchizedek, without father, without mother, without genealogy, having neither beginning of days nor end of life, but made like unto the Son of God—would be free from the principle of private property. And in the first form of Christianity the brethren had all things common. Sons without fathers share everything and own nothing. The brethren, as Plato saw, should have all things in common, including wives. Locke's commitment to brotherhood is deep enough to produce another inner contradiction: communism and private property. The world was given to the children of men in common, he says. In one sentence he affirms both principles: "Though the things of Nature are given in common, man (by being master of himself and proprietor of his own person, and the actions or labour of it) had still in himself the great foundation of property."

Hebrews VII, 3; Acts II, 44. Locke, *Two Treatises of Civil Government*, 138; cf. 136.

As in Locke and Filmer, so in Plato and Aristotle, the two giant forms, fatherhood and brotherhood, enjoy another incarnation and another phantom battle. In these reincarnations the archetypes wear different masks; in Plato and Aristotle we can discern fatherhood and brotherhood in the guise of the family and the division of labor as alternative principles of social organization.

Aristotle displays the state as the final and perfected expression of the same principle of organization which constructs the patriarchal family. First, "a house, and a wife, and an ox"; then a collection of households in a village, then a collection of villages (synoecism) into a polis. The cement which binds the wider collection together is the same which binds the family: "kinship." The patriarchal family supplies the primal model for political government: the first form of government is kingship, "because families are always monarchically governed"; the essence of government is domination, "rule"—in the family the domination of male over female, parent over child, master over slave.

Cf. Aristotle, *Politics,* I, ii–v.

Plato hears a different drummer. In his analysis of the elements of social organization, he never even mentions the family. Instead, his basic principle of social organization is the division of labor and professional specialization, "each doing the one thing for which he is naturally fitted," and united with others by mutual exchange and organic interdependence. And the perfect realization of the potentialities inherent in this principle of social organization, Plato's ideal state, requires the abolition of the family.

Cf. Plato, *Republic* II, 367E-372A.

In Plato the abolition of the family accompanies the abolition of property: property is patriarchal, communism fraternal. So also in Marxism: Engels connected the family with private property and the state; society has been patriarchal and will become fraternal. Marxism, in succession to Locke, picked up the cause of brotherhood. The history of Marxism shows how hard it is to kill the father; to get rid of the family, private property, and the state.

What is the division of labor? Durkheim in his book on the division of labor saw two distinct principles, antagonistic and complementary, as warp and woof of human social organization, which he called mechanical and organic solidarity. Mechanical solidarity is union based on likeness; and it finds its clearest expression in kinship. Organic solidarity is union based on differentiation and organic interdependence; its expression is the division of labor. Durkheim associates mechanical solidarity not only with the family but also with the collective conscience and with criminal law as a repressive system —in Freudian terms, the super-ego and the father. Organic solidarity on the other hand he associates with the civil law which sustains persons, properties and contracts on the basis of equity and equality.

Cf. Durkheim, *The Division of Labor.*

•

In *Group Psychology and the Analysis of the Ego* Freud adumbrated the distinction between two archetypes of social psychology: the individual psychology which in the primal horde belonged to the father alone, and the group psychology of the sons, or brothers. Fatherhood and brotherhood are the archetypes brooding in the background of such sociological abstractions as Durkheim's mechanical and organic solidarity; or Gierke's *Herrschaft* and *Genossenschaft*, the imperial and fraternal principles, which dialectically combine to weave the changing fabric of Western social corporate bodies. It is the specific gift of psychoanalysis to see behind these sociological abstractions the human face; and their name is fatherhood and brotherhood.

Cf. Freud, *Group Psychology*, 92. Brophy, *Black Ship to Hell*, 73. Gierke, *Das deutsche Genossenschaftsrecht*, I, 12–16.

Locke suggests that the fraternity is formed not by birth but by election, by contract; Plato's fraternity based on the division of labor excludes the family; Durkheim's organic solidarity is the opposite of kinship. This brotherhood is not made inside the family, nor by the father; is not born of the flesh, but of the spirit; is not natural, but artificial. Rousseau would say it is based on will; in the vocabulary of Freud's *Totem and Taboo* it is totemic brotherhood. In totemic brotherhood the bond which unites the brothers is not family relationship or blood kinship. The totem clan is defined by a peculiar relation to its particular totem animal, plant, or object; by virtue of which they are of one body, and have one common totem ancestor. The body is mystical, and the ancestor mythical.

Cf. Cornford, *From Religion to Philosophy*, 56–57.

Only in the latest of his tellings of the story, in *Moses and Monotheism*, does Freud distinguish the brotherhood from the natural relation among the sons inside the family. In that version the brotherhood comes into being after the sons are expelled from the family, when they "club together" in the wilderness; the social contract perpetuates "the attachment that had grown up among them during the time of their exile." They club together in the fatherless wilderness; it is a fraternity of young men in college, away from home. The artifice that makes the brotherhood, the social contract, is initiation.

Freud, *Moses and Monotheism*, 131–132.

If the story is to be told in the form of anthropology, then the sons and brothers are to be found not inside the family, but in the clubs or fraternities or secret societies, which are not merely outside the family but rather diametrically contradict it. In the family there is a natural symbiosis of those who have a natural need for each other: male and female; parent and child. The fraternity, or club, or secret society strives to put asunder what is joined in the family—male and female, parent and child. In primitive secret societies, in puberty rites, in *Altersklassen und Männerbünde*, the persistent tendency is to separate the sexes and the generations; to form homosexual and coeval groupings. Besides the natural union of the sexes in the family of which Aristotle speaks, there is also unconscious hostility between the sexes; "an archaic reaction of enmity"; taboos which prescribe sexual separation, mutual avoidance; the castration complex. Without an understanding of the seamy side of sexuality there is no understanding of politics.

Cf. Freud, "The Taboo of Virginity," 234. Reik, "Couvade," 50; "The Puberty Rites of Savages," 154–155. Crawley, *Mystic Rose* I, 44–45, 54–55, 171. Blüher, *Die Rolle der Erotik in der männlichen Gesellschaft*. Webster, *Primitive Secret Societies*. Schurtz, *Altersklassen und Männerbünde*.

Conventional Anglo-Saxon political theory, dismissing Nazism as an irrelevant aberration, a lunatic episode, in the history of the West, is all patriarchal. In the Greek polis, where it all begins, historians and philosophers see only fatherhood and the family. The theory is Aristotle's, modernized by Fustel de Coulanges. The minority opposition to the orthodox line of patriarchal interpretation has clustered round the hypothesis of a contrary matriarchal factor. There is a connection between matriarchy and fraternity, even as there is an alliance between Mother Earth and the band of brothers led by Cronus to castrate Father Sky. But Freud directs us to the idea that the true, the only contrary of patriarchy is not matriarchy but fraternity.

Cf. Bachofen, *Das Mutterrecht*, 869–871.

Fraternity, which is the governing principle of Plato's ideal state, was the governing principle of one real state—Sparta. And Aristotle's emphasis on fatherhood and the family corresponds to the reality of Athens. Just as the antithesis of Aristotle and Plato incarnates the battle of fatherhood against brotherhood, so does the antithesis Athens vs. Sparta. And Sparta is a constellation in the horoscope of Western culture as fixed, as recurrent, as Athens.

According to the current patriarchal orthodoxy, Sparta is a "land-holding aristocracy," and then the great war is between progressive, democratic, and commercial Athens and reactionary, aristocratic, and agrarian Sparta. The truth is that the indispensable basis for a "land-holding aristocracy"—the house-and-land-holding patriarchal family—is lacking at Sparta. Fustel de Coulanges, with a candor and clarity not imitated by his followers, admits that his theoretical construction does not apply to Sparta. At the time of the Dorian invasion, he says, "the old rule of the gens had already disappeared. We no longer distinguish among them this ancient organization of the family; we no longer find traces of the patriarchal government, or vestiges of the religious nobility, or of hereditary clientship; we see only warriors, all equal, under a king."

Fustel de Coulanges, *The Ancient City*, Book IV, ch. XIII, 459.

"Warriors, all equal" is fraternal organization. The Spartan educational system sent the boys away from home at the age of seven, into the wilderness, to be initiated in boy scout or wolf cub packs, in which each boy lived, ate, and slept together with his coevals. The adult military organization prolonged these groupings and the principle of being boys together (the "peers" or *homoioi*) into a total way of life. The mess halls, *syssitia*, where the Spartan warrior lived, ate, and slept together with his comrades, correspond to the primitive institution of the men's house. Spartan society was a hierarchy not based on either property or blood, but on graduated degrees of initiation—initiation into secret societies. Thucydides named secrecy as the distinctive principle of their polity.

Cf. Jeanmaire, *Couroi et Courètes*. Thucydides V, 68.

The men's house and the home are mutually antagonistic institutions; the Spartan bridegroom had to spend the night of his marriage in the men's house, and could visit his wife only if he could slip away from his comrades by stealth. One might expect the homosexual emphasis of fraternal organization to degrade the status of women; but it was at Sparta that women had freedom and dignity, while the women of the Athenian patriarchal family were degraded into nonentity. The fraternal style of sexual separation maintains a relation of mutuality, with equality and exchange, between the sexes. While the man spent his life in the men's house, the Spartan woman was mistress of the household: the fraternal style of sexual separation naturally results in a matriarchy of the household as well as a sexual morality free from patriarchal jealousies. It is in this sense that we should understand the claim that there was no adultery at Sparta.

Cf. Bachofen, *Das Mutterrecht*, 255–260. Nilsson, "Die Grundlage des spartanischen Lebens."

The energy which builds fraternal organization is in rebellion against the family and the father; it is youthful energy. Ortega y Gasset can see that the primeval political association is the secret society, not the gray-bearded senate, because he is willing to acknowledge the youthful, or sportive, or playful origin of the state. "It was not," he says, "the worker, the intellectual, the priest, properly speaking, or the businessman who started the great political process, but youth, preoccupied with women and resolved to fight—the lover, the warrior, the athlete." The ideology of utilitarianism which in the origin of the state and everywhere in life sees only obedience to necessity and the satisfaction of elementary vital needs, is senile, and in politics sees only senatorial activity. Youthful energy has that exuberance which overflows the confines of elementary necessity, and rises above labor into the higher, or is it lower, sphere of play.

Ortega y Gasset, "The Sportive Origin of the State," 32.

Academic orthodoxy, senile and senatorial, is against fraternities; against Sparta; against Plato; against athletics; against play; against sex; against youth. "The fate of the sons," says Freud, "was a hard one; if they excited the father's jealousy they were killed or castrated or driven out." *Virginibus puerisque canto.* The Voice of the Ancient Bard, saying,

Youth of delight, come hither,
And see the opening morn,
Image of truth new born.

Folly is an endless maze,
Tangled roots perplex her ways.
How many have fallen there!
They stumble all night over bones of the dead,
And feel they know not what but care,
And wish to lead others, when they should be led.

Freud, *Moses and Monotheism,* 131. Blake, "The Voice of the Ancient Bard," *Songs of Innocence.*

"Youth preoccupied with women and resolved to fight": politics as juvenile delinquency. Ortega is thinking, as Freud did also, of a connection between fraternal organization and exogamy, conceived as form of "marriage by capture." The band of brothers feel the incest taboo and the lure of strange women; and adopt military organization (gang organization) for purposes of rape. Politics as gang bang. The game is juvenile, or, as Freud would say, infantile; and deadly serious; it is the game of Eros and Thanatos; of sex and war.

To know the reality of politics we have to believe the myth, to believe what we were told as children. Roman history is the story of the brothers Romulus and Remus, the sons of the she-wolf; leaders of gangs of juvenile delinquents (*collecta juvenum manu hostilem in modum praedas agere; crescente in dies grege juvenum seria ac jocos celebrare*); who achieved the rape of the Sabine women; and whose festival is the Lupercalia; at which youth naked except for girdles made from the skins of victims ran wild through the city, striking those whom they met, especially women, with strips of goatskin; a season fit for king killing, *Julius Caesar*, Act I.

Livy, I, 4–5.

Politics made out of delinquency. All brothers are brothers in crime: all equal as sinners. "To expand the population, Romulus followed the model of other founders of cities: he opened an asylum for fugitives. The mob that came in was the first step to the city's future greatness." "The remission of sins which makes us citizens of the Heavenly City was faintly adumbrated when Romulus gathered the first citizens of his city by providing a sanctuary and immunity for a multitude of criminals." The Heavenly City is also only an asylum for fugitives. Or as social contract thinkers see it, the social contract establishes corporate virtue as an asylum for individual sin, making a moral society out of immoral men; men whose natural inclination, according to Hobbes and Freud, is murder. The social contract establishes the general will to counter the will of each—that general will which Freud called the super-ego. The super-ego is supra-individual; even as the crime, so also conscience is collective.

Livy, I, 7. Augustine, *De Civitate Dei,* V, 17.
Cf. Freud, *Group Psychology,* 80.

The foundation of the fraternity or state is itself a crime, or rather the primal crime. The brothers club together in a criminal (Catilinarian) conspiracy: "society was now based on complicity in the common crime." Freud says that the sense of guilt can be allayed only by the solidarity of the participants. Actually, it is the common crime that creates the solidarity. Athenian political clubs, which were organized as secret societies, guaranteed their own solidarity by common participation in religious sacrilege; as in the parody of the Eleusinian mysteries (a Black Mass) or the mutilation of the Hermae.

Freud, *Totem and Taboo,* 146.
Cf. Calhoun, *Athenian Clubs in Politics and Litigation,* 34–37.

The social contract, in the form of a sworn covenant, is itself such a socializing sacrilege. On the Day of Atonement the Jews, the people of the Covenant, repent and cancel all the covenants they will make in the coming year until the next Day of Atonement. The people of the Covenant know that covenants are crimes. In origin and in essence the oath is a curse. An oath is a conditional curse; a suspended sentence. The oath mobilizes the powers of punishment by being itself a crime, a sin, a sacrilege; wherefore it is written swear not at all. An oath lays violent hands upon the power invoked; and so is blasphemy, or taking the divine name in vain. Thus every oath plays with fire—is an ordeal. Men swear by the greater, that is to say the father. Every oath is sacred sacrilege, like the primal crime itself. In ancient Syracuse the official oath they called "the great oath" was taken dressed in purple and wielding a fiery bolt—a sacrilegious usurpation of the attributes of the all-father Zeus.

Matthew V, 34. Hebrews VI, 16.
Cf. Cornford, *From Religion to Philosophy*, 23. Reik, "Kol Nidre," 169–195. Glotz, "Le Serment," 111. Goitein, *Primitive Ordeal and Modern Law*, 49. Freud, *Totem and Taboo*, 140.

Brotherhood is always a quarrel over the paternal inheritance. "After the killing of the father a time followed when the brothers quarrelled among themselves for the succession." Justice is the solution and the perpetuation of the quarrel; as Heraclitus said, justice is the strife. Equals are rivals; and the dear love of comrades is made out of mutual jealousy and hate. "Observation has directed my attention to several cases in which during early childhood feelings of jealousy derived from the mother-complex and of very great intensity arose against rivals, usually older brothers. This jealousy led to an exceedingly hostile aggressive attitude against brothers (or sisters) which might culminate in actual death-wishes, but which could not survive farther development. Under the influence of training—and certainly not uninfluenced also by their own constant powerlessness—these wishes yielded to repression and to a transformation, so that the rivals of the earlier period became the first homosexual love-objects." Brotherhood is an agonal relation between competing brothers.

Freud, *Moses and Monotheism,* 132; "Certain Neurotic Mechanisms in Jealousy," 242.

The Rule of Law is the Rule of Force. Justice is Strife; and in the arbitrament of battle Ares is just. In the ordeal of battle is a divine judgment: Rome won world rule by ordeal, and hence by right; it was by divine will that the Romans prevailed in the athletic contest for world rule. Jehovah is a man of war; deeds of justice hath he loved. The question could only be decided by an appeal to heaven, that is, by war and violence. The violence vindicates (*vim dicare*).

Cf. Dante, *De Monarchia,* II, 8, 9. Goitein, *Primitive Ordeal and Modern Law,* 64. Hume, *Political Essays,* 57.

The fraternal principle of equality, the paternal principle of domination; division of power (federation) or monopoly; coordination or subordination; reciprocity (interdependence) or sovereign self-sufficiency. "Sinful man hates the equality of all men under God and, as though he were God, loves to impose his sovereignty on his fellow men." Fraternity was the relation between the elements in pre-Socratic philosophy—those antagonistic pairs, the hot and the cold, the moist and the dry; and then Anaxagoras brought back the paternal and monarchical principle of *nous.* And at the same time Anaxagoras' friend Pericles, *nous* in action, sought to establish a monarchy among the Greek cities. In the archaic age, the age of the pre-Socratic philosophers, the sixth century B.C., the century of Spartan hegemony, the relations between cities were fraternal and agonal; a *concordia discors*, out of opposites the fairest harmony. Like the balance of power in the old brotherhood of nations, or "concert of Europe," in which, Ranke said, "The union of all must rest upon the independence of each single one. Out of separation and independent development will emerge true harmony."

Augustine, *De Civitate Dei*, XIX, 12. von Laue, *Leopold Ranke, The Formative Years*, 218.
Cf. Schaefer, *Staatsform und Politik*. Vlastos, "Equality and Justice in early Greek cosmologies."

The old agonal warfare was between brothers; conducted according to rules; limited in objectives, and limited in time, in a necessary alternation of peace and war; the brothers need each other in order to fight again another day. The new warfare is total: it seeks an end to war, an end to brotherhood.

The quarrel is over the paternal inheritance. Fraternities are moieties, or segments, into which the body of the world is divided; giving to each a property, a lot (Moira); a system of provinces marked off by boundaries, i.e., fenced by taboo. The myths represent totemism as what remains of a diminished totality, or what results from a separating out from each other of what was previously united. Here is the origin of the division of labor—something that Freud did not know. The division of labor is established by distributing the parts among the clans as their totems. " 'The plan, or order, which was carried out when all the people camped together, was that of a wide circle. This tribal circle was called Hudhu-ga, and typified the cosmos. . . . The circle was divided into two great divisions or halves' (the exogamous phratries). 'The one called In-shta-sun-da represented the

Heavens; and the other, the Hun-ga-she-nu, denoted the Earth. . . . Each of the two great divisions was subdivided into clans, and each of the ten clans had its particular symbol' (totem) 'representing a cosmic force, one of the various forms of life on the Earth.' "

Cornford, *From Religion to Philosophy,* 69; cf. 55–56.
Cf. Lévi-Strauss, *Totemism,* 26.

That is why the body politic, for example in ancient Athens, Rome, or Israel, is composed of artificially symmetrical parts. According to Aristotle's scheme, rejected as "artificial" by the modern revisionists, the Athenians were distributed into four tribes, corresponding to seasons, each of the four tribes being divided into three parts so that there would be altogether twelve, corresponding to months, called trittyes or phratries; with thirty clans going to make up each phratry, as days make up the month. In Rome a mystic interplay between three and ten produced three tribes, thirty curies (the Roman equivalent of the Greek phratry), three hundred gentes, three thousand households each supplying one footsoldier. It is a military organization of *Quirites*; and when assembled, it consists of, and votes by, groups—*comitia curiata*—not individuals.

Cf. Aristotle, *Constitution of Athens,* 208–209. Mommsen, *History of Rome,* I, 101–102. Sinaiski, *La Cité quiritaire.* Brandon, *History, Time and Deity,* 62, 73–74. Ortega y Gasset, "The Sportive Origin of the State," 33–40.

The quarrel is over the paternal inheritance. But the paternal inheritance is the paternal body itself. "All partook of his body," says Freud. The body of the world which is broken into pieces is the body of the god. As the Christians say: others bequeath to their heirs their property, but he bequeathed himself, that is the flesh and blood of his body. The fall is the Fall into Division of the one universal man. Civil strife is dismemberment:

> O let me teach you how to knit again
> This scattered corn into one mutual sheaf,
> These broken limbs again into one body.

Freud, *Moses and Monotheism*, 131. Shakespeare, *Titus Andronicus*, V, iii.
Cf. Lubac, *Corpus Mysticum*, 77. Blake, *Night I*, l. 21.

The body of the world which is broken into pieces is the body of the god. This is Freud's "cannibalistic act." "The 'native bear' when slain is thus divided. The slayer has the left ribs: the father the right hind leg, the mother the left hind leg, the elder brother the right fore-arm, the younger brother the left fore-arm, the elder sister the backbone, the younger the liver, the father's brother the right ribs, the mother's brother of the hunter a piece of the flank." "The various totems were only the name given to the different parts of Baiame's [the Great Spirit] body." The body is divided equally: no one came away from the feast without his fair share. A Thyestean banquet: "the fathers shall eat the sons in the midst of thee, and the sons shall eat their fathers."

Freud, *Moses and Monotheism*, 132. Harrison, *Themis*, 141; *Epilegomena*, XXXI. Ezekiel V, 10.

Fraternities are moieties or segments of one body. But the segments are sexes; "the prototype of all opposition or contrariety is the contrariety of sex." Fraternal organization is a separating out of opposites which must forever seek each other out: contrary and complementary halves; sexes. "The two exogamous sections are opposed as male and female, since the male belonging to one phratry must marry a female from the other. This contrariety is reconciled in marriage—the union of opposites." The marriage combines Eros and Thanatos, Love and Strife.

Cornford, *From Religion to Philosophy*, 65; cf. 68.

Division, duality, two sexes; in a sense there are always two brothers. "There is in every act a sociological dualism; two parties who exchange services and functions, each watching over the measure of fulfillment and the fairness of conduct of the other." Dual organization. There is something here that Freud did not know. There are always two fraternities, not one; and exogamy is not marriage by capture but part of the ritual of Eros and Thanatos in the dual organization. Totemism is not based on an analogy between man and animal, but on an analogy between the differentiation of men into fraternities and the differentiation of animals into species. Lévi-Strauss quotes Bergson: "When therefore they [the members of two clans] declare that they are two species of animals, it is not on the animality but on the duality that they place the stress." The resemblances presupposed by so-called totemic systems is between two systems of differences—animals as a kingdom divided into species, and men as a kind divided into segments which are each one a species.

Malinowski, *Crime and Custom*, 25–26.
Cf. Huizinga, *Homo Ludens*, 55. Hocart, *The Progress of Man*, 238–242. MacLeod, *Origin and History of Politics*, 213–214, 218–219. Roheim, *War, Crime and the Covenant*, 99–100. Lévi-Strauss, *Totemism*, 95.

Dual organization is sexual organization. The structural principle is the union of opposites. "The most general model, and the most systematic application, is to be found perhaps in China, in the opposition of the two principles of Yang and Yin, as male and female, day and night, summer and winter, the union of which results in an organized totality (*tao*) such as the conjugal pair, the day, or the year." The agon, contest, between winter and summer, night and day, is coitus. "The efficacy of the ceremonies seemed to depend upon the participants confronting each other face to face and performing alternate gestures. There must sit a party of hosts—here a party of guests. If some were supposed to represent the sun, heat, and summer, the principle *yang*, others embodied the moon, cold, winter, the principle *yin*. . . . The seasons were imagined as belonging to one or the other sex. Nevertheless the actors were all men."

Lévi-Strauss, *Totemism*, 89. Granet, *Chinese Civilization*, 169.

The prototype of all opposition or contrariety is sex. The prototype of the division into two sexes is the separation of earth and sky, Mother Earth and Father Sky, the primal parents. The primal one body that was divided among the brothers was parental and bisexual—the two become one flesh—the parents in coitus; in psychoanalytical jargon, the "combined object." The primal crime is also the crime of Cronus, the youngest of the brothers, severing the member that joined Father Sky and Mother Earth. The fraternity comes together, on a contract, or covenant, "when they cut the calf in twain and passed between the parts thereof." "It was an ancient custom for allies to pass between severed parts, that being enclosed within the sacrifice, they might be the more sacredly united in one body."

Jeremiah XXXIV, 18. Calvin on Genesis XV, 10.
Cf. Roheim, "Covenant of Abraham," 452–459; *War, Crime and the Covenant*, 19–20; "Some Aspects of Semitic Monotheism."

At this point we go beyond Freud, with Melanie Klein: the body that the brothers partook of was not the body of the father, but the body of the father and mother combined. "In Peter's second hour my interpretation of the material he had brought had been that he and his brother practised mutual masturbation. Seven months later, when he was four years and four months old, he told me a long dream. . . . '*There were two pigs in a pig-sty and in his bed too. They ate together in the pig-sty. There were also two boys in his bed in a boat; but they were quite big, like Uncle G——* (a grown-up brother of his mother) *and E——* (a girl friend whom he thought almost grown-up).' Most of the associations I got for this dream were verbal ones. They showed that the pigs represented himself and his brother and that their eating meant mutual *fellatio.* But they also stood for his parents copulating together. It turned out that his sexual relations with his brother were based on an identification with his mother and father, in which Peter took the role of each in turn." Compare the case of two brothers, Franz and Günther, age five and six. "The brothers got on very badly together, but on the whole Günther seemed to give way to his younger brother. Analysis was able to trace back their mutual sexual acts as far as the age of about three and a half and two and a half respectively, but it is probable that they had begun even earlier. . . . An analysis of the phantasies accompanying the acts showed that they not only represented destructive onslaughts upon his younger brother, but that the latter stood for Günther's father and mother joined in sexual intercourse. Thus his behavior was in a sense an actual enactment, though in a mitigated form, of his sadistic masturbatory phantasies against his parents." The material of the analysis; of *Finnegans Wake*; of World History.

Klein, *Psychoanalysis of Children,* 49, 167.

The brothers introject the parents in coitus, in a new coitus, a new covenant or coming together. In dual organization, in exogamous phratries between whom there is intercourse and antagonism, the brothers perpetually reënact in their mutual relations what Freud calls the primal scene; their wrestling is sexual as well as aggressive, in imitation of the parental copulation.

Cf. Calif, "Justice and the Arbitrator."

Moieties in reciprocal exchange are to each other as male and female; and also as mother and child. "We are here in the midst of a society which overcomes its retribution anxiety by a kind of division of labor. . . . The fundamental idea common to all of the tribes is that the men of any totemic group are responsible for the maintenance of the supply of the animal or plant which gives its name to the group. . . . Each group by its ceremonial attitude serves as a guarantee for the permanent existence of 'good objects' for the other group." Each group is to the other a breast; but, as we know from Melanie Klein, the breast is equated with the penis. Thus copulation is always oral. One of Melanie Klein's discoveries in the world of the unconscious is the archetypal—primordial and universal—fantasy of (parental) coitus as a process of mutual devouring—oral copulation; or rather, cannibalistic; and therefore combining in one act the two Oedipal wishes, parental murder and incest; and including sexual inversion, since the male member is seen as a breast sucked. The contest or coitus is always a funeral feast (game) on or beside a grave; "A Christian Altar, by the requirements of Canon Law, should contain relics of the dead." It is always *Hamlet,* Act I, Scene ii:

> The funeral baked meats
> do coldly furnish forth the marriage tables.

Freud's vision and Melanie Klein's finally meet and merge into one. *Consummatum est.*

Roheim, *Eternal Ones of the Dream*, 150. Jones, *Anathémata*, 51. Cf. Klein, *Psychoanalysis of Children*, 68, 188, 213, 269; "The Early Development of Conscience," 273.

There are always only two brothers: Romulus and Remus, Cain and Abel, Osiris and Set; and one of them murders the other. Or rather they both accuse each other of fratricide and put each other to death for the crime; as the Christian identifies the Jew with Cain, for having killed Christ, and accordingly punishes the Jew with crucifixion. The mutual relations of the brothers reënact the primal scene, the cannibalistic intercourse, and the primal crime, the dismemberment. The brothers are brothers to dragons, dragon seed sown (Spartoi); that comes up as young men armed for a Pyrrhic dance in which they mow each other down. All fraternity is fratricidal.

Cf. Ambrose, *Cain and Abel*, I, ii. Cornford, *Origins of Attic Comedy*, 19–20. Harrison, *Themis*, 23–25. Sartre, *Critique de la raison dialectique*, 455, 479. Warren, *Brother to Dragons.*

> Was it (as it must look to any god of cross-roads) simply a fortuitous intersection of life-paths, loyal to different fibs,
>
> or also a rendezvous between accomplices who, in spite of themselves, cannot resist meeting
>
> to remind the other (do both, at bottom, desire truth?) of that half of their secret which he would most like to forget,
>
> forcing us both, for a fraction of a second, to remember our victim (but for him I could forget the blood, but for me he could forget the innocence)
>
> on whose immolation (call him Abel, Remus, whom you will, it is one Sin Offering) arcadias, utopias, our dear old bag of a democracy, are alike founded:

For without a cement of blood (it must be human, it must be innocent) no secular wall will safely stand.

Auden, "Vespers," *Shield of Achilles*, 79–80.

The reason for the civil war that destroyed the Roman Republic is the one given by Horace. For the reality of politics, we must go to the poets, not to the politicians; and believe the stories we were told as children.

Sic est: acerba fata Romanos agunt
scelusque fraternae necis,
ut immerentis fluxit in terram Remi
sacer nepotibus cruor.

"The truth is that avenging furies plague the Romans, and the guilt of fratricide, ever since the earth was soaked with innocent Remus' blood, a curse on his posterity."

Horace, *Epodes*, VII.
Cf. Wagenvoort, "The Crime of Fratricide."

The fratricide which killed the Roman Republic was only the final fulfillment of the symbolic and attenuated fratricide which had been its life. Roman liberty—the fraternity carved out of the cadaver of royal despotism—is despotism divided and set forever at war with itself. The *imperium* of the republican magistracy is the same royal *imperium*, now subdivided in time (made annual) and divided between colleagues. "The collegiate principle," says Mommsen, "assumed [in the case of the consuls] an altogether peculiar form. The supreme power was not entrusted to the two magistrates conjointly, but each consul possessed it and exercised it for himself as fully and wholly as it had been possessed and exercised by the king. Each of the colleagues was legally at liberty to interfere at any time in the province of the other. When therefore supreme power confronted supreme power and the one colleague forbade what the other enjoined, the consular commands neutralized each other." Mommsen thought that the legend of Remus was an etiological reflection of the institution of the double consulate. There is reflection, or rather recurrence, of the archetype in the institution. Remus jumped over his brother's wall, and his brother killed him, saying, "So perish whoever else shall leap over my battlements." As we can see in any playground; or in Berlin.

Mommsen, *History of Rome* I, 323–324; cf. "Die Remuslegende." Cf. Livy, I, 6.

As colleague confronts colleague, so also do the constituent orders of the Roman Republic: the sovereignty (*imperium*) of the magistracy confronts the sovereignty (*majestas*) of the people not on a line of vertical subordination but horizontally coordinate (*SPQR—Senatus Populusque Romanus*). The Roman body politic is not one, but two. The two principles cannot operate except as they cooperate; so that, as Mommsen says, "law was not primarily, as we conceive it, a command addressed by the sovereign to the community as a whole, but primarily a contract concluded between the constitutive powers of the state by address and counter-address." The schism in the body politic known as the secession (not rebellion) of the plebs is only an aggravation of the inherent separation of the constituent orders. The extraordinary institution to which that secession gave rise, the tribunate of the people, with its veto over the acts of the magistracy, amounted to legalized, and institutionalized, civil war. Hence it was properly used later to bestow Republican legality on the actual civil war. In the end, in accordance with the Freudian law of the return of the repressed, the murdered father returned and put an end to the quarreling of the brothers; it came to a choice between *libertas* and *pax; omnem potentiam ad unum conferri pacis interfuit.* Truly these were sons of Mars or of a she-wolf.

Mommsen, *History of Rome,* I, 111. Tacitus, *Histories,* I, i.

Like all good archetypes the story can also take the form of a comedy. As Karl Marx observed in the *Eighteenth Brumaire of Louis Bonaparte,* there is eternal recurrence in history; events and personalities reappear, "on the first occasion they appear as tragedy; on the second, as farce." Like the satyr play after the trilogy of tragedies; or the modern dual organization, the two-party system.

Marx, *Eighteenth Brumaire of Louis Bonaparte,* ch. I, *ad init.*

Political parties are primitive secret societies: Tammany's Wigwam; caucus; mafia; cabal. The deals are still always secret, in a smoke-filled room. Political parties are conspiracies to usurp the power of the father, "a taking of the sword out of the hand of the Sovereign." Political parties are antagonistic fraternities, or moieties; a contest between Blues and Greens in the Hippodrome; an agon between Leather Seller and Sausage Seller to seduce and subvert Old Man Demos; an Eskimo drumming contest; organized not by agreement on principle, but by confusing the issues to win; in a primitive ordeal or lottery in which the strife is justice, might makes right, and the *major* is the *sanior pars.*

Hobbes, *Leviathan,* 202.

Cf. Heckethorn, *Secret Societies.* Schattschneider, *Party Government,* 39–41, 44. Calhoun, *Athenian Clubs in Politics and Litigation.* Cornford, *Origins of Attic Comedy.* Ostrogorski, *Democracy and the Organization of Political Parties.* Headlam, *Election by Lot,* 19, 26, 33. Washington, *Farewell Address. The Federalist,* nos. 9 and 10. Huizinga, *Homo Ludens,* 85, 65–67, 207.

It is the tale of Shem and Shaun in North Armorica. "Bostonians sometimes seemed to love violence for its own sake. Over the years there had developed a rivalry between the South End and the North End of the City. On Pope's Day, November 5, when parades were held to celebrate the defeat of Guy Fawkes' famous gunpowder plot, the rivalry between the two sections generally broke out into a free-for-all with stones and barrel staves the principal weapons. The two sides even developed a semimilitary organization with recognized leaders, and of late the fighting had become increasingly bloody. In 1764 a child was run over and killed by a wagon bearing an effigy of the pope, but even this had not stopped the battle. Despite the effort of the militia, the two sides had battered and bruised each other until the South End finally carried the day. When Boston had to face the problem of nullifying the Stamp Act, it was obvious that men who fought so energetically over the effigy of a pope might be employed in a more worthy cause"—to dress up as Indians and hold a Boston Tea Party, the *Finnegans Wake* of American History, the foundation legend.

Morgan, *The Stamp Act Crisis,* 121.
Cf. Forbes, *Paul Revere,* 97–98.

The comic wearing of the Indian mask, in the Boston Tea Party, or Tammany's Wigwam, is the lighter side of a game, a ritual, the darker side of which is fraternal genocide. Indians are our Indian brothers; one of the ten lost tribes of Israel; the lost sheep we came to find; now unappeased ghosts in the unconscious of the white man.

Cf. Lawrence, *Studies in Classic American Literature,* 44–45. Allen, *The Legend of Noah,* ch. VI.

This could go on forever; there is eternal recurrence. Even on the other side of the Wall, in a one-party system. From the statement of the Chinese Communists on the Sino-Soviet dispute:

> It is a very very bad habit of yours thus to put on the airs of a patriarchal party. It is entirely illegitimate. The 1957 declaration and the 1960 statement clearly state that all Communist parties are independent and equal. According to this principle, the relations among fraternal parties should under no circumstances be like the relations between a leading party and the led, and much less like the relations between a patriarchal father and his son . . . the attitude that Comrade Khrushchev has adopted is patriarchal, arbitrary, and tyrannical. He has in fact treated the relationship between the great Communist party of the Soviet Union and our party not as one between brothers but as one between patriarchal father and son.

The New York Times, September 14, 1963.

II
Nature

Fraternity comes into being after the sons are expelled from the family; when they form their own club, in the wilderness, away from home, away from women. The brotherhood is a substitute family, a substitute woman—alma mater.

In puberty rites the boys are detached from their mothers, and given a new mother by initiation. In one of the Chinese secret societies in Singapore the oath was, "I swear that I shall know neither father nor mother, nor brother nor sister, nor wife nor child, but the brotherhood alone." "And one said unto him, Behold, thy mother and thy brethren stand without, desiring to speak with thee. But he answered and said, Who is my mother? And who are my brethren? And he stretched forth his hand toward his disciples, and said, Behold my mother and my brethren!" *Habere non potest Deum patrem, qui ecclesiam non habet matrem.*

Heckethorn, *Secret Societies,* II, 132. Matthew XII, 47–50. Cyprian quoted in Willis, *St. Augustine and the Donatist Controversy,* 96n.

Initiation is rebirth. By rebirth birth from one's "real" mother is nullified. At the marriage in Cana "the mother of Jesus said unto him, They have no wine. And Jesus said unto her, Woman, what have I to do with thee?" By being born again, the original sin is canceled. "Verily, verily, I say unto thee, Except a man be born again, he cannot see the kingdom of God." Birth from the mother is nullified, and a new spiritual mother found.

John II, 3–4; III 3.
Cf. Reik, "Puberty Rites of Savages," 145–146.

Who is my real mother? It is a political question. The two sons of King Tarquin, and Brutus, the future Liberator, were on a mission to the Delphic Oracle. "A desire sprang up in the hearts of the youths to find out which one of them should be king at Rome. From the depths of the cavern this answer, they say, was returned. 'The highest power at Rome shall be his, young men, who shall be first among you to kiss his mother.' The two sons of Tarquin gave orders that the incident should be kept strictly secret, and, as between themselves, they cast lots to determine which should be the first, upon their return to Rome, to give their mother a kiss. The Liberator thought the Pythian utterance had another meaning: pretending to stumble, he fell and touched his lips to the earth, regarding her as the common mother of all mortals."

Livy, I, 56.

In Plato's *Republic* the fraternity of guardians are to think of the land they dwell in as mother and nurse. They are to think of their former experience as a dream: "in reality they were the whole time down inside the earth, being fostered and moulded while their arms and all their equipment were being fashioned also; and at last, when they were complete, the earth sent them up from her womb into the light of day." Men of the golden age were earth-born and not born of human parents: a race formed from men dead and laid in earth, made new in that womb and thence returning to life once more, in a resurrection of the dead.

Plato, *Republic,* III, 414; cf. *Politicus,* 269–272.
Cf. Bachofen, *Das Mutterrecht,* 258.

As in the "Marseillaise":

s'ils tombent, nos jeunes héros,
la terre en produit de nouveaux–

"Ma mère, c'est la République," says a character in Victor Hugo's *Les Misérables;* a motto for Swinburne, in one song to the Earth Mother, who is

Maiden most beautiful, mother most bountiful, lady of lands,
Queen and republican—

She is our real mother:

Hast thou known how I fashioned thee,
Child, underground?

Swinburne, "Song of the Standard," "Hertha"; cf. "Litany of Nations," "Mater Dolorosa," "Mater Triumphalis."

The fraternity is itself the mother. "The journey of initiation is ended. It goes from the mothers to the mothers. Although in reality the young man is henceforth to be separated from the mother, symbolically he is brought back to her. . . . The young man is put into a hole and reborn—this time under the auspices of his *male mothers.*" Male mothers; or vaginal fathers: when the initiating elders tell the boys "we two are friends," they show them their subincised penis, artificial vagina, or "penis womb." The fathers are telling the sons, "leave your mother and love us, because we, too, have a vagina." Dionysus, the god of eternal youth, of initiation, and of secret societies was the twice-born: Zeus destroyed his earthly mother by fire, and caught the baby to his thigh, saying: "Come, enter this my male womb."

Roheim, *Eternal Ones of the Dream,* 123, 164, 166. Euripides, *Bacchae,* 518.
Cf. Harrison, *Themis,* ch. II.

Male mothers; "shield-bearing nurses"; the political authorities. Authority, *auctoritas,* is from *augeo,* to grow. Margaret Mead tells how an Arapesh boy gets authority over his future wife by "growing her," with gifts of food. The authorities are authors; they are the "nursing fathers" of the Old Testament and of the New England Puritan political theorists. From the mothers to the mothers. The transition from matriarchy to patriarchy is always with us, and gets us nowhere.

Cf. Harrison, *Themis,* ch. I. Mead, *Sex and Temperament,* 65.

All of human culture is our alma mater; every polis a metropolis. What we enter in our initiation is a womb; and stay there (no exit). It is the birth trauma: trauma or separation not accepted, and the mind regresses to the time before the separation took place. It is as though we had never been born.

The world is our mother: The outside world is "the mother's body in an extended sense." "If you have chanced to wonder at the frequency with which landscapes are used in dreams to symbolize the female sexual organs, you may learn from mythologists how large a part has been played in the ideas and cults of ancient times by 'Mother Earth' and how the whole conception of agriculture was determined by this symbolism." "From mythology and poetry we may take towns, citadels, castles and fortresses to be further symbols for women." Jerusalem, "a City, yet a Woman."

Klein, "The Importance of Symbol Formation," 250.
Freud, *General Introduction*, 170–171.
Blake, *Night* IX, l. 222.

To explore is to penetrate; the world is the insides of mother. "The entry into the world of knowledge and schoolwork seemed to be identified with the entry into the mother's body." "The child's epistemophilic instincts . . . together with its sadistic impulses, have been directed toward the interior of its mother's body." "The whole scene on the water was the inside of his mother—the world." "Sadistic phantasies directed against the inside of her body constitute the first and basic relation to the outside world and to reality." "In the imagination of the small child these multiple objects are situated inside the mother's body." The interior of the mother's body "becomes the representative of her whole person as an object, and at the same time symbolizes the external world and reality." Geography is the geography of the mother's body: "his sense of orientation, which had been strongly inhibited, but now developed in a marked manner, was determined by the desire to penetrate the mother's body and to investigate it inside, with the passages leading in and out and the processes of impregnation and birth." Geography; or geometry, as in *Finnegans Wake*. Melanie Klein made her discoveries by interpreting the gestures of children playing with toys. Already in childhood symbolic equivalents for the inside of the mother's body are discovered in external objects, the toys. Growing up consists in finding new toys, new symbolic equivalents; so that in all our explorations we are still exploring the inside of our mother's body.

Klein, *Psychoanalysis of Children*, 208, 247; "Infant Analysis," 109; "The Importance of Symbol Formation," 238; "The Theory of Intellectual Inhibition," 256; cf. "The Role of the School in the Libidinal Development."

And what the child is doing in the inside of his mother's body is scooping it out: "this desire to suck and scoop out, first directed to her breast, soon extends to the inside of her body." Excavation. The child is hollowing out a cave for himself inside his mother's body. We are still unborn; we are still in a cave; Plato's cave. "Behold, men live in a sort of cavernous underground chamber, with a long passage stretching towards the light all down the cave. Here they have lived from childhood, chained by the leg and by the neck, so that they cannot move and can look only straight forwards, the chains preventing them from turning their heads. At some distance higher up there is the light of a fire burning behind them; and between the fire and the prisoners there is a raised track, with a parapet built along it, like the screen at a puppet-show, which hides the men who work the puppets."

Klein, *Psychoanalysis of Children*, 185. Plato, *Republic*, VII, 514 A–C.

The world a cave for Melanie Klein's infants, Plato's prisoners, and Spengler's Magian soul. In the early Christian catacombs, in the domes and cupolas of Byzantine churches, space is experienced as cavernous; the world a world cavern; a darkness in which the light shines, in which the faithful are concealed; in which the Church, like a seed, is buried.

Cf. Spengler, *Decline of the West,* I, 184, 200; II, 233, 238.

Porphyry says that Zoroaster was the first to consecrate a natural cave to the worship of Mithra, the maker and father of all things, a cave bearing the image of the cosmos which Mithra fashioned. But actually it begins in the paleolithic caves. Human history begins in caves. Inside the caves are labyrinthine passages. The paleolithic caves, which revealed, or concealed, the paleolithic paintings, are labyrinths of twisting, narrow slippery corridors and galleries along which intruders have to grope, often on hands and knees, before reaching the hall where the paintings are. "Les Trois Frères needs half an hour's walk through a succession of corridors to the chamber whose principal figure is wholly visible only after the crawl through a pipe-like tunnel and negotiation of a rock-chimney, with a foot on either side of the chasm. The descent to Labastide is a vertical pit. The cave opens from its side, a hundred feet down, into another pit that leaves only a narrow ledge by which passage can be made to vast corridors."

Porphyry, *Cave of the Nymphs,* 6. Levy, *Gate of Horn,* 13.

Meandering or labyrinthine paths, spirals, mazes, actually followed in ritual (initiation) dances, or symbolically represented in ritual objects, represent the archetypal endeavors of the divine ancestor, the prototypical man, to emerge into this world, to be born. In the ceremony of the Dog totem in Northern Australia, "a winding path is cut through the bush for a processional march, which represents at the same time the flounderings of the ancestral beast through the primeval mud, and also the rope by which it was drawn onto dry land by the human companion." This is what Freud meant by anal birth: "I cannot help mentioning how often mythological themes find their explanation through dream interpretation. The story of the Labyrinth, for example, is found to be a representation of anal birth; the tortuous paths are the bowels, and the thread of Ariadne is the umbilical cord." Mother is mold, *modder*, matter; *Mutter* is mud.

Levy, *Gate of Horn*, 51–52; cf. 36–37. Freud, *New Introductory Lectures*, 38–39.
Cf. Roheim, *Eternal Ones of the Dream*, 102.

The history of mankind goes from the natural cave to the artificial cave, from the underground cave to the above-ground underground. Mr. and Mrs. Antrobus are getting nowhere. The pyramid, with its winding corridors and labyrinthine galleries inside, is an artificial cave; the ziggurat an artificial or architectural mountain with spiral stairs on the outside. The megalithic maze at Stonehenge or Carnac is an alternative architectural embodiment of the same idea. The palace is a labyrinth. King Lakengu of the Bakuba and his eight hundred wives: "His palace is guarded by an impenetrable labyrinth of raffia screens, which the wives built and repaired. To reach the king, a visitor is passed from one guide to another to be led through the maze." The palace was the nucleus of the city: the Cretan cities, their archetype was the labyrinth. Troy, the archetypal city, is the archetypal maze. The spiral is the entrails; and the entrails are "the palace."

Cf. Knight, "Myth and Legend at Troy," 98–121. Kerényi, *Labyrinth-Studien*, 14.

The labyrinth, or maze, is also a dance; the dance of life.

> Then as all actions of mankind
> Are but a labyrinth or maze,
> So let your dances be entwined—

The Cretan labyrinth was Ariadne's dancing ground. After their victory, Theseus and the young Athenians danced a dance consisting of certain measured turnings and re-turnings imitative of the windings and twistings of the labyrinth. The mazes in Medieval Europe, called walls of Troy, were the scene of dancing games called the game of Troy: a penetration of the maze, to win or capture a maiden. The game of Troy, a military game of evolutions by two groups on horseback, a mock battle of alternate flight and pursuit; just like the Cretan labyrinth, says Virgil. The game of Troy is the siege of Troy, to capture a maiden. The Trojans themselves danced the labyrinth dance as they pulled the Trojan horse inside their walls; that Trojan horse which is itself another image of civilization, pregnant in its cavernous bowels with armed men; entered in the Dream Life of Ballso Snell from the rear.

Jonson, "Pleasure reconciled to Virtue."
Cf. Knight, "Myth and Legend at Troy."

The dance of life, the whole story of our wanderings; in a labyrinth of error, the labyrinth of this world. We wandering in the wilderness: Israel; Aeneas and his band of brothers to find Rome; Brute and his band of brothers to find Britain; the band of Pilgrims, compact together in one ship, to fly into the wilderness from the face of the dragon, from England to New England. The exodus is an initiation. The two brothers in Australian aborigine totemic myths have two functions: to wander from place to place and to initiate young men; and their wanderings are imitated in the bush wandering of the newly circumcised young men.

Cf. Voegelin, *New Science of Politics*, 45–46. Miller, *American Puritans*, 14, 24. Roheim, "Some Aspects of Semitic Monotheism," 173; *Eternal Ones of the Dream*, 11, 13.

The exodus is an initiation; the wandering is a rite of passage, from Troy to New Troy, from England to New England. From the mother to the mother; we are getting nowhere. And the wandering is all in the mother: the churinga which the initiate takes with him on the way, marked with the concentric maze pattern, symbolizes and magically achieves the unity of the infant with the mother. Thus "they always stay where they were born, so that the individual compelled by reality to eternal wanderings, in this his supernatural form has never left his mother."

Roheim, *Eternal Ones of the Dream*, 239.

The labyrinth of this world; Satan's labyrinth; this world as underworld, the inferno of Dante's wanderings; night with his ninefold coils; the meandering Stygian waters. At the Cumaean gates, at the mouth of Hades, a representation of the Cretan labyrinth. This labyrinthine cave in which we live is the world of the dead; *où le spectre en plein jour accroche le passant*. This metropolis is necropolis.

Cf. Kerényi, *Labyrinth-Studien*, 32.

The beehive tomb, or treasury (of Atreus); the circular dome, the home of Dis or Pluto, wealth or death. The tomb is the architectural prototype of palace and house; the ancestral grave, the lares and penates in the hearth, is the nucleus of the house. Every house is a house of Hades. And every city a city of Dis; marked, like a paleolithic cave, with the sign of the labyrinth.

les mystères partout coulent comme des sèves
dans les canaux étroits du colosse puissant

The dream of a sleeping giant; the circulation in a labyrinth of alimentary canals.

Baudelaire, "Les Sept Vieillards."
Cf. Roheim, *Eternal Ones of the Dream,* 144. Levy, *Gate of Horn,* esp. 133, 234, 254–255. Schreuer, *Das Recht der Toten,* II, 100, 114. Fustel de Coulanges, *The Ancient City,* Book I, chs. ii-iv. Roheim, *Gates of the Dream,* 124–125. Harrison, *Themis,* 153.

This cave is grave; this womb is tomb. We are not yet born: we are dead. The souls of children not yet born are the souls of ancestors dead. The underlying idea is reincarnation. Of the public magicians among the Australian aborigines Frazer says: "Their most important task is to take charge of the sacred storehouse, usually a cleft in the rocks or a hole in the ground, where are kept the holy stones and sticks (*churinga*) with which the souls of all people, both living and dead, are apparently supposed to be in a manner bound up." Among the Murngin "the most unifying concept of the whole clan ideology is that of the sacred waterhole in which reposes the spiritual unity of clan life. It is the fundamental symbol of clan solidarity. From it come all the eternal qualities, and to it those qualities return when they have been lived or used by members of the clan."

Frazer, *The Golden Bough,* 84. Roheim, *Eternal Ones of the Dream,* 150.

The wanderings of the soul after death are prenatal adventures; a journey by water, in a ship which is itself a Goddess, to the gates of rebirth. In Vao the newly dead man is believed to arrive before the entrance to a cave on the sea shore, where he encounters a terrible female monster, seen as spider woman, man-devouring ogress, crab woman with immense claws, or a giant bivalvular mollusk, clam, which when opened resembles the female genital organ, and which shuts to devour. In front of the cave mouth is a mazelike design called "the Path," traced on the sand by the monster. As the dead man approaches, she obliterates half of the design, and he has to restore it, or else be devoured. "The Path" is the same one that he has trodden many times in the ceremonial dances, and his knowledge of it proves him to be an initiate. After completing the design, he must tread its mazes to the threshold of the cave.

Cf. Levy, *Gate of Horn*, 95, 156–157, 174. Neumann, *The Great Mother*, 176–177.

We dwell in Night, the dungeonlike heaven the lid of our coffin; like the vaulted chamber in which the dead Egyptian kings lay, a representation of the heavens as a firmament, or lid.

Cf. Blake, *First Book of Urizen*, pl. 25. Hugo, "Horror."

The labyrinth is also a spreading tree: "a Cave, a Rock, a Tree deadly and poisonous."

> The Tree spread over him its cold shadows, (Albion groan'd)
> They bent down, they felt the earth, and again enrooting
> Shot into many a Tree, an endless labyrinth of woe.

The tree of mystery, the tree of knowledge: *serpentina sapientia*, "pursuing matter through its infinite divisions"; the serpentine deity which is the wisdom of this world.

Blake, *Jerusalem*, pl. 43, l. 60; pl. 28, ll. 17–19. Servetus in Williams, *Radical Reformation*, 315. Taylor in Raine, "Blake's Debt to Antiquity," 415.

"For man has closed himself up, till he sees all things thro' narrow chinks of his cavern." The cave is the self-enclosure of the self; self-imprisonment; in a shell—the shellfishness of selfishness, the cave of separation and the self. Our cosmos is a cosmic shell, the "Mundane Shell"—

> The Mundane Shell is a vast concave Earth, an immense
> Harden'd shadow of all things upon our Vegetated Earth, . . .
> In Twenty-seven Heavens and all their Hells, with Chaos
> And Ancient Night and Purgatory. It is a cavernous Earth
> Of labyrinthine intricacy, twenty-seven folds of opakeness.

Blake, *Marriage of Heaven and Hell,* pl. 14; *Milton,* pl. 17, ll. 21–26.

And the shellfishness of selfishness is the reluctance to be born. *Mein Leben ist das Zögern vor der Geburt.*

> Embryos we must be, till we burst the shell
> You ambient, azure shell, and spring to life.

Weinberg, *Kafkas Dichtungen,* 34. Young, *Night Thoughts,* I, 132–135; quoted in Frye, *Fearful Symmetry,* 168.

> The natural man is, speaking in terms of conscious vision, an imaginative seed. Just as the seed is a dry sealed packet of solid "matter," so the natural mind is a tight skull-bound shell of abstract ideas. And just as the seed is surrounded by a dark world which we see as an underworld, so the physical universe, which surrounds the natural man on all sides, and is dark in the sense that he cannot see its extent, is the underworld of the mind, the den of Urthona, the cave of Plato's *Republic.* The majority of seeds in nature die as seeds, and in human life all natural men, all the timid, all the stupid and all the evil, remain in the starlit cavern of the fallen mind, hibernating in the dormant winter night of time. They are embryos of life only, infertile seeds, and die within the seed-world. The possibility of life within them remains in its embryonic form of abstract ideas, shadows and dreams. Some of the dreams are troubled visions of the real world of awakened consciousness; others are the night-

mares of paralyzing horror which all minds in a stupor of inertia are a prey to. Here and there a seed puts out a tentative shoot into the real world, and when it does so it escapes from the darkness of burial into the light of immortality. Such a seed, however, would only have begun its development, for the vegetable life is not the most highly organized form of life, because it is still bound to nature. The animal symbolizes a higher stage of development by breaking its navel-string, and this earth-bound freedom of movement is represented in our present physical level.

The bird is not a higher form of imagination than we are, but its ability to fly symbolizes one, and men usually assign wings to what they visualize as superior forms of human existence. In this symbolism the corresponding image of nature would be neither the seed-bed of the plant nor the suckling mother of the mammal, but the egg, which has been used as a symbol of the physical universe from the most ancient times. . . . In Blake the firmament is the Mundane Shell, the indefinite circumference of the physical world through which the mind crashes on its winged ascent to reality. To the inexperienced eye the egg appears to be a geometrical stone, but the imagination within the egg soon demonstrates that it is something much more fragile. The same is true of the Newtonian universe, the rock rolled against the tomb of divine humanity.

Frye, *Fearful Symmetry*, 347–348.

In the cave of separateness the self curls up in sleep. In the Mundane Shell the unborn sleep. The human condition is that of Albion at the beginning of Jerusalem: the Sleep of Ulro. And sleep is uterine regression, a reactivation of the intra-uterine situation. "Our relationship with the world which we entered so unwillingly seems to be endurable only with intermission; hence we withdraw periodically into the condition prior to our entrance into the world: that is to say, into intra-uterine existence. . . . One third of us has never been born at all."

Freud, *General Introduction*, 92.
Cf. Roheim, *Gates of the Dream*, 1, 116, 132.

The underworld cave is the cave of sleep and dreams; Aeneas comes back up by the gate of dreams. In the ancient world disturbed persons went, for a dream and a cure, to the cave of Trophonios; like paleolithic man. At the cave of Trophonios the dreamer was swaddled like an infant, then descended by a ladder to a cave, then crawled through a narrow passage where he can barely squeeze through, and is finally drawn as it were into a whirlpool. The psychoanalytic session is "an improved maternal womb" in which the patient incubates.

Cf. Roheim, *Gates of the Dream*, 8, 279–292. Meier, *Antike Inkubation und moderne Psychotherapie.*

The cave of dreams and the cave of the dead are the same cave. Ghosts are dreams, and dreams are ghosts: shades, *umbrae*. Sleep is regressive; in dreaming we return to dream time—the age of heroes and ancestors; Roheim's *Eternal Ones of the Dream;* or the primal parents. In the idea of reincarnation, the father finds his child in a dream: i.e., finds the child pre-existent, in spirit or ancestral form; in some cave or water hole.

Cf. Roheim, *Gates of the Dream*, 110–112; 279.

Where life is still within the cave, and we still unborn, the beginning of life (birth) is not exit from the womb, but entry into the cave (womb), the descent of the soul into the world of matter, the "world of generation" (Porphyry). When Empedocles says "we have come down into this roofed cave," he is referring to the moment of reincarnation. Life is seen as beginning, not at birth, but at conception. The life of the individual is identified with the seed of life; or with his father's penis. "The spirit child seen in his [the father's] dream is his own penis."

Porphyry, *Cave of the Nymphs*, 6, 8. Roheim, *Gates of the Dream*, 111.

The spirit children called their prospective mother's vagina "rock hole"; when they say "I am going into a rock hole," they intend to be born. Porphyry says that souls proceeding into generation are nymphs ready for marriage; the pleasure of sex is the honey in the bowl by which they are seduced and fall into the world of generation. So too in the *Tibetan Book of the Dead* the compulsion to be reborn takes the form of a sexual attraction to the mother's womb. The men of the primitive tribe behave as though the birth of the boy out of his mother was because of the erotic attraction between him and her. The first act of the individual is incest with his mother.

Cf. Porphyry, *Cave of the Nymphs,* 16. Roheim, *Gates of the Dream,* 111. Reik, "The Puberty Rites of Savages," 145. Evan-Wentz, *Tibetan Book of the Dead,* xli.

Copulation is uterine regression. "The purpose of the sex act can be none other than an attempt to return to the mother's womb." "The sex act achieves this transitory regression in a three-fold manner: the whole organism attains this goal by purely hallucinatory means, somewhat as in sleep; the penis, with which the organism as a whole has identified itself, attains it partially or symbolically; while only the sexual secretion itself possesses the prerogative, as representative of the ego and its narcissistic double, the genital, of attaining *in reality* to the womb of the mother."

Ferenczi, *Thalassa,* 18.

Birth, copulation, and death, equated. The basic structure of the dream, the basic dream, is a reaction to being asleep. And "we can distinguish three stages in this basic dream: (a) Sleep is death. (b) Sleep is uterine regression. (c) Sleep is coitus." The crux is the equation of coming out and going in; forwards and backwards; progression and regression; life and death. Birth is to come out of a womb; and to go into a womb. "For, 'flinging oneself into the water' read 'coming out of the water.'" The birth of the hero is the death of the hero. "In dreams, as in mythology, the delivery of a child from the uterine waters is commonly represented, by way of distortion, as the entry of the child into water." Sleep is both uterine regression and emergence into a new world; as soul leaves body; i.e., being born. "The dream-body-phallus while it is going in is at the same time coming out of the womb."

Roheim, *Gates of the Dream,* 16, 58. Freud, "Interpretation of Dreams," 394, 395.

The woman penetrated is a labyrinth. You emerge into another world inside the woman. The penis is the bridge; the passage to another world is coitus; the other world is a womb-cave. Cave man still drags cave woman to his cave; all coitus is fornication (*fornix,* an underground arched vault). And the cave in which coitus takes place is the grave; a cthonic fertility rite; Antigone buried alive, together with her ancestors, her bridal chamber the tomb. Death is coitus and coitus is death. Death is genitalized as a return to the womb, incestuous coitus.

Cf. Levy, *Gate of Horn,* 104. Roheim, *Animism,* 44–46, 56, 233, 259–260. Porphyry, *Cave of the Nymphs,* 16. Ferenczi, "The Symbolism of the Bridge."

Life and death, equated. Every coitus repeats the fall; brings death, birth, into the world. It is Sky descending into Mother Earth, ejaculating his powers, suffering castration. The staff that cleaves the waters is the dead man's body, the corpse; the stiff that ejaculates the soul or semen is the penis. Penis or corpse, stiff as stone; a perpetual erection, or monument. "The Dieri have a number of long cylindro-conical stones which are supposed to temporarily contain the male element of certain ancestral spirits now residing in the sky as their recognized deities. . . . The virility of the tribe is dependent upon the preservation of the stones." To be turned into stone symbolizes not only erection but also castration. This is the Rocky Law of Condemnation and double Generation and Death; which makes the Loins the place of the Last Judgment.

Roheim, *Eternal Ones of the Dream,* 85; cf. *Gates of the Dream,* 101, 264.
Cf. Freud, "Medusa's Head." Blake, *Jerusalem,* pl. 30, ll. 37–38.

Unborn—in the womb, then; asleep; and dreaming. Withdrawn from the environment, or split from the environment; as in schizophrenia. As Blake saw, there is a fission, a duplication, a division. Withdrawn into a cave (or womb) which is himself; as Blake would say, the Selfhood. The womb into which the sleeper withdraws is at the same time his own body. The dreamer sinks into himself. And makes himself a whole new world; a man-made world, in the deepest sense. A whole new world out of the body of the dreamer, a world which is his cave.

Cf. Roheim, *Gates of the Dream,* 7, 18, 36, 49, 58, 62, 95, 105, 116; *Eternal Ones of the Dream,* 213, 217.

To make a world out of himself the dreamer must not only split with the world, but also split himself into both self and world, self and environment, mother and child. But inside the womb self and environment is penis in vagina. Out of the body of the dreamer is made both a phallus and a womb; and the basic dream is of phallic movement in a female environment (space).

Cf. Roheim, *Gates of the Dream,* 62, 116, 439.

The wandering heroes are phallic heroes, in a permanent state of erection; pricking o'er the plain. The word coition represents genital sexuality as walking; but the converse is also true: all walking, or wandering in the labyrinth, is genital-sexual. All movement is phallic, all intercourse sexual. Hermes, the phallus, is the god of roads, of doorways, of all goings-in and comings-out; all goings-on.

Cf. Roheim, *Eternal Ones of the Dream,* 10, 11, 13, 16, 17, 79, 177, 202, 208, 249; *Gates of the Dream,* 9.

All walking, or wandering, is from mother, to mother, in mother; it gets us nowhere. Movement is in space; and space (χώρα), as Plato says in the *Timaeus,* is a receptacle, a vessel (ὑποδοχή—"undertaker"); a matrix (ἐκμαγεῖον); as it were the mother (μήτηρ) or nurse (τιθήνη), of all becoming. Space is a sphere or spheres containing us; ambient and embracing; the world-mothering air as atmosphere. Also a chaos or chasm (χώρα), a yawning pit, a devouring mother. Without form; void; and dark. And then there is light walking in darkness: the son-sun-hero in the mother-dragon night.

Cf. Plato, *Timaeus,* 49A–52B. Whitehead, *Adventures of Ideas,* ch. xi, §19. Roheim, "The Dragon and the Hero: Part Two," 90. Ferenczi, "Gulliver Fantasies," 46–47. Spitzer, "Milieu and ambiance," *Essays.*

Mundus, this world; as a yawning pit, *mundus patet*; abode of the dead. *Mundus,* the circular ceremonial trench, *urbi et orbi,* that represents the vulva or uterus of the mother, the *sulcus primigenius.* Both the jaws of death and a storehouse, *penus,* for the penis, the *lapis manalis.* But also the decoration, the female adornment, which conceals the yawning pit, *mundus muliebris.*

Cf. Roheim, *Gates of the Dream,* 131. Neumann, *The Great Mother,* 283. Patai, *Man and Temple,* 106.

Both the phallic hero and the female space are made out of the one body of the dreamer. It is then true, after all, that Eve came from Adam's rib, that the separation of the sexes (a fission, division, duplication) occurs in Adam's sleep, or dream. The Eve that comes from Adam's rib is not just a woman but the Emanation, the world as a woman. "Time and Space are Real Beings, a Male and a Female. Time is a Man, Space is a Woman, and her Masculine Portion is Death." He the Priest and She the Tabernacle. In the sleep of Adam the church is born: *in somno Adae ecclesia nascitur.*

Blake, *A Vision of the Last Judgement,* 614. Hilary in Daniélou, *From Shadows to Reality,* 49.
Cf. Roheim, *Animism,* 336.

The split of self from environment, and of self into both self and environment, is also the split of self or soul from body. The essence of dreaming is duplication, division; as in schizophrenia. The dreamer sees himself, a double of himself; "The moment of falling asleep is the moment in which the soul is born, that phallic personification of the body." "The formation of a double in the dream is the moment when animism originates." Primitive animism says that in dreaming the soul leaves the body; in Blake the separating off of the Emanation is accompanied by the separating off of the Spectre.

Roheim, *Gates of the Dream,* 58, 59; cf. 116.

This soul is a penis. The hero of the dream is a phallic double, or phallic personification of the whole body. Having a soul, the hero with a thousand faces, is the same as having genital organization—to take the penis as the "narcissistic representative of the total personality."

Ferenczi, *Thalassa,* 28; cf. 16, 18.
Cf. Roheim, *Gates of the Dream,* 58, 116, 439; *Animism,* 19, 25.

The uterine regressive trend—Ferenczi's thalassal regressive trend—is the same thing as genital organization. For those not yet born, their whole person is in the womb. But what belongs in the womb is the penis. The whole person is identified with the penis—the basic equation of body and phallus. "The phantasy originates in the intra-uterine (mother's body) complex and usually has the content of the man's desire to creep completely into the genital from which he came. . . . The entire individual is in this case a penis." The little man in the enormous room: the ego which explores his cave and penetrates its secrets is a penis. This identification of the whole person with the penis is genital organization.

Tausk, "The 'Influencing Machine' in Schizophrenia," 554.
Cf. Ferenczi, "The Symbolism of the Bridge," "Gulliver Fantasies." Klein, "The Theory of Intellectual Inhibition." Roheim, *Gates of the Dream,* 96.

We have not yet been born; we are still in the womb; asleep; we are such stuff as dreams are made on. Life begins with a fall; a falling into the womb; a fall into sleep. Our birth is but a sleep and a forgetting. Adam's fall is Adam's fall into sleep; or Osiris' descent to the underworld. The descent to the underworld is what happens to every human being when he goes to sleep. The question what is life turns out to be the question what is sleep; Freud is the master of those who know.

Cf. Roheim, *Gates of the Dream,* 259–312.

To sleep; to die. Sleep is the twin brother of Death. "Sleep is death stirred by dreams, death is dreamless sleep." The womb then is a tomb. To be born is to die, and life is really death-in-life. Psychoanalysis is the rediscovery of the Orphic or Oriental vision of life as sleep disturbed by dreams, of life as a disturbance in death. In the philosophy of Freud's *Beyond the Pleasure Principle* and Ferenczi's *Thalassa,* life itself is a catastrophe, or fall, or trauma. The form of the reproductive process repeats the trauma out of which life arose, and at the same time endeavors to undo it. The "uterine regressive trend in the sex act" is an aspect of the universal goal of all organic life—to return to lifeless condition out of which life arose. "The goal of all life is death." In this philosophy life and the main stages in biological evolution (sexual differentiation, adaptation to dry land) are catastrophes excited by external forces: these catastrophes create "tension"; and the aim of life (or of evolutionary adaptation) is to get rid of the tension, and so die. Life is a temporary (accidental) disturbance in a lifeless (and thus peaceful) universe. It is best, then, never to have been born; and second best, quickly to die. Nirvana is release from the cycle of rebirth.

Roheim, *Gates of the Dream,* 3. Freud, *Beyond the Pleasure Principle,* 50. Ferenczi, *Thalassa,* 69.

The conclusion of the whole matter—Blake: "We are in a world of Generation and death, and this world we must cast off." The Sleep of Ulro; the passage through Eternal Death; the awakening to Eternal Life. And then we shall see that Generation is not the reality but a shadow of the reality: Generation is only an image of Regeneration. The real birth would be birth from the womb of the dream world. The real death is the death we are dead with here and now. Real life can only be life after death, or resurrection; life other than the life whose goal is death, and whose pattern is the repetition-compulsion, karma.

Blake, *A Vision of the Last Judgement,* 613; cf. *Jerusalem,* pl. 4.

Here is the point where we have to jump, beyond psychoanalysis: They know not of Regeneration, but only of Generation. Therapy must be rebirth; but psychoanalysis does not believe that man can be born again; and so it does not believe that man is ever born at all; for the real birth is the second birth.

Cf. Blake, *Jerusalem*, pl. 7, ll. 61–65.

The awakening to eternal life; free from the cycle of rebirth; satori, the experience of the unborn. Unborn, but not in a womb; before the fall, into a womb. "'United with Sakti, be full of power,' says the *Kulacūdāmani-Tantra*. 'From the union of *Siva* and *Sakti* the world is created.' The Buddhist, however, does not want the creation and unfoldment but the coming back to the 'uncreated, unformed' state of *sunyata* from which all creation proceeds."

Govinda, *Foundations of Tibetan Mysticism*, 97.
Cf. Fromm *et al.*, *Zen Buddhism and Psychoanalysis*, 19.

"The 'sin' in the sex act is not that of love but that of parentage. It is the father and the mother, not the lover and the beloved, who disappear from the highest Paradise. In the resurrection Jesus is a Melchizedek, without father, mother or descent." This Melchizedek; King of Salem, which is King of peace; without father, without mother, without descent; having neither beginning of days, nor end of life; but made like unto the Son of God. A Son of God who is without a father; a son without a father; the Oedipus Complex transcended. Without descent, without genealogy; no more generations; the world of generation and death transcended.

Frye, *Fearful Symmetry*, 388.
Cf. Hebrews VI, 20; VII, 1–3.

The son without a father in the resurrection; in the resurrected body; a body that is not genitally organized.

> These are the sexual garments, the Abomination of Desolation,
> Hiding the Human Lineaments as within an Ark and Curtains
> Which Jesus rent and now shall purge away with Fire
> Till Generation is swallow'd up in Regeneration.

Blake, *Milton,* pl. 41, ll. 25–28.

Without mother. "Today the Virgin gives birth to the maker of the universe. The Cave brings forth Eden." Adam wakes from his sleep and there is no longer any separate Eve. No longer any mother Eve; no longer any mother Nature. "The Pope supposes Nature and the Virgin Mary to be the same allegorical personages, but the Protestant considers Nature as incapable of bearing a Child." No more nature; no more nascence. Unborn; or virgin birth. Beyond nature; supernatural.

Greek liturgy in Ladner, *Idea of Reform,* 291. Blake, note in Cennini's "Trattato Della Pittura"; cf. *A Vision of the Last Judgement,* 613.
Cf. Augustine, *De Civitate Dei,* XII, 26. Frye, *Fearful Symmetry,* 74–76.

III
Trinity

Turning and turning in the animal belly, the mineral belly, the belly of time. To find the way out: the poem.

Paz, "Hacia el poema," *Aguila o Sol,* 93.

"The sleeper turns into himself and falls back into the womb." "Sleep is a combination of regression and introversion. The dream space is both the mother's womb and the dreamer's body." In the dream, in magic, in schizophrenia we return to the dual unity, mother and child, as one body. "The representation of the dual unity as one body and the libidinization of the separation situation is just the essence of magic."

Roheim, *Gates of the Dream,* 7, 116; *Eternal Ones of the Dream,* 177; cf. *Magic and Schizophrenia,* 109.

The churinga, the holy stones with which the life of the tribe is bound up, the stone body or mystical body of the individual, incised with patterns of concentric circles: *"the body that is identical with environment;* here we have struck rock bottom. What the tjurunga symbolizes and magically achieves is *the unity of the infant with the mother.* The tjuranga, although it represents the body of an individual, also stands for the environment in which he moves."

Roheim, *Eternal Ones of the Dream,* 243; cf. *Gates of the Dream,* 106.

And like the baseless fabric of the dream, so also the cloud-capp'd towers, the gorgeous palaces: "The house or town which the boy is so keen to build up again in his play signifies not only his mother's renewed and intact body, but his own." Or the machine, as in the dream of the self-service elevator in the big house, a symbol both of the mother and of the man's own erection.

Klein, *Psychoanalysis of Children,* 340; cf. "The Theory of Intellectual Inhibition," 261.
Cf. Roheim, *Magic and Schizophrenia,* 113.

The basic dream is of self as embryo in womb = penis in womb = parents in coitus; the primal scene. The penis that is in mother's womb is father's. It is via identification with the father that the subject achieves incest. "The act of entry is transferred from the father to the dreamer herself"; "father (or father's penis) disappears into mother = I disappear into mother."

Roheim, *Gates of the Dream,* 40; cf. 29. Freud, *New Introductory Lectures,* 39.

In genital organization we identify with the penis; but the penis we are is not our own, but daddy's; or at least, in it we and the father are one. In genital organization body and soul are haunted, possessed, by the ghost of father; coitus is performed in a dream, by the ghost. The retention of the primal scene as an endopsychic element makes present the past and derealizes the present. The self is present with "father's penis in mother's womb." "Phantasies of meeting father's penis in mother's womb and of witnessing copulation between the parents, or of being damaged by it, during intra-uterine life." "It is as though, when he [the father] entered the mother's body sexually, he found the children there."

Brophy, *Black Ship to Hell*, 209. Klein, *Psychoanalysis of Children*, 189n.

"Complete analysis must reveal the primal scene." The super-ego is the introjected parents: but the parents introjected were in coitus; the nucleus of the super-ego is the introjected primal scene. It comes to the same thing to say, as Roheim said, that the parent killed in the primal crime was the combined parent, or parents in coitus.

Klein, "Infantile Anxiety Situations," 230; cf. *Psychoanalysis of Children*, 189n.
Cf. Roheim, *Riddle of the Sphinx*, 209–210, 225; *Gates of the Dream*, 39–40.

The parents in coitus, the two snakes copulating that Teiresias saw. The two snakes are one snake, a phallic snake which also bites and swallows like a vagina: the uroboric snake, which is both a pole and a hole. A Dragon red and hidden Harlot. Sitting on the waters: the rainbow serpent of the Australian aborigines "—this ambisexual symbolism of the snake is associated with the rainbow." The ambisexual sea serpent Leviathan in the Jewish tradition, whose castration and separation into two sexes is the creation of this world, when God separated the upper male waters from the lower female waters. "What then did the Holy One blessed be He do? He castrated the male and killed the female . . . as it is written 'And he will slay the dragon that is in the sea.'" As the separation of male and female is the creation of this world, their union is its destruction by flood: "they united and grew mighty to destroy the world." And in the final end: "He will open all the chambers of waters which are above the heavens, and of the fountains which are beneath the earth. And all the waters shall be joined with the waters: that which is above the heavens is the masculine, and the water which is beneath the earth is the feminine. And they shall destroy all who dwell on the earth and those who dwell under the ends of the heaven."

Patai, *Man and Temple*, 64, 65. Roheim, *Eternal Ones of the Dream*, 196; cf. 165–166, 176, 182.
Cf. Frye, *Fearful Symmetry*, 301. Blake, *Jerusalem*, pl. 89.

The Holy of Holies is a Nuptial Chamber, "though not until a comparatively late period do we find the express statement that the couple whose Nuptial Chamber it was, were God and the Holy Matrona personifying the Community of Israel." "On great festivals the curtain of the sanctuary was shown to the people and on the curtain the image of cherubim entwined in each other's arms. And the priests said: 'See, God loves his people as a man loves a woman.' Jehovah in the temple is a combined object, the parents in coitus. "A male within a Female hid as in an Ark and Curtains." "The staves that were used to carry the Ark during the wanderings grew longer in the sanctuary, and caused the Veil to protrude as the two breasts of a woman." Breasts, or penises—who knows?

Roheim, *Animism*, 336; cf. *Riddle of the Sphinx*, 209–210, 225. Blake, *Jerusalem*, pl. 76, l. 15.
Cf. Patai, *Man and Temple*, 89, 91.

The parents in coitus make one flesh; not a juxtaposition of two separatenesses, but a genuine Two-in-One, incorporated; making one corporate body. "The father's penis incorporated in the mother"; "at this early stage of development the principle of *pars pro toto* holds good and the penis represents the father in person." "Combined parent figures such as: the mother containing the father's penis or the whole father; the father containing the mother's breast or the whole mother; the parents fused inseparably in sexual intercourse." "They incorporate each other." "The penis inside the mother represents a combination of father and mother in one person."

Klein, *Psychoanalysis of Children,* 189, 190; "The Emotional Life of the Infant," 219–220. Heimann, "Functions of Introjection and Projection," 164.

The combined object: "The tjurunga which symbolizes both the male and the female genital organ, the primal scene and combined parent." The penis which is also a vagina, the circle squared, or swastika: *Roma Quadrata.* The omphalos or navel stone which is womb and tomb and phallus. The rock in the temple: "This rock, called in Hebrew *Ebhen Shetiyyah,* the Stone of Foundation, was the first solid thing created, and was placed by God amidst the as yet boundless fluid of the primeval waters. Legend has it that just as the body of an embryo is built up in its mother's womb from its navel, so God built up the earth concentrically around this stone, the Navel of the Earth."

Roheim, *Riddle of the Sphinx,* 120.
Cf. Neumann, *Great Mother,* pls. 106–107. Patai, *Man and Temple,* 85. Harrison, *Themis,* 396–424. Roheim, *Eternal Ones of the Dream,* 250.

The stone (tjurunga) becomes the house of the Lord, Beth-El. The house, the pillared gateway, the trilithic dolmen or lintel on two pillars: a combined object. Like the altar, which is both post erected and table spread.

Cf. Genesis XXVIII, 18–19. Levy, *Gate of Horn,* 98–102, 119–120, 126, 153. Roheim, *Magic and Schizophrenia,* 113.

Incorporation (introjection) seen with the inward eye, is always eating or swallowing. In the primal scene a regression takes place: "genital desires in the infant of either sex coalesce with oral desires," and copulation is seen as oral copulation. The two giants are cannibals in mutual manducation.

Klein, "Early Development of Conscience," 273; "The Emotional Life of the Infant," 218.
Cf. Roheim, *Animism,* 48; *Gates of the Dream,* 96.

In oral copulation the vagina is a devouring mouth. The combined object (parents in coitus) becomes the mother with a penis. The father is castrated; the mother retains his penis. "The horrible woman who thrusts her long nose into the room through the window at night to alarm the cobbler is clearly the dream apparition of the old woman with a penis, that is the primal scene in the abbreviated form of the combined parent."

Roheim, *Riddle of the Sphinx,* 55; cf. *Animism,* 357.
Cf. Klein, *Psychoanalysis of Children,* 103–104, 189. Heimann, "Functions of Introjection and Projection," 165.

Father and mother together is a mother with a penis. And so Hamlet calls Claudius his mother: "Father and mother is man and wife, man and wife is one flesh; and so, my mother." The city on a hill, the world mountain, is the great mountain mother, the Niobe of Nations; a great rock on which the temple or church is built, a rock of ages which is nevertheless cleft for me. Cybele's towered head: the phallus in whose bosom I can hide. No laughing matter, *Agelastos Petra*; for the mountain above is the cave below.

Cf. Jones, *Anathémata,* 56. Patai, *Man and Temple,* 106. Levy, *Gate of Horn,* 89, 95, 101, 119.

The woman is a penis. "The symbolic equation, Girl =Phallus." Aphrodite, the personification of femininity, is just a penis, a penis cut off and tossed into the sea; the penis which Father Sky lost in intercourse with Mother Earth.

Cf. Fenichel, "The Symbolic Equation: Girl=Phallus." Roheim, "Aphrodite or the Woman with a Penis."

Mother and child as one body is mother with a penis. The symbolic equation, penis=child. The king entering the arch; the priest in the tent or tabernacle: "He is the Lamb and I the fold"; both a penis and a child.

Cf. Levy, *Gate of Horn,* 100; cf. 119, 127, 153–154. Freud, "On the Transformation of Instincts," 170.

The tree of life, with both rising trunk and spreading branches bearing fruit, both a penis and a breast, is also the tree of death on which the son is hung; the mother with a penis.

> Thus was the Lamb of God condemn'd to Death.
> They nailed him upon the Tree of Mystery, weeping over him
> And then mocking and then worshipping, calling him Lord
>   and King.
> Sometimes as twelve daughters lovely, and sometimes as five
> They stood in beaming beauty, and sometimes as one, even
>   Rahab
> Who is Mystery, Babylon the Great, the Mother of Harlots.

Blake, *Night* VIII, 325–330.

The vagina as a devouring mouth, or vagina dentata; the jaws of the giant cannibalistic mother, a menstruating woman with the penis bitten off, a bleeding trophy.

Cf. Roheim, *Riddle of the Sphinx,* 41; "The Dragon and the Hero: Part Two," 80–81.

The dying gods, Attis, Adonis, Osiris, die in or on a mother. Her privates we; privates in her armies; in her battles we are mowed down; the flower of a nation cut off. Mater Triumphalis; Ishtar, Athena, Queen of Battles.

> A Female hidden in a Male, Religion hidden in War,
> A Dragon red and hidden Harlot which John in Patmos saw.

Blake, *Milton,* pl. 40, ll. 20, 22. Cf. Brophy, *Black Ship to Hell,* 48–50.

Coitus as a battle, in which the prize is a penis: "The infantile notion of coitus as a fight between two phalloi, in which the weaker one is castrated and becomes a female." Ferenczi's theory of genitality: "Both [sexes] developed the male sexual organ, and there came about, perhaps, a tremendous struggle, the outcome of which was to decide upon which sex should fall the pains and duties of motherhood and the passive endurance of genitality. In this struggle the female sex succumbed." Psychoanalysis is still looking at the primal scene.

Roheim, *Riddle of the Sphinx,* 47. Ferenczi, *Thalassa,* 103.

Love and War in the Western World: how they are similar. Mars and Venus; their daughter is Harmony, the peg that joins, an arm or armor. *Arma virumque:* not two subjects but one. Mars is masculine, "a god of fertility," marital as well as martial. The spear is a bridge; and intercourse invasion.

Cf. Rougemont, *Love in the Western World,* Book V. Roheim, *Animism,* 103.

"In deadly combat, i.e., in destructive copulation." Locked in battle, in holy deadlock. Wedlock is the continuation of war by other means.

Bella gerant alii, tu, felix, Austria nube;
Quodque aliis Mars, dat tibi regna Venus.

Women are the gift, which makes peace; the fatal gift, which leads to war. The diplomatic joust begins with the insidious present of a woman.

Klein, *Psychoanalysis of Children,* 322.
Cf. Roheim, *Magic and Schizophrenia,* 65; *War, Crime and the Covenant,* 78. Granet, *Catégories matrimoniales,* 125–136. Lévi-Strauss, *Les Structures élémentaires de la parenté,* 77, 80. Turney-High, *Primitive War,* 224, 247.

The two giant figures are cannibals, in mutual manducation. "The dangerous tapeworm represented the two parents in a hostile alliance (actually in intercourse) against him." Oral copulation is the prototype for all the ramifications of the sado-masochistic perversions, sexual and social. "They fight in the sky for the nation," aerial combats of witches or air forces. The latent content is the primal scene. Those dogfights are dog copulations; the Milky Way, "a pair of dogs connected by the male dog's penis and tail, which are permanently fixed in the bitch's anus. They are thus a married pair. When they bite, their victim is immediately cut in two."

Klein, "The Psychogenesis of Manic-Depressive States," 293. Roheim, *Riddle of the Sphinx,* 115; cf. 28.
Cf. Roheim, *Gates of the Dream,* 171–172, 376.

Oral copulation, or the equation of penis and breast, the crux in sexual inversion. Coitus as castration. To be castrated is to be a woman; but the woman is a devouring mouth which castrates. Those who have been castrated must castrate others to incorporate their penis; but to receive into themselves a penis is again to be a woman, to be castrated. The solution to the castration-complex is genital organization. But genital organization is the basic equation of body (self) and penis; and "the sexual aim of a person who has in phantasy eaten the penis and become the penis is—to be eaten."

Lewin, "The Body as Phallus," 33.
Cf. Roheim, *Gates of the Dream*, 244, 366, 372; *Riddle of the Sphinx*, 65. Freud, "Splitting of the Ego," 375. Fenichel, "Trophy and Triumph," 145.

The aim is to be penis of the mother with a penis. In Central Australia, "the Milky Way is a very great mystery or tjurunga. A boy was being initiated and the women danced in his honor. But a demon woman was hidden in the bush and she seized the boy's penis and inserted it into her vagina, holding it tight with her labia. They were thus stuck together, with the woman riding on the boy's penis. They went up higher and higher into the sky and were transformed into the Milky Way." "The Milky Way is really a mother and her son, stuck forever in the act of copulation. . . . 'Stuck in the Milky Way' means eternal coitus and union with mother." Milky Way, or Great Bear:

> Petit Poucet rêveur, j'égrenais dans ma course
> Des rimes. Mon auberge était à la Grande-Ourse.

Roheim, *Eternal Ones of the Dream*, 165, 193. Rimbaud, "Ma Bohème."
Cf. Bachelard, *La Poétique de l'espace*, 143–144.

To be the penis of the mother with a penis: both erection and castration. The primal scene seen is Medusa's head seen: a trophy, decapitated, and still potent; the female genitals with no penis, but with snakes for hair—"a confirmation of the technical rule according to which a multiplication of penis symbols signifies castration." "It is a remarkable fact that, however frightening they may be in themselves, they (the snakes) nevertheless serve actually as a mitigation of the horror, for they replace the penis, the absence of which is the cause of the horror." Multiplication here signifies both division, dismemberment, bits instead of unity, castration; and also fruitful multiplication, reproduction, many where there had been only one. We are in a world oscillating between the one and the many, a world of fission and fusion, the world of schizophrenia; the world of the schizophrenic patient whose "primary function in life, as he saw it, was to restore people who had been *multilated.*"

Freud, "Medusa's Head," 105. Roheim, *Magic and Schizophrenia,* 96; cf. 137–138, 140, 150.
Cf. Freud, "Splitting of the Ego with Defensive Process"; "Fetichism."

The sight of Medusa's head makes the spectator (of the primal scene) stiff with terror, turns him to stone. The stiff is a corpse, and an erection. The stone phallus, an abbreviation for all kingship; the final goal of all monumental aspiration; the Stylites complex. Both castration and erection achieved, in a genitalization of death.

Cf. Freud, "Medusa's Head." Fenichel, "Scoptophilic Instinct and Identification," 389–392.

The stone phallus, a permanent erection. The Milky Way is really a mother and her son stuck together forever in the act of copulation; a pair of dogs connected by the male dog's penis and tail, which are permanently fixed in the bitch's anus. But to be stuck (in a rut) is also castration. "In connection with this he had the association that he had been warned that, if one made faces and the clock struck, one's face would stay so. Thus he was afraid that he might actually 'remain stuck' in his feminine role, and this would involve his forfeiting his penis."

Fenichel, "The Psychology of Transvestitism," 174.
Cf. Roheim, *Riddle of the Sphinx*, 28, 64, 71; *Eternal Ones of the Dream*, 193.

To be stuck; stuck together in eternal coitus; wedlock as deadlock; coitus and covenant; stuck together in the social compact, bound by their oath, the waters of the River Styx that freeze a man and make him stiff.

The stone phallus—of royal majesty; or pillared martyrdom—exists to be exhibited. The demonstrative factor in sado-masochism. "Patience on a monument, smiling at tears," needs to be seen. Exhibitionism is a denial of castration; it says, see, I do have a penis.

Cf. Reik, *Masochism in Modern Man*, 79.

The monumental immobility of the stone phallus is a recapitulation of the primal scene. "In our patient's associations there constantly recurred the fairytale of the stone prince in the Arabian Nights. . . . The purpose of these fantasies was simply to repress or psychically master her childhood observations of the genitals of adults in childhood. Now the rigidity of the stone prince, his disability, and his immobility were stressed in a very remarkable fashion. They signified something more than an erection. . . . The idea of being turned into stone reminds us of the strange immobility of the wolves in the Wolf-Man's dream. Freud interprets this as 'representation through the opposite'; i.e., the immobility stands for the vigorous movement which the child must have witnessed in the primal scene. Now there was one person, who, as Freud also has noted, actually was rigid during this scene: the child who witnessed it. So 'to be turned to stone' by the sight of something means to be fascinated by it." The child is stiff, with the actual inability to move, the rigidity which comes over someone who suddenly sees something terrifying. But the rigidity is also the erection of his penis. The child is petrified. "Petrification as death represents erection seen through the mirror of anxiety."

Fenichel, "Scoptophilic Instinct and Identification," 389, 390. Roheim, "The Dragon and the Hero: Part Two," 80.

Parental coitus interrupted, immobilized. The immobility; no end-pleasure; coitus interruptus. The erection is also the magic staff which intervenes to freeze the status quo, to hold the parents in suspended animation with an intervening space between them. The great rock on which the temple of Jerusalem was built was regarded not only as the navel of the world but also as separating the waters above from the waters below, the male waters above from the female waters below. "The ritual offers another form of gratification to the son, that of interrupting the father in the sexual act"; as in *Finnegans Wake*. And at the same time, *verweile doch, du bist so schön.*

Roheim, *Riddle of the Sphinx,* 116.
Cf. Jones, *Anathémata,* 58. Patai, *Man and Temple,* 54–71.

The dungeonlike heaven between sky and earth is between father sky and mother earth in coitus. The children make space for themselves in the Maori myth by pushing Father Sky up from Mother Earth; by cutting off the penis of Sky in the Greek myth. The children are stuck between heaven and earth: not to touch the earth or see the sun, as in the taboos of kings and of young girls at puberty, means to be in the womb.

Cf. Seidenberg, "Dual Organization and Kingship," 338–339. Frazer, *The Golden Bough*, ch. LX.

Under the influence of the primal scene, he masturbates: "I have lost the mother but I can masturbate." "I am not castrated, I can go on masturbating." The eternal coitus of mother and son is really masturbation; genitality in which fantasy (a scene seen; a dream) takes the place of reality is masturbation—a castrated genitality. "The child introjects the primal scene with the pleasure of ideal participation, and the prohibition of actual participation": a eunuch in the harem. "She turns herself in phantasy into a man, without herself becoming active in a masculine way, and is no longer anything but a spectator of the event which takes the place of the sexual act."

Roheim, *Riddle of the Sphinx*, 283; cf. 120, 48; Freud, " 'A Child is being Beaten,' " 196; cf. "Splitting of the Ego with Defensive Process," 374–375. Cf. Roheim, *Eternal Ones of the Dream*, 79, 177; *Gates of the Dream*, 365–366; 398.

Both castration and erection; both the terror and the excitement of the primal scene; both the fear and the wish. Stuck together in eternal coitus is both eternal passion and eternal pain; both coitus and the punishment for it. The origin of the theater of sado-masochism: the primal scene is transformed into onanistic scenarios in which "a child is being beaten." "This being beaten is now a meeting-place between the sense of guilt and sexual love. It is not only the punishment for the forbidden genital relation, but also the regressive substitute for it, and from this latter source it derives the libidinal excitation which is from this time forward attached to it, and which finds its outlet in onanistic acts. Here for the first time we have the essence of masochism." "Boys being chastised and beaten, and especially being beaten on the penis; the heir to the throne being shut up in a narrow room and beaten." *La vida es sueño.*

Freud, "'A Child is being Beaten,'" 184; "From the History of an Infantile Neurosis," 494.

Sado-masochism is an endless, a vicious cycle; in which subject and object are confused; active and passive, male and female roles are exchanged, in the desire and pursuit of the whole, the combined object. Roles or clothes are exchanged: transvestitism. In the desire to be beaten by a woman, the woman is both father and mother; a composite figure, a Sphinx. The dreamer takes part in the pleasure of both parents; as an observer, or in fantasy; in an endless web of passive identifications. In a spectral world of onanistic gratification, "the child who produces the phantasy appears at most as spectator." Both the victim and the executioner; the spectator thrilled at his own execution.

Freud, "'A Child is being Beaten,'" 186.
Cf. Reik, *Masochism in Modern Man,* 23, 55. Fenichel, "The Psychology of Transvestitism."

Stuck together in eternal coitus: eternal lust and eternal punishment; eternal lust as eternal punishment. Tityos' punishment for raping Leto, an ever-growing liver forever being eaten up by vultures. Or Ixion's wheel; "the rotating movement clearly symbolizes coitus." The wheels of Enitharmon, "wheel without wheel, with cogs tyrannic." Or at the mill, the dark Satanic mills: "It is now clear why mills are frequently haunted. The revolving motion of the mill is coitus, the mill itself is the vagina." A permanent orgasm is an endless task, like carrying water in a sieve. The dream of work (*Beschäftigungstraum*), really endless work, is a dream of coitus as work, and therefore punishment. The unfinished task, the residue of the previous day, an ingredient in all dreams, in the basic dream.

Blake, *Jerusalem,* pl. 15, pl. 18. Roheim, *Gates of the Dream,* 507, 527; cf. 493–528.

Dreams of work (to do accounts, to learn a foreign language) are masturbation dreams. "Scrubbing the water-faucet till it is spotless": the punishment for self-pollution is masturbation. In the endless task there is no end-pleasure; it is sublimated coitus, that is to say work. So too the (onanistic) scenarios of masochism, with no definite termination, and the avoidance of end-pleasure (Reik's "suspense factor" in masochism). Souls that are not good enough for heaven and not bad enough for hell must keep riding till doomsday. Or the flying Dutchman —"The flying is an erection or masturbation dream with the body as phallus." But flight is also fright: "the flight of birds, the genitalization of anxiety."

Roheim, *Gates of the Dream,* 13, 492; cf. 493–495.

The endless task: to achieve the impossible, to find a male female (vaginal father) or a female male (phallic mother). It is to square the circle; the desire and pursuit of the whole in the form of dual unity or the combined object; the Satanic hermaphroditism of Antichrist. "A Wine-press of Love and Wrath, double, Hermaphroditic"; the sado-masochistic witches' brew.

> The plates and screws and wracks and saws and cords and fires and cisterns,
> The cruel joys of Luvah's Daughters, lacerating with knives
> And whips their Victims, and the deadly sport of Luvah's Sons.

They dance around the dying and they drink the howl and groan,
They catch the shrieks in cups of gold, they hand them to one another:
These are the sports of love, and these the sweet delights of amorous play.

Blake, *Jerusalem*, pl. 89, l. 4; *Milton*, pl. 27, ll. 34–39.
Cf. Roheim, *Gates of the Dream*, 517.

The endless task: psychoanalysis interminable. "Man is constitutionally attempting the constitutionally impossible" (Roheim). "We are born with a conflict between our older and our more recent heritage, and something in us that is rather vaguely defined in psychoanalysis as the ego is the organic defense against this inherent conflict. The struggle is eternal, the result never stable." Squaring the circle; the ego, like Atlas, stuck in between Father Sky and Mother Earth; trying to push the superego a little further up and away: working through the repressed material. "Where id was, there shall ego be. It is reclamation work, like the draining of the Zuyder Zee" (Freud).

Roheim, *The Origin and Function of Culture*, 99. *Gates of the Dream*, 545–546; Freud, *New Introductory Lectures*, 112.
Cf. Freud, "Analysis Terminable and Interminable."

The penis that is also a vagina, the subincised penis; a penis-womb and a penis-wound. The wholeness of the combined object is castration denied. Work is endless work, women's work. A man loses his manhood when he has to work. And gets it back again: until I labor, I in labor lie.

Cf. Roheim, *Eternal Ones of the Dream*, 164, 174. Feldman, "The Illusions of Work."

Squaring the circle, finding a male female or female male; incessantly renewed denial of the fact that there are human beings without a penis; it is the big lie, which makes the world go round. Or masturbation: "it is not true that I am deprived of pleasure (mamma), since I have my penis."

Roheim, *Gates of the Dream*, 398.
Cf. Fenichel, "The Psychology of Transvestitism," 180.

Castration denied. The big lie, a phony penis, a fetish. "He created a substitute for the penis which he missed in women, that is to say, a fetish. In so doing it is true that he had given the lie to reality, but he had saved his own penis." Or cutting of women's plaits of hair; "the action contains within it two incompatible propositions: the woman has still got a penis, and the father has castrated the woman."

Freud, "Splitting of the Ego," 374; "Fetichism," 203–204.
Cf. Brunswick, "The Accepted Lie," 458–464.

Cutting off women's hair woven into plaits; weaving a lie, a veil, a fetish; weaving a non-existent penis. "The Emperor's New Clothes": "We held that in a woman's dream a cloak stood for a man." Weaving the woman's pubic hair into a non-existent penis. "People say that women contributed but little to the discoveries and inventions of civilization, but perhaps after all they did discover one technical process, that of plaiting and weaving. If this is so, one is tempted to guess at the unconscious motive at the back of this achievement. Nature herself might be regarded as having provided a model for imitation, by causing pubic hair to grow at the period of sexual maturity so as to veil the genitals. The step that remained to be taken was to attach the hairs permanently together, whereas on the body they are fixed in the skin and only tangled with one another. If you repudiate this idea as being fantastic, and accuse me of having an *idée fixe* on the subject of the influence exercised by the lack of a penis upon the development of feminity, I cannot of course defend myself." But as it says at the end of the Greek tragedy, the fantastic turns out to be true.

Freud, *New Introductory Lectures,* 37, 170.

A tangle of hair, a tissue of lies. The web of social action. The complexities of intellectual systems; a web of deceit, a woof wove called Science. *Hyphen, hymen, hymn, hypnos.* The net or nexus. Networks of affiliation: the filial relation is not natural but artificial, threaded (*filum*). The binding ties or obligations. The close-knit groups. The seamless garment of the church or state. The shining looms of vegetation, where the tissue of the body is woven as a garment for the soul. Dürer's knots and Leonardo's concatenations. In the ascent of the soul, the doffing of garments, the slipping of knots, the loosing of bonds, disaffiliation: "the sum of these knots is called 'psyche'"—the complexes, or complications.

Jonas, *Gnostic Religion,* 166.
Cf. Govinda, *Foundations of Tibetan Mysticism,* 167. Eliade, "The 'God Who Binds' and the Symbolism of Knots." Blake, *First Book of Urizen,* pl. 19; *Night* I, 121–122. Dante, *De Monarchia,* III, 10. Augustine, *De Civitate Dei,* XVI, 41. Porphyry, *Cave of the Nymphs,* 14. Coomaraswamy, "Dürer's knots and Leonardo's concatenations," 109–125.

Woman, wife, thy name is weaving (*Weib, weben*).

Thou'rt my Mother from the Womb,
Wife, Sister, Daughter, to the Tomb,
Weaving to Dreams the Sexual strife
And weeping over the Web of Life.

Great Mother, Maya, Weaver of the World, the veil.

Blake, *The Gates of Paradise,* 771.
Cf. Zimmer, *The King and the Corpse,* 240; Swinburne, "Mater Triumphalis."

In the Apocalypse the chief thing to be unveiled is the great whore, Babylon, that great city which reigneth over the kings of the earth. Babylon is a whore: she it is with whom the kings of the earth have committed fornication. The mother of harlots is the mother of kings. In the Apocalypse, pomp, power and politics is discovered to be sex. Perverted sex; sado-masochistic sex; the inhabitants of the earth have been made drunk with the wine of her fornication, and she is drunken with the blood of the saints. Perverted sex; Satanic mills and looms: "The Male is a Furnace of beryll; the Female is a golden Loom." "A Wine-Press of Love and Wrath, double, Hermaphroditic." She is a phallic woman; Rahab, a Dragon red and hidden Harlot.

Revelations XVII, 2, 5. Blake, *Jerusalem*, pl. 5, l. 34.

Rahab, Babylon the Great, and all her Twenty-seven Heavens, now hid and now reveal'd.

> And these the names of the Twenty-seven Heavens & their
> Churches:
> Adam, Seth, Enos, Cainan, Mahalaleel, Jared, Enoch,
> Methuselah, Lamech: these are the Giants mighty,
> Hermaphroditic.
> Noah, Shem, Arphaxad, Cainan the Second, Salah, Heber,
> Peleg, Reu, Serug, Nahor, Terah: these are the Female Males,
> A Male within a Female hid as in an Ark & Curtains.
> Abraham, Moses, Solomon, Paul, Constantine, Charlemaine,
> Luther: these Seven are the Male Females, the Dragon Forms,
> The Female hid within a Male; thus Rahab is reveal'd,
> Mystery, Babylon the Great, the Abomination of Desolation,
> Religion hid in War, a Dragon red & hidden Harlot.
> But Jesus, breaking thro' the Central Zones of Death & Hell,
> Opens Eternity in Time & Space, triumphant in Mercy.

Blake, *Jerusalem*, pl. 76; cf. *Milton*, pl. 40.

The great whore is to be stripped. Her name is Mystery; to see her naked is to destroy the mystery. The mystery of sex is the mystery of kingship. The mystery is the deception, the non-existent penis, the clothes. "He substituted for her her clothes, which did away with the dreadful nakedness." Take away her clothes, the Emperor's New Clothes.

Fenichel, "The Psychology of Transvestitism," 173.

Political power is a web woven, a politic well-wrought veil; a veil of deceit, the veil of Maya. It is a non-existent cloth, the Emperor's New Clothes, made by the imperial fiat, the fiat of Marduk: "Open thy mouth: the cloth will vanish! Speak again, and the cloth shall be restored!" It is an endless task, as King Alfred learned from the spider.

Cf. Mendelsohn, *Religions of the Ancient Near East*, 31.

> Now that all classes of arts active in the government of the state have been distinguished, shall we go onto scrutinize Statesmanship and base our scrutiny of it on the art of weaving which provides our example for it?
>
> Most certainly.
>
> Then we must describe the kingly weaving-process.

The king in council is weaving the sacred robe, the royal *pallium* or palliative. The king in council is weaving a cloak of deceit, lying counsels, *metis* (μῆτιν ὑφαίνειν). Odysseus (as well as his wife) is a most ingenious weaver, *polymetis* Odysseus; so is Prometheus. Metis is a Lady, Mrs. Tweedy, Maya, the big lie. Metis was the first consort of King Zeus, whom Zeus swallowed, so that he might himself, in couvade, give birth to Athena (no slouch she either at weaving, as the spider-woman Arachne learnt to her cost). But the cloth is a fetish, the mother's penis. The word *metis* is the word *medea,* which means both "counsels" and male genitals. Both meanings are combined in a Homeric phrase where the image is of cutting, castrating, the *medea* of battle. Political power is a plait in the pubic hair, and the woman who plaits it is the king. In his royal robes he is a transvestite, Achilles hid among women, or Hercules, a knot tied in Omphale's apron or navel string.

Plato, *Politicus,* 305E. *Iliad,* XV, 467; XVI, 120.

Politics as transvestitism. "The content of the perversion was 'Phallic girls do exist: I myself am one.'" Political power is Athena, the phallic girl. Political power is a male female and a female male: Pallas Minerva, phallus Minerva, *mascula virgo* or virago, springing fully armed from the head of Zeus: the very personification of an erection, the embodiment of Fenichel's equation: girl = phallus, the equation contained in the root vir-go, or in the idea of maiden-head or virgin knot.

Fenichel, "The Psychology of Transvestitism," 175.

Zeus has an erection, in the head; and bears a child. And he bears a child via castration; his head is split by the blow of an axe. The father produces children from his head. Paternal power is not natural virility or paternity but castration denied; a lie, a veil made of the pubic hair of mother. "The father-image is a thin mask covering the image of the pre-Oedipal mother." "A great advance was made in civilization when men decided to put their inferences upon a level with the testimony of their sense and to make the step from matriarchy to patriarchy. The prehistoric figures which show a smaller person sitting upon the head of a larger one are representations of patrilineal descent; Athena had no mother, but sprang from the head of Zeus. A witness who testifies to something before a court of law is still called '*Zeuge*' [literally, 'begetter'] in German, after the part played by the male in the act of procreation; so too in hieroglyphics a 'witness' is represented pictorially by the male genitals." But the witness that stands up in the court is denying castration; the testimony is false testicles; and civilization a lie. "The concept of fatherhood is the beginning of idealistic thinking"; born from the head.

Feldman, "The Illusions of Work," 269. Freud, "A Case of Obsessional Neurosis," 368–369n.

All work is women's work. Every commodity is, as Marx says, a fetish, that is to say a non-existent penis. An investment. From feudal investiture to capitalistic investment, the manufacture of clothes for their own sake, not to be worn but to be saved in the hope chest. Instead of fixed robes and roles, fashion design and the endless search for identity: new personalities for old, turn in last year's model. The industrial revolution. Work is a masturbation dream, punishment for the Fall, which is falling asleep; and also a fall into division of the sexes.

> Locke sank into a swoon;
> The Garden died;
> God took the spinning-jenny
> Out of his side.

Yeats, "Fragments."

The work is endless, as on Penelope's loom, because the web of deceit is unbuilt even as it is upbuilded; dismantled every night. "It is not true that the child emerges from his experience of seeing the female parts with an unchanged belief in the woman having a phallus. He retains this belief but he also gives it up."

Freud, "Fetichism," 200.

This mantle covers the ends of the earth, *Weltenmantel und Himmelszelt.* It is the star-inwrought veil of the heavens, God's garment, reproduced in the robes of God's representatives in earth, the priest and the king. The spinning sisters, at the humming looms of time, weave a mantle of pestilence and war, concealing the divine humanity. It is the veil of the temple which the Savior born and dying rends; the clothes to be abandoned at the empty tomb. The frozen net, the rooted tree; the tree of Mystery, that spreads dismal shade and bears fruits of Deceit—

> The Gods of the earth and sea
> Sought thro' Nature to find this Tree;
> But their search was all in vain:
> There grows one in the Human Brain.

A rock, and a veil: woven on the rocky looms in the cave of the nymphs—

> The Twelve Daughters of Albion united in Rahab and Tirzah,
> A Double Female; and they drew out from the Rocky Stones
> Fibres of Life to Weave, for every Female is a Golden Loom,
> The Rocks are opake hardnesses covering all Vegetated things.

Blake, "The Human Abstract," *Songs of Experience; Jerusalem,* pl. 67, ll. 2–5.

Cf. Fyre, *Fearful Symmetry,* 136, 381. Porphyry, *Cave of the Nymphs,* 14. Eisler, *Weltenmantel und Himmelszelt.*

IV
Unity

Is there a way out; an end to analysis; a cure; is there such a thing as health?

To heal is to make whole, as in wholesome; to make one again; to unify or reunify: this is Eros in action. Eros is the instinct that makes for union, or unification, and Thanatos, the death instinct, is the instinct that makes for separation, or division.

Crazy Jane in William Butler Yeats—Crazy Jane who is both the student and the teacher—says,

> Nothing can be sole or whole
> That has not been rent.

We have been rent; there is no health in us. We must acknowledge the rents, the tears, the splits, the divisions; and then we can pray, as Freud prays at the end of *Civilization and Its Discontents*, "that the other of the two heavenly forces, eternal Eros, will put forth his strength so as to maintain himself alongside his equally immortal adversary."

Yeats, "Crazy Jane Talks with the Bishop."

There is only one political problem in our world today: the unification of mankind. The Internationale shall be the human race. That they may be one—*ut unum sint.* This is Christ's last prayer before the crucifixion, which was also the last prayer of the late Pope John; it must be set beside Freud's prayer in *Civilization and Its Discontents.* For indeed they will not be one until Freud and Pope John are found to speak in unison; or Freud and Marx and Pope John: the thing is to bring them together. John X, 16: Other sheep I have, which are not of this fold: them also must I bring, and they shall hear my voice; and there shall be one fold, and one shepherd.

John XVII, 21.

The unification of the human race: a mental fight, a struggle in and about men's minds. The rents, the tears, splits and divisions are mindmade; they are not based on the truth but on what the Buddhists call illusion, what Freud calls unconscious fantasies. The prevailing sense of reality, the prevailing forms of knowledge, are ruled by the instinct of aggression and division, are under the dominion of the death instinct. We are in Satan's kingdom; to build a Heaven in Hell's despite is to construct an erotic sense of reality.

To make in ourselves a new consciousness, an erotic sense of reality, is to become conscious of symbolism. Symbolism is mind making connections (correspondences) rather than distinctions (separations). Symbolism makes conscious interconnections and unions that were unconscious and repressed. Freud says, symbolism is on the track of a former identity, a lost unity: the lost continent, Atlantis, underneath the sea of life in which we live enisled; or perhaps even our union with the sea (Thalassa); oceanic consciousness; the unity of the whole cosmos as one living creature, as Plato said in the *Timaeus.*

Cf. Freud, "Interpretation of Dreams," 370.

Union and unification is of bodies, not souls. The erotic sense of reality unmasks the soul, the personality, the ego; because soul, personality and ego are what distinguish and separate us; they make us individuals, arrived at by dividing till you can divide no more—atoms. But psychic individuals, separate, unfissionable on the inside, impenetrable on the outside, are, like physical atoms, an illusion; in the twentieth century, in this age of fission, we can split the individual even as we can split the atom. Souls, personalities, and egos are masks, spectres, concealing our unity as body. For it is as one biological species that mankind is one—"the species-essence" that Karl Marx looked for; so that to become conscious of ourselves as body is to become conscious of mankind as one.

Cf. K. Marx and F. Engels, *Kleine ökonomische Schriften,* 42–166.

It is the erotic sense of reality that discovers the inadequacy of fraternity, or brotherhood. It is not adequate as a form for the reunification of the human race: we must be either far more deeply unified, or not at all. The true form of unification—which can be found either in psychoanalysis or in Christianity, in Freud or Pope John, or Karl Marx—is: "we are all members of one body." The true form of the unification of the human race is not the brothers, Cain and Abel, but Adam the first man, and Christ the second man: for as in Adam all die, even so in Christ shall all be made alive.

I Corinthians XV, 22. Cf. Daniélou, *Origen*, 205: "When we expound the dogma of the Mystical Body we do not take the dogma itself from Karl Marx but we do bring out the factors in it that correspond to what Karl Marx taught."

Christ is the second Adam; these two are one; there is only one man. This is not a new idea, but part of the great tradition, to be made new and alive today. St. Thomas Aquinas says, "many men are derived from Adam, as members of one body"—*tanquam membra unius corporis;* and, "the human race is to be considered as one body, which is called the mystical body, whose head is Christ himself, both with regard to the souls and with regard to the bodies"—*et quantum ad animas et quantum ad corpora.* The mystical body is not, because mystical, therefore non-bodily. And St. Augustine: "the whole human race which was to become Adam's posterity through the first woman, was present in the first man." "We all existed in that one man, since, taken together, we were the one man who fell into sin." Even as in Hebrew *adham* is man and mankind in one; and the man Adam. "All mankind, whose life from Adam to the end of this world is as the life of one man."

St. Thomas Aquinas in Gierke, *Political Theories of the Middle Age*, 103, n.7. Augustine, *De Civitate Dei*, XIII, 3–14, *de vera religione*, 27, 50. Cf. Pedersen, *Israel*, I, 110. Ladner, *The Idea of Reform*, 264–265.

And the resurrection is the resurrection of the body; but not the separate body of the individual, but the body of mankind as one body. The fall of man is the fall into division of the human race, the dismemberment of the first man, Adam; and the resurrection or rebirth through the second man, Christ, is to reconstitute the lost unity. "His fall into Division & his Resurrection to Unity"; till we all come to one perfect man. St. Athanasius, commenting on Christ's last prayer, "that they may be all one, as Thou in Me, and I in Thee," says it means that "born as it were by Me, they may all be one body and one spirit, and may combine to form one perfect man . . . so that, made divine, they may be one in us." The unification of mankind into one is also the unification of humanity and divinity; St. Gregory of Nyssa says, "Christ, by whom all mankind was united into divinity." Unification is deification.

Blake, *Night* I, l. 21. Scheeben, *Mysteries*, 367n., 386n.
Cf. Augustine, *De Civitate Dei*, XXII, 17–18. Dante, *De Monarchia*, I, 8.
Ephesians IV, 13; John XVII, 21.

If we are all members of one body, then in that one body there is neither male nor female; or rather there is both: it is an androgynous or hermaphroditic body, containing both sexes. In this way St. Augustine explains that other old story: the creation of Eve out of the rib of Adam. "God did not wish to create the woman who was to be mated with man in the same way that He created man, but, rather, out of him, in order that the whole human race might be derived entirely from one single man." The division of the one man into two sexes is part of the fall; sexes are sections.

Galatians III, 28. Augustine, *De Civitate Dei*, XII, 21.

Hence according to the Epistle to the Ephesians the true meaning of the mystery of sexual intercourse is that it is a symbolic representation, or adumbration, of that mystical body in which we are all members of one body.

So ought men to love their wives as their own bodies. He that loveth his wife loveth himself.

For no man ever yet hated his own flesh; but nourisheth and cherisheth it, even as the Lord the church.

For we are members of his body, of his flesh, and of his bones.

For this cause shall a man leave his father and mother, and shall be joined unto his wife, and they two shall be one flesh.

This is a great mystery: but I speak concerning Christ and the church.

Ephesians V, 28–32.

The fantastic hypothesis of Freud in *Beyond the Pleasure Principle* and Ferenczi in *Thalassa* turns out to be right after all. The tendency of the sexual instinct is to restore an earlier state of things, an earlier state of unity, before life was sexually differentiated; ultimately going back to a state "before living substance was torn apart into separate particles." Freud illustrated his hypothesis with the myth in Plato's *Symposium*, deriving sexual differentiation from the bisection of a primal hermaphroditic body.

Freud, *Beyond the Pleasure Principle*, 79–80.

What else is to be found in psychoanalysis, by those determined to find, about the one body, the mystical body? The truth, the healing truth, the wholesome truth, the truth that will make us whole, is not in individual psychology, nor in the currently so fashionable ego psychology, but in what the later Freud called "mass-psychology." Freud said his last work, *Moses and Monotheism*, was an attempt "to translate the concepts of individual psychology into mass-psychology." "Mass-psychology" is not mob psychology, but the psychology of mankind as a whole, as one mass, or one body. Mass, then, in the same sense as Augustine's *massa perditionis; universa massa in vitiata radice damnata.* The word "en-masse."

Cf. Augustine, *De Civitate Dei,* XIV, 26. Whitman, "One's-Self I Sing."

Psychoanalysis is always the discovery of the unconscious; the turn to mass-psychology corresponds to the discovery that the unconscious is collective. As early as *Totem and Taboo* (1913), Freud took as the basis of his whole position the existence of a "collective mind," or "mass-psyche"—the German is *Massenpsyche*—and he remained steadfast to that basis in *Massenpsychologie* (1921) and *Moses* (1937): "a mass-psyche in which psychological processes occur as they do in the psyche of an individual." The defect in this statement is the implication that individual minds, as well as a group mind, are real. In *Moses and Monotheism* Freud disallows the term "collective unconscious," because it suggests that there might be some other kind of unconscious which is not collective; then comes his statement: "The content of the unconscious is collective anyhow, a general possession of all mankind." Since the true psychic reality is the unconscious, the true psychic reality is collective; there is only one psyche, a general possession of mankind.

Freud, *Moses and Monotheism,* 208; *Totem and Taboo,* 157.

The goal of psychotherapy is psychic integration; but there is no integration of the separate individual. The individual is obtained by division; integration of the individual is a strictly self-contradictory enterprise, as becomes evident in the futile attempts of the therapists to define "what we mean by mental health" in the individual person. The goal of "individuation," or of replacing the ego by the "self," deceitfully conceals the drastic break between the *principium individuationis* and the Dionysian, or drunken, principle of union, or communion, between man and man and between man and nature. The integration of the psyche is the integration of the human race, and the integration of the world with which we are inseparably connected. Only in one world can we be one. The inner voice, the personal salvation, the private experience are all based on an illusory distinction. Consciousness is as collective as the unconscious; there is only one psyche, ego-cosmic, in relation to which all conflict is endopsychic, all war intestine. Hence, when Cain slew Abel he slew himself: "for the soul, not belonging to the category of things separate from each other but under the category of things which form a single whole, must necessarily suffer what it seems to do."

Philo, *That the Worse is wont to Attack the Better,* XV.
Cf. Klein and Riviere, *Love, Hate and Reparation,* 61, 66, 68.

In the collective unconscious Freud finds what he calls an "archaic heritage," or "phylogenetic inheritance." "Phylogenetic inheritance," i.e., belonging to the "species-essence" of the human species. "Archaic heritage," i.e., archetypes; at any rate the phylogenetic factor is the symbolic factor, the former identity or lost unity which symbolic consciousness recovers. "There probably exists in the mental life of the individual not only what he has experienced himself, but also what he brought with him at birth, fragments of a phylogenetic origin, an archaic heritage." Not in entire forgetfulness do we come. Freud comes to the conclusion that "the archaic heritage of mankind includes not only dispositions, but also ideational contents, memory traces of the experiences of former generations." The nucleus of neurosis turns out to be precisely in this phylogenetic factor: not in the individual's own murderous impulses against his individual father, but in the primal crime against the primal parent or parents. For Freud, then, in the end, as for Christianity, in Adam's fall we sinned all, and there is just that one collective sickness of the human race in all its generations: we are all in the same boat, or body.

Freud, *Moses and Monotheism,* 157, 159; cf. 208–209.

Another signpost pointing in the same direction is the term *id,* which, in the later Freud, is the opposite of the term *ego;* as, in the earlier Freud, consciousness is the opposite of the unconscious. The *id* is instinct; that Dionysian "cauldron of seething excitement," a sea of energy out of which the ego emerges like an island. The term "*id*"—"it"—taken from Nietzsche (via Groddeck), is based on the intuition that the conduct through life of what we call our ego is essentially passive; it is not so much we who live as that we are lived, by unknown forces. The reality is instinct, and instinct is impersonal energy, an "it" who lives in us. I live, yet not I, but it lives in me; as in creation, *fiat.* Let it be; no "I," but an it. The "I-Thou" relationship is still a relation to Satan; the old Adversary; the Accuser; to whom we are responsible; or old Nobodaddy in the garden, calling, Adam, where art thou? Let there be no one to answer to.

Freud, *New Introductory Lectures,* 98; *The Ego and the Id,* 27. Cf. Wilhelm and Jung, *Secret of the Golden Flower,* 131–132. Galatians II, 20.

The unconscious, then, is not a closet full of skeletons in the private house of the individual mind; it is not even, finally, a cave full of dreams and ghosts in which, like Plato's prisoners, most of us spend most of our lives—

The unconscious is rather that immortal sea which brought us hither; intimations of which are given in moments of "oceanic feeling"; one sea of energy or instinct; embracing all mankind, without distinction of race, language, or culture; and embracing all the generations of Adam, past, present, and future, in one phylogenetic heritage; in one mystical or symbolical body.

Cf. Freud, *Civilization and Its Discontents,* ch. I.

V
Person

Hobbes, *Leviathan,* ch. XVI, "Of Persons, Authors, and things Personated"—

> The word Person is latine: instead whereof the Greeks have πρόσωπον, which signifies the Face as *Persona* in latine signifies the *disguise*, or *outward appearance* of a man, counterfeited on the Stage; and sometimes more particularly that part of it, which disguiseth the face, as a Mask or Visard: And from the Stage, hath been translated to any Representer of speech and action, as well in Tribunalls, as Theaters. So that a *Person,* is the same that an *Actor* is, both on the Stage and in common Conversation.

Hobbes, *Leviathan,* 133–134.

Personality is *persona,* a mask. The world is a stage, the self a theatrical creation: "The self, then, as a performed character, is not an organic thing that has a specific location, whose fundamental fate is to be born, to mature, to die: it is a dramatic effect arising diffusely from a scene that is presented." The self does not belong to its possessor. "He and his body merely provide the peg on which something of a collaborative manufacture will be hung for a time. The means for producing and maintaining selves do not reside inside the peg. . . . There will be a team of persons whose activity on stage in conjunction with available props will constitute the scene from which the performed character's self will emerge, and another team, the audience, whose interpretive activity will be necessary for this emergence."

Goffman, *The Presentation of Self in Everyday Life,* 252–253.

It is all psychodrama. The symptom is a dramatized wish; neurosis endows reality with a special meaning and a secret significance. "'I have a little dog and they want to take it away from me." "The dog was his disease, his personality, and his penis." Sickness is all shamming, role-playing, acting-out. And so is therapy; in the transference, the patient is acting out, reënacting, new editions of old conflicts. Social groups are theatrical groups, for group therapy.

Roheim, *Magic and Schizophrenia,* 101; cf. 10.
Cf. Freud, "Loss of Reality in Neurosis and Psychosis," 282; "Recollection, Repetition and Working Through," 369.

Masks, or names—

This loam, this rough-cast, and this stone doth show
That I am that same wall; the truth is so—
Thus have I, Wall, my part discharged so;
And, being done, thus Wall away doth go.

The name makes it so; *vocare est invocare.* It's all in a name. I'm a noun, the schizophrenic girl said—Crazy Jane said—noun, none, nun. I'm a nomen or no man; my name is no man, Odysseus, Everyman, said.

Cf. Laing, *Divided Self*, 223.

Names are taboo; primitive man regards his name not as an external label but as an essential part of his personality. Neurotics likewise: "One of these taboo patients of my acquaintance had adopted a rule against writing her own name for fear that it might fall into the hands of someone who would then be in possession of a portion of her personality." "Our children do the same." It is not that children, neurotics, and primitives are so stupid as to be unable to discriminate between words and things; it is that they are not so repressed as to be unaware that personality is a social fiction, and a name a magical invocation of a particular role in the social drama.

Freud, *Totem and Taboo*, 56.

The mask is magic. Character is not innate: a man's character is his *demon*, his tutelar spirit; received in a dream. His character is his destiny, which is to act out his dream.

> When a boy is to be thus initiated, he is put under an alternate course of physic and fasting, either taking no food whatever, or swallowing the most powerful and nauseous medicines, and occasionally he is made to drink decoctions of an intoxicating nature, until his mind becomes sufficiently bewildered, so that he sees visions and has extraordinary dreams, for which, of course, he has been prepared beforehand. He will fancy himself flying through the air, walking under ground, stepping from one ridge or hill to the other across the valley beneath, fighting and conquering giants and monsters and defeating whole hosts by his single arm. . . . When a boy has been initiated, a name is given to him analogous to the visions he has seen, and to the destiny that

is supposed to be prepared for him. The boy, imagining all that happened to him while under perturbation to have been real, sets out in the world with lofty notions of himself, and animated with courage for the most desperate undertakings.

Roheim, *Magic and Schizophrenia,* 54–55, quoting Frazer, *Totemism and Exogamy,* III, 395.

The dream-stuff out of which personality is made is not private, but social; a collective dream.

In each clan is to be found a set of names called the names of childhood. These names are more of titles than of cognomens. They are determined upon by sociologic and divinistic modes, and are bestowed in childhood as the verity names or titles of the children to whom given. But this body of names relating to any one totem—for instance, to one of the beast totems—will not be the name of the totem beast itself, but will be names both of the totem in its various conditions and of various parts of the totem, or of its functions, or of its attributes, actual or mythical. Now these parts or functions, or attributes of the parts or functions, are subdivided also in a six-fold manner, so that the name relating to one member of the totem—for example, like the right arm or leg of the animal thereof—would correspond to the north, and would be the first in honor in a clan (not itself of the northern group); then the name relating to another member—say to the left leg or arm and its powers, etc.—would pertain to the west and would be second in honor; and another member—say the right foot—to the south and would be third in honor; and of another member—say the left foot—to the east and would be fourth in honor; to another—say the head—to the upper regions and would be fifth in honor; and another—say the tail—to the lower region and would be sixth in honor; while the heart or the navel and center of the being would be first as well as last in honor. . . .

With such a system of arrangement as all this may be seen to be, with such a facile device for symbolizing the arrangement (not only according to number of the regions and their subdivisions in their relative succession and the succession of their elements and seasons, but also in colours attributed to them, etc.) and, finally, with such an arrangement of names correspondingly classified and of terms of relationship significant of rank rather than of consanguinal connection, mistake in the order of a ceremonial, a procession or a council is simply impossible, and the people employing such devices may be said to have written and to be writing their statutes and laws in all their daily relationships and utterances.

F. H. Cushing cited in Mauss, "La notion de personne," 338–339.

The fund of personality, the fund of soul-stuff available, is fixed and collective. The only soul is the group-soul, and this consists of nothing but group functions.

Cf. Cornford, *From Religion to Philosophy*, 95.

Personality is not innate, but acquired. Like a mask, it is a thing, a fetish, a fetishistic object or commodity. "I consent that Isis shall search into me, and that my name shall pass from my breast into hers." The real name of the god, with which his power was inextricably bound up, was supposed to be lodged, in an almost physical sense, somewhere in his breast, from which Isis extracted it by a sort of surgical operation and transferred it with all its supernatural powers to herself. In the famous potlatch cultures of the Indians of the northwest coast, what is wagered, won, and lost, is personality, incorporated not only in the name but also in a variety of emblematic objects; in masks; also blankets, and bits of copper.

Frazer, *The Golden Bough*, 261.
Cf. Mauss, "La notion de personne," 342, 344–345.

The fund of personality types in a given culture is fixed and hereditary. "They never change their names from the beginning, when the first human beings existed in the world; for names cannot go out of the family of the head chiefs of the numayms, only to the eldest one of the children of the head chief." "Earth-maker, in the beginning, sent four men from above, and when they came to this earth everything that happened to them was utilized in making proper names. . . . As they had come from above so from that fact has originated a name Comes-from-above. . . . When they came, there was a drizzling rain and hence the names Walking-in-mist, Comes-in-mist, Drizzling-rain. . . . Now the thunderbirds come with terrible thunder-crashes. Everything on the earth, animals, plants, everything, is deluged with rain. Terrible thunder-crashes resound everywhere. From all this a name is derived and that is my name—Crashing-Thunder."

P. Radin cited in Mauss, "La notion de personne," 342.

Fixed personalities; unchanging masks; character is carving. When Marcus Aurelius says, "carve your mask," he means "develop your character." Stereotypes. All personality is rigid—"This is the way to do things, and this is the only way"—magical, and mechanical; a mechanization of a particular way of reacting"; a repetition-compulsion. A compulsion to perpetuate an identity established in previous incarnations: character is karmic.

> At the death of the human incarnation, the divine spirit transmigrates into another man. The Buddhist Tartars believe in a great number of living Buddhas, who officiate as Grand Lamas at the head of the most important monasteries. When one of these Grand Lamas dies his disciples do not sorrow, for they know that he will soon reappear, being born in the form of an infant. Their only anxiety is to discover the place of his birth. . . . When at last they find the child they fall down and worship him. Before, however, he is acknowledged as the Grand Lama whom they seek he must satisfy them of his identity. He is asked the name of the monastery of which he claims to be the head, how far off it is, and how many monks live in it; he must also describe the habits of

the deceased Grand Lama and the manner of his death. Then various articles, as prayer-books, tea-pots, and cups, are placed before him, and he has to point out those used by himself in his previous life. If he does so without a mistake his claims are admitted, and he is conducted in triumph to the monastery.

Frazer, *The Golden Bough,* 102–103.
Cf. Ferenczi, "The Adaptation of the Family to the Child," 66. Roheim, *Magic and Schizophrenia,* 81, 83.

Thus names and personalities are fixed by archetypal persons and situations; the voices coming through the masks are always ancestral voices. The masquerade or carnival is a *danse macabre,* a visit of ancestral spirits, represented by the authorized bearers of their persons. The life of the clan consists in the perpetual reincarnation of ancestors—a reincarnation achieved by magic, by imitation (identification), by dramatic representation.

Cf. Eliade, *The Myth of the Eternal Return,* ch. I.

Ancestral voices prophesying war; ancestral spirits in the *danse macabre* or war dance; Valhalla, ghostly warriors who kill each other and are reborn to fight again. All warfare is ghostly, every army an *exercitus feralis,* every soldier a living corpse. The dead and the living who fought together at Marathon are indistinguishable.

Cf. Höfler, *Germanisches Sakralkönigtum,* I, 160–167, 188, 220, 242. Roheim, *Gates of the Dream,* ch. X, I. "Feralis Exercitus."

Larva means mask; or ghost. *Larvatus,* masked, a personality—*larvatus prodeo* (Descartes); it also means mad, a case of demoniacal possession. *Larva* is also "the immature form of animals characterized by metamorphosis"; in the grub state; before their transformation into a pupa, or pupil; i.e., before their initiation. Children are reincarnated ghosts.

Cf. Descartes, *Cogitationes privatae,* 213.

> Among the Lapps, when a woman was with child and near the time of her delivery, a deceased ancestor or relation used to appear to her in a dream and inform her what dead person was to be born again in her infant, and whose name the child was therefore to bear. If the woman had no such dream, it fell to the father or the relatives to determine the name by divination or by consulting a wizard. Among the Khonds a birth is celebrated on the seventh day after the event by a feast given to the priest and to the whole village. To determine the child's name the priest drops grains of rice into a cup of water, naming with each grain a deceased ancestor. From the movements of the seed in the water, and from observations made on the person of the infant, he pronounces which of his progenitors has reappeared in him, and the child generally, at least among the northern tribes, receives the name of that ancestor. Among the Yorubas, soon after a child has been born, a priest of Ifa, the god of divination, appears on the scene to ascertain what ancestral soul has been reborn in the infant. As soon as this has been decided, the parents are told that the child must conform in all respects to the manner of life of the ancestor who now animates him or her, and if, as often happens, they profess ignorance, the priest supplies the necessary information. The child usually receives the name of the ancestor who has been born again in him.

Frazer, *The Golden Bough,* 256.

We are such stuff as dreams are made on. "The *altjira* (ancestor of the mythical period), the *ngantja* (hidden double), the *kuruna* (soul), and the *rella ndurpa* (real person), are all identical in one sense though different in another." The *altjira,* the ancestors with whom we are identical, are "the people of the dream" or the Eternal

Ones of the Dream. And, "a father always 'finds' his child in a dream. . . . In his dream he sees the spirit child standing on his head and catches it in his hand after which it enters his wife."

Roheim, *Eternal Ones of the Dream,* 98; cf. 149, 210–211; *Gates of the Dream,* 111; cf. 105, 112–113.

"A PERSON, is he, *whose words or actions are considered, either as his own, or as representing the words or actions of another man. . . .* When they are considered as his owne, then he is called a *Naturall Person:* And when they are considered as representing the words and actions of another, then is he a *Feigned* or *Artificiall person.*" A person is always a feigned or artificial person, *persona ficta.* A person is never himself but always a mask; a person never owns his own person, but always represents another, by whom he is possessed. And the other that one is, is always ancestors; one's soul is not one's own, but daddy's. This is the meaning of the Oedipus Complex.

Hobbes, *Leviathan,* 133.

From the primitive mask to the modern personality, through three intermediate reorganizations of the theater: Roman law, Stoic ethics, Christian theology.

Cf. Mauss, "La notion de personne."

Roman law, the Roman jurists say, is concerned with three things only, persons, things, and actions. Roman law is a set of rules for a new theater of judicial and political process, the *respublica* or public realm. "The organization of the *polis,* physically secured by the wall around the city and physiognomically guaranteed by its law—lest the succeeding generations change its identity beyond recognition—is a kind of organized remembrance. It assures the mortal actor that his passing existence and fleeting greatness will never lack the reality that comes from being seen, being heard, and, generally, appearing before an audience." "Action, in so far as it engages in founding and preserving political bodies, creates the condition for remembrance, that is, for history." "That is why the theater is the political art par excellence." Solon and Thespis, these two, are one: a new theatricality, a new histrionic sensibility.

Arendt, *The Human Condition*, 10, 167, 176–177.
Cf. Else, "The Origin of Τραγῳδία."

Action is what takes place in front of the camera, with the lights turned on, to throw the rest of reality into darkness (scotomisation, repression); action takes place in Plato's cave. Those for whom not to be seen is non-existence are not alive; and the kind of existence they seek, the immortality they seek, is spectral; to be seen is the ambition of ghosts, and to be remembered the ambition of the dead. The public realm is the stage for heroic action, and heroes are spectres of the living dead. The passport which grants access to the public realm, which distinguishes master from slave, the essential political virtue, is the courage to die, to commit suicide, to make one's life a living death. "One must pay dearly for immortality: one has to die several times while still alive."

Nietzsche, *Ecce Homo* (*The Portable Nietzsche*), 660.

Heroic individualism is identification with ancestors in a new space and a new time: the new space is the public realm; the new time is history. Greek Tragedy is the imitation of an action; Roman real action, as opposed to the childish stage plays of the Greeks, is what takes place on the stage of history. Identification with ancestors, instead of being an occasional ritual, is now a life destiny, is enacted in a whole life (of public service). Instead of the cyclic recurrence of a temporary role, the historical personage offers a continuous performance and achieves a continuous existence; not for a moment but for all time; an individual embodiment of the ancestral soul or dream.

Cf. Arendt, *The Human Condition,* 8–9. Roheim, *Animism,* 143. Kris, *Psychoanalytic Explorations in Art,* 81–83. Bentzen, *King and Messiah,* 32–38.

And in legal actions: Kant says, "If I look at public law and abstract from its matter or empirical elements, then there remains the form of publicity. The possibility of this publicity, every legal title implies. Without it there could be no justice, which can only be thought of as before the eyes of men." The action, in the courtroom, or in the political arena, is a trial or contest, an agon, as in the Greek stage plays, in which "the parties litigant are not definite individuals, but abstract persons in the mask of plaintiff and defendant."

Kant, *Perpetual Peace,* 44–45. Ihering in J. Frank, *Law and the Modern Mind,* 218.

Those entitled to stage an appearance in the public realm, the actors as opposed to the chorus, are juristic persons. A slave, the Roman jurists say, has no *persona;* the Greek jurists say he is without face (απρόσωπος) and hence is represented—the Greeks say "characterized"—by his master. There is a vestige of this distinction in the requirement of a property qualification for voters: "The true reason," says Blackstone (quoted by Alexander Hamilton), "of requiring any qualification, with regard to property in voters, is to exclude such persons as are in so mean a situation, that they are esteemed to have no will of their own." No substance, no soul, no suffrage. The ego is public relations.

Hamilton cited in Scott, *Political Thought in America*, 58–59.

The new juristic personality created by the Romans is, like a Kwakiutl mask, hereditary. Roman law showed subsequent civilizations how to accomplish the magical metamorphosis of living persons into reincarnations of the dead by new, even more binding methods. In the Roman law of inheritance, says Henry Maine, "the notion was that, though the physical person of the deceased had perished, his legal personality survived and descended unimpaired on his Heir or Co-Heirs, in whom his identity (so far as the law was concerned) was continued." This is the principle of "universal succession," whereby the heir "is invested with the legal clothing of another," is "instantly clothed with his entire legal person"; so that "in the old Roman Law of Inheritance, the notion of a will or testament is inextricably bound up, I might almost say confounded, with the theory of a man's posthumous existence in the person of his heir—the elimination of the fact of death." Compare Roheim: "What is the basis of inheritance? A retention of the past. The great man is not dead; his psychological identification with his son is taken to be real."

Maine, *Ancient Law*, 179, 181, 189–190. Roheim, *Riddle of the Sphinx*, 233.

The king never dies (Kantorowicz). "The temple of the Baganda kings, with their hereditary courts, keeping the past alive by perpetual reënactment." "For purposes of Roman Testamentary Jurisprudence each individual citizen was a Corporation sole," like the English king.

Everything turns on the continuity of succession. The immortal corporation, the *universitas juris* of universal succession, never dies: *universitas non moritur.* The legal fictions of the West correspond to the metaphysical fictions of the East. The immortal corporation corresponds to the immortal soul which carries the succession to the Grand Lama of Tibet. In both cases there is the man's posthumous existence in the person of his heir, the elimination of the fact of death. The Western legal fiction, with its fetishism (personification) of the property, its reification of persons, eliminates the facts more completely, by eliminating the moment of truth, the interregnum, the search for the new incarnation. Modern (Western) legalistic rationalism does not get away from magic: on the contrary, it makes the magical effects so permanent and so pervasive that we do not notice them at all. But only God can make an heir.

Maine, *Ancient Law,* 187, 182. Chadwick, *Poetry and Prophecy,* 44. Cf. Kantorowicz, *The King's Two Bodies,* chs. VI and VII.

"God planted in men a strong desire also of propagating their kind, and of continuing themselves in their posterity"; this is the basis of inheritance, according to Locke. Patrilineal inheritance is not for the sake of the sons, but for the sake of the defunct father—*hereditas non heredis personam sed defuncti sustinet.* This the classical Western patriarchy. In "universal succession" the family is a corporation of which the paterfamilias is the representative, its public officer, or head. The paterfamilias in his own person incorporates the corporation, embodies its soul (dream) stuff. In patriarchy the living father is the incarnate ancestors; *praesens deus;* an ever present godhead; an owner: for a king, to be a god is to own land instead of being merely the god's steward. The result is an immortal corporation, with an ever present representative, and continuity of succession. "Immediately on the death of the father ownership is, so to say, continued"; and the gloss on this passage of Justinian's *Institutes* says, "Father and son are one according to the fiction of the law"—*pater et filius unum fictione juris sunt.*" Father and son are *identified.*

Locke, *Treatise of Civil Government*, 62. Kantorowicz, *The King's Two Bodies*, 338.
Cf. Maine, *Ancient Law*, 184, 186. Noyes, *Property*, 101–104.

In fraternal organization, in the primitive mask culture, the ancestors, the Eternal Ones of the Dream, are distinct from the living. The son is an ancestor reincarnated, but not a continuation of his father; he is his grandfather (reincarnated), but not his father. The distinction between generations, the unity of the generations (the brothers) is preserved. The rhythm is not continuity but alternation (oscillation) between generations; my son is my father reborn, and as such to be respected by me; the integrity of the separate generations is preserved. In patrilineal inheritance my son is a continuation of me; I incorporate him, swallow him (Cronus swallowing his children). In fraternal organization my son was my father; in swallowing him I have swallowed my father. So in patriarchy I become my own father, *pater sui;* by parricide; and deny the deed: the king never dies.

Cf. Granet, *Chinese Civilization*, Bk II, ch. V. Roheim, *Riddle of the Sphinx*, 233. Bachofen, *Das Mutterrecht*, 435–436.

The Stoic reorganization of the theater is contained in the word conscience; *conscientia* (συνείδησις); literally, "joint-knowing"; as in complicity; or witnessing. Conscience is what Freud in his later writings called the super-ego; which in earlier writings he more eloquently called the "watching-institution." The construction of the super-ego moves the open-air theater indoors. Action, which is action only if displayed, is now displayed to an internal observer; a super-ego looking down from above; the god in the gallery, watching his children play. In the primitive mask culture, the person makes visible the other that one is (is not), namely, ancestors. The super-ego is constructed by internalizing the ancestors. The self unifies itself with the other by splitting itself into both self and other; withdrawing the imitation of ancestors into its own invisible interior. And the process of withdrawing the external drama into the interior is itself dramatic. The process which Freud calls identification with parents, or incorporation of parents, is an imitation of them, a mimesis of them. Freud says that the condition for giving up an external love-object is to make out of oneself a substitute for the lost object; part of the ego dresses up as father and says to the id, "Look, I am so like father, you can just as well love me instead." So Roheim can say, "By personality we mean that each individual grows up by wearing a mask, by imitating one of his parents."

Roheim, *Psychoanalysis and Anthropology,* 12; cf. *Magic and Schizophrenia,* 45.
Cf. Freud, "On Narcissism," 54n; *The Ego and the Id,* 37.

Some capital texts in the New Testament tell us that God is no respecter of persons—*οὐ προσωπολήπτης*; "not taken by masks"; not captivated, not crazy about them; not taken in, not deceived by them. This is the God in whom "there is neither Jew nor Greek, there is neither bond nor free, there is neither male nor female, for ye all are one in Christ Jesus." This God cares not for visible distinctions; or visible achievements, outer works. The faith that saves is internal and invisible. Christian virtue, St. Augustine says, is of a kind that "cannot be displayed before men's eyes"; "take heed that ye do not your alms before men, to be seen of them." Here is the deeper root of the Augustinian and Puritanical opposition to the theater. But the theatrical is the political; this Christianity is subversive of the public realm. Hannah Arendt quotes Tertullian: *nec ulla magis res aliena quam publica,* no concern is more alien to us than the public concern or republic. My kingdom is not of this world: not of this world of outward appearance, this vain show. It is a real kingdom, not a spectral theatrical show.

Acts X, 34; Romans II, 11; Galatians III, 28; Ephesians VI, 9; Colossians III, 25; Matthew VI, 1. Arendt, *The Human Condition,* 65–66. Augustine, *De Civitate Dei,* I, 28.

God does not go for personalities; nor does the Last Judgment consist in the award of prizes to personalities for the performance of their parts. The performance principle must go; the show must not go on. The parts are not real: for ye are all one in Christ Jesus; he is not your personal Saviour. In the Last Judgment the apocalyptic fire will burn up the masks, and the theater, leaving not a rack behind. Freud came to give the show away; the outcome of psychoanalysis is not "ego psychology" but the doctrine of "anatta" or no-self: the ego is a "me-fabrication" (*ahamkara*), a piece of illusion (*Maya*), which disintegrates at the moment of illumination: "the self has been completely understood, and so ceases to be." And with the doctrine of no-self goes the doctrine of non-action: action is proper only to an ignorant person, and doing nothing is, if rightly understood, the supreme action.

Cf. Powell, *Zen and Reality,* 49, 69. Nikhilananda, *Bhagavad Gita,* 15. Durckheim, *The Japanese Cult of Tranquillity,* 88–89. Marcuse, *Eros and Civilization,* 44, 75, 89. Mauss, "La notion de personne," 348.

But I Samuel XVI, 7: "For Jehovah seeth not as man seeth; for man looketh on the outward appearance, but Jehovah looketh on the heart." Christian virtue is displayed to an even more exacting audience than the Stoic conscience. Jeremiah XVII, 10: "I, Jehovah, search the heart, I try the reins, even to give every man according to his ways, and according to the fruit of his doings." Christian personality remains a self-dramatization of the son enacted before the eyes of the heavenly father. In the sight of this spectator, personality ceases to be a social or political role (we take from our earthly fathers to give to our heavenly father); all performers are immediate and unique; the distinction between public and private disappears; we are on stage all the time. Christianity will not be rid of the performance principle, will not become a pure principle of invisible grace, until it gets rid of the spectre of the Father, Old Noboddady, the watching institution.

The God who is no respecter of persons is yet himself God in three Persons. The Athanasian Creed says that we worship One God in Trinity, and Trinity in Unity; neither confounding the Persons, nor dividing the Substance. God is three Persons: the Father is God, the Son is God, and the Holy Ghost is God. For like as we are compelled by the Christian verity to acknowledge every Person by himself to be God and Lord; So are we forbidden by the Catholic religion to say, There be three Gods, or three Lords. And of Christ it says that he is God and Man: God, of the Substance of the Father, begotten before the worlds; and Man, of the Substance of his Mother, born in the world; Who although he be God and Man—yet he is not two, but one Christ; One; not by conversion of the Godhead into flesh, but by the taking of the Manhood into God; One altogether: not by confusion of Substance, but by unity of Person.

Cf. Schlossmann, *Persona und πρόσωπον im Recht und im Christlichen Dogma.*

The Athanasian Creed is a doctrine of representation, or impersonation. Hobbes: "A Person, (as I have shewn before, chapt. 13) is he that is Represented, as often as hee [*sic*] is Represented; and therefore God, who has been Represented (that is, Personated) thrice, may properly enough be said to be three Persons; though neither the word *Person*, nor *Trinity* be ascribed to him in the Bible. . . . For so God the Father, as Represented by Moses, is one Person; and as Represented by his Sonne, another Person; and as Represented by the Apostles, and by the Doctors that taught by authority from them derived, is a third Person, and yet every Person here, is the Person of one and the same God." The Trinity is a doctrine of the masks of God. In this play God is one, but three actors take his part; and yet it is not a part but the whole of God that they represent.

Hobbes, *Leviathan*, 430.

The complicated dramaturgy of the Athanasian Creed is a new interpretation of the old story—the drama of the incarnation (or reincarnation) of God in Man. What it seems to assert is the mystical transformation of the actor into the part—the absorption of the Manhood into the Godhead; the Son into the Father (I and my Father are one); and the mystical transformation of the part into the whole. But if the actor is really transformed into the part, and the part is the whole; then mask is reality, and persona finally acquires the modern sense of the personality as the real self. *Persona est substantia rationalis individua:* "a person is a rational individual substance." Substance, Latin *substantia,* is what stands underneath (the mask); but also that which stands by itself or in itself and not in another. A person is a mask which has grown into the body, grown one with the body; which became permanent when the drama was internalized: which became indivisible from the body when it became invisible; a part which is a whole: "some things can exist apart and some cannot, and it is the former that are substances" (Aristotle); an individual, a part which is a whole; that finite substance which Spinoza exposed as a nonentity.

John X, 30. Cassiodorus cited in Mauss, "La notion de personne," 358. Cf. Wolfson, *The Philosophy of Spinoza*, I, 63.

The black fellows of Australia, the rudest savages we know, make themselves a temporary personality by the simple application of "make-up," paint; and the mask is gone as quickly as it is made. Permanent masks, preserved as heirlooms, represent a deeper occupation of the individual by ghosts, a deeper investment of the present by the past; but the mask is worn only on ritual occasions. The juristic personality never dies, and, incorporated in the property, never disappears. The invisible internal drama of conscience never ceases; and, finally, the mystery of Christianity is its abolition of the distinction between person and substance.

The incomprehensibility of the Athanasian Creed corresponds to our unconsciousness of the magic in personality. "Where primitives have magic, we have the unconscious magic which is personality." "What we fail to recognize is that all symptoms, defense mechanisms, in fact, personality itself, are a form of magic. . . . Primitives have magic in a conscious form, whereas with us it can function only (except in certain forms of neurosis or psychosis) if it is unconscious." Except in certain forms of neurosis and psychosis: the insane are closer to the truth.

Roheim, *Magic and Schizophrenia*, 84; *Gates of the Dream*, 132.

VI
Representative

When the problem in psychoanalysis becomes not repression, but symbolism; when we discover that even if there were no dream-censor we should still have symbolism; then personality (soul, ego) becomes not substance, but fiction, representation; and the primal form of politics becomes not domination (repression), but representation.

Cf. Freud, *General Introduction,* 156.

Representation, or personality: for these two notions are one; for the Essence of the Commonwealth is (to define it) "*One Person, of whose Acts a great Multitude, by Mutuall Covenants one with another, have made themselves every one the Author.*" And "a Multitude of men are made *One* Person, when they are by one man, or one Person, Represented." Representation is the essence of the social contract: "To conferr all their power and strength upon one Man, or upon one Assembly of men, that may reduce all their wills, by a plurality of voices, unto one Will: which is as much as to say, to appoint one Man, or Assembly of men, to bear their Person." The essence of representation is the mysterious relation, "bearing the Person of them all."

Hobbes, *Leviathan,* 136, 143, 146.

"A Multitude of men are made *One* Person." The idea of a people is the idea of a corporation, and the idea of a corporation is the idea of a juristic person. "This is more than Consent, or Concord: it is a reall Unitie of them all, in one and the same Person." Out of many, one: a logical impossibility; a piece of poetry, or symbolism; an enacted or incarnate metaphor; a poetic creation. The Commonwealth is "an Artificiall Man," a body politic, "in which, the *Soveraignty* is an Artificiall *Soul;* the Magistrates, and other *Officers* of Judicature and Execution, artificiall *Joynts,*" etc. Does this "Artificiall Man," this "Feigned or Artificiall Person," make "a real Unitie of them all"? Are juristic persons real, or only legal fictions, *personae fictae?* "Analogy with the living person and shift of meaning are the essence of the mode of legal statement which refers to corporate bodies." Is the shift of meaning real? Does the metaphor accomplish a metamorphosis? "The Pacts and Covenants, by which the parts of this Body Politique were at first made, set together, and united, resemble that *Fiat,* or the *Let us make man,* pronounced by God in the Creation." Or like that *hoc est corpus meum,* This is my body, pronounced by God in the Redemption. Is there a real transubstantiation? Is there a miracle in the communion of the mortal God, the great Leviathan; a miracle which gives life to the individual communicants also? For so-called "real," "living," "natural" persons, individual persons, are not natural but juristic persons, *personae fictae,* social creations, no more real than corporations.

Hobbes, *Leviathan,* 3–4, 136, 143.
Cf. Wolff, "On the Nature of Legal Persons." Hart, "Definition and Theory in Jurisprudence."

The Commonwealth is a Person; the representative, or "*Publique* Person," is a person. But "A PERSON is he, *whose words are considered, either as his own, or as representing the words or actions of another man* . . . a *Person,* is the same that an *Actor* is, both on the Stage and in common Conversation; and to *personate,* is to *Act,* or *Represent* himselfe, or an other; and he that acteth another is said to bear his Person, or act in his name; . . . and is called on diverse occasions, diversly: as a *Representer,* or *Representative,* a *Lieutenant,* a *Vicar,* an *Attorney,* a *Deputy,* a *Procurator,* an *Actor,* and the like." Political representation is theatrical representation. A political society comes into existence when it articulates itself and produces a representative; that is to say, organizes itself as a theater, addressed to a stage, on which their representative can perform. The "real Unitie of them all" is made out of the identification of the group with the actor on the stage. In Hobbes's words, "it is the *Unity* of the Representer, not the *Unity* of the Represented, that maketh the Person *One.*" In Freud's words, "I have in mind the situation of the most ancient Greek Tragedy. A company of individuals, named and dressed alike, surrounded a single figure, all hanging upon his words and deeds: they were the chorus and the impersonator of the Hero." "A primary group of this kind is a number of individuals who have substituted one and the same object for their ego ideal and have consequently identified themselves with one another in their ego."

Hobbes, *Leviathan,* 133–134, 136, 359. Freud, *Totem and Taboo,* 155; *Group Psychology,* 80.

The stage produced by political articulation is the stage of history. "As a result of political articulation, we find human beings, the rulers, who can act for society, men whose acts are not imputed to their own persons but to the society as a whole." Representation is "the form by which a political society gains existence for action in history." The nations obtain access to the stage of history through their representatives, the kings who strut the stage. Voegelin illustrates from the *History of the Lombards* by Paulus Diaconus. The active history of the Lombards begins when the people decided that they no longer wanted to live in small federated tribes, and "established for themselves a king like the other nations." And the consequence of having a king is having a history, that is to say, wars; the purpose of which is to put down the historical action, the kings, of other peoples. First the Herules and next the Gepids were defeated and their power broken to the degree that "they no longer had a king." Peaceful existence, existence without historical action, needs no kingship: the Alans and Suebes preserved their kingship in Spain for a long time, "though they had no need of it in their undisturbed quiet."

Voegelin, *New Science of Politics,* 37, 46–47, 49.

Theater is ritual; representation is a form of ritual. Representation is the organizing principle in religion: "The guiding principle in redemptive history is the election of a minority for the redemption of the whole. Otherwise expressed, it is the principle of representation." Political representation and religious representation, these two, are one; being united in the archetypal pattern underlying both—divine kingship. All rule is royal in essence, and all royalty by grace of God. "Sacral or divine kingship is the accepted term for an institution, simultaneously of a religious and a political kind, found in a majority of different cultural areas, and meaning that the king 'by the Grace of God' in his own person incarnates the god and in the cult plays the part of the god. At the same time, however, he also represents, in a special manner, the Collective, the Whole, the People, and so stands between man and god as the Mediator on whom everything and everybody depends."

Cullmann, *Christ and Time,* 116. Engnell in Bentzen, *King and Messiah,* 36.

Hobbes says, "The Kingdome of God is a Civil Commonwealth, where God himself is Soveraign, by vertue first of the *Old,* and since of the *New,* Covenant, wherein he reigneth by his Vicar, or Lieutenant." The representative of the people is the representative of God. The thrust of the social group to make itself visible on the stage of history is at the same time the thrust of a transcendent reality to make itself visible; to be represented on earth; to be impersonated, or incarnated; for, in the last resort, the transcendent reality is the social group itself. Therefore, in the social contract, which is the divine *Fiat* which incorporates the group, the *vox populi* is the *vox dei;* and this mythology is the only basis for popular suffrage. "The people make," and "only God can make," a representative. It is precisely in the voluntary consent of the Governed that Government displays its divine origin (Cusanus); in the republican theory of American Puritanism, "There are not two several and distinct actings, one of God, another of the people; but in one and the same action God, by the people's suffrages, makes such an one governor, or magistrate, and not another."

Hobbes, *Leviathan*, 393; cf. 357, 496, 499. Miller, *American Puritans*, 90. Cf. Gierke, *Political Theories of the Middle Age*, 47, 146.

Every king is an image of God; a representation on earth of the divine majesty. But, Thou shalt not make unto thee any graven image. Hobbes interprets the Second Commandment, "That they *should not make any Image to represent him;* that is to say, they were not to choose to themselves, neither in heaven, nor in earth, any Representative of their own fancying." In Locke, "the public person vested with the power of the law . . . is to be considered as the image, phantom, or representative of the commonwealth." In Locke royalty is reduced to mere effigy and show; revolutionary republicanism seeks to abolish effigy and show: "The old idea was that man must be governed by effigy and show, and that a superstitious reverence was necessary to establish authority"; "The putting of any individual as a figure for a nation is improper" (Paine). "Democracy has no monuments. It strikes no medals. It bears the head of no man on a coin. Its very essence is iconoclastic" (John Quincy Adams). The old idea was that man must be governed by effigy and show; the new idea is—modern representative government. An end to idolatry is not so easy.

Hobbes, *Leviathan*, 452. Locke, *Treatise*, 193–194. Adams, *Memoirs*, VIII, 433. Paine, *Major Writings*, II, 683.
Cf. Frazer, *The Golden Bough*, 99. Gierke, *Political Theories of the Middle Age*, 141.

A ritual approach is a historical approach. Ritual is, simply, a reënactment of the past. The great revolutions in human society are changes in the form of symbolic representation; reorganizations of the theater, of the stage for human action. The matter remains the same: the "seasonal pattern of ritual"; the basic dream; the old, old story; old unhappy far-off things—the matter of Troy, or Brittany, or Britain—which are also familiar matter of today; as in *Finnegans Wake*. But the form changes, the form of the public enactment. In one of these great revolutions, the principle of representation itself emerges; there was a time before there were kings. "Up to this point we have been considering the seasonal ceremonies as rites performed collectively by the community as a whole. In course of time, however, the tendency grows up to concentrate them in a single individual who is taken to personify and epitomize the entire group. . . . Consequently all the things which were previously done by the group as a whole in order to ensure and maintain its existence, now tend to be done representatively by the king." The king incorporates the ritual; makes it a one-man show.

Gaster, *Thespis*, 48.

The (royal) representative needs a new space and a new time for his act. The sacred center is now incarnate, in the king: "His person is considered, if we may express it so, as the dynamical centre of the universe." And from his own person sacredness radiates everywhere: "Polynesian chiefs, by extending the application of the taboo on their own persons, bring everything into the sphere of ritual." This extension of the realm of the sacred gives rise to the secular order: the king became the supreme judge in all matters throughout the land, thus embodying, enacting in his own person, the universal sun-order. The whole world becomes their sepulcher, or pyramid; the scene of their actions; their memorable actions. As an individual embodiment of the group-soul, the royal performance must be continuous; and must tell the whole story; in a whole life devoted to acting out the dream, the ritual, the ancestral destiny; and therefore obtaining individual immortality. When public dreaming is no longer limited to a restricted sacred space and time, but has become a full-time activity of our special representative, ritual and myth are "historicized." The ritual battle against the primal Chaos monster becomes an actual battle against the hordes of heathens. Often it is difficult to say whether a hymn celebrates a ritual "victory" or an "actual" battle: the word for "heathens" is also the word for "devils." History is the enactment of ritual on a permanent and universal stage; and its perpetual commemoration.

Frazer, *The Golden Bough*, 168. Hocart, *Kings and Councillors*, 136–137; cf. 139, 153.
Cf. Bentzen, *King and Messiah*, 16–17, 30–33, 37–38, 57–59. Gaster, *Thespis*, 38–39.

The urban revolution in the Ancient Near East was to make a world fit for kings to perform in, the city of the great king; a city and a tower that would reach unto heaven. And in Oriental despotism is the origin of modern individualism. Those kings were the first historical embodiments of the group-soul, the first incarnations of the group-soul in an individual. The further revolution of the iron age in the West—in Greece, in Rome, in Israel—was to establish popular sovereignty, monarchy inverted; magistrates, among whom royal power was distributed; and a leisure class to take up the dreams, the holy sports of kings. The ceremonial life of royalty is diffused in bourgeois etiquette: every lass a queen (once a week, at any rate; or once in a lifetime); and every man an individual soul, entitled to royal immortality (Osirification).

Durkheim, *Division of Labor*, 195. Gordon Childe, *What Happened in History*, ch. IX.

Political society articulates itself and produces a representative; and is then ready for history; tragedy; even as the chorus, the dance group, articulates itself and produces the hero, the dying god. The chorus has a leader of the dance; the Couretes, the young men of the war dance, have a Leading Man. More and more they differentiate him from themselves, make him their vicar. Their attitude becomes more and more one of contemplation. More and more they become spectators, of his action. Theatrically speaking, they become an audience; religiously speaking, they become worshipers; he becomes a god. Gradually they lose all sense that the god is themselves. "He is utterly projected."

Harrison, *Themis,* 46.

The hero is a "collective ego" of the same substance as the chorus. "A primary group is a number of individuals who have substituted one and the same object for their ego-ideal and have consequently identified themselves with one another in their ego" (Freud); "By Covenant of every man with every man, in such a manner, as if every man should say to every man, '*I Authorize and give up my Right of Governing my selfe to this Man*'" (Hobbes). The ego-ideal of every man is projected into the representative, who becomes the "authorized bearer of their Persons"; the "publique Soule." The self-projection is a split in the self, or schizophrenia; a self-alienation, "to confer all their power and strength upon one Man," and "therein to submit their Wills, every one to his Will, and their Judgements, to his Judgement." It is a mental alienation; a permanent reduction of the self to a condition of tutelage, as in minors or madmen. And the madness is the self-commitment to an asylum. The representative body is an asylum for the soul-substance of the group; a safety deposit bank, "bearing the Person of them all." "Primitive man takes his soul out of his body and deposits it for security in some snug spot," just as people deposit their money with a banker rather than carry it on their persons. "If he should discover some place of absolute security, he may be content to leave his soul there permanently. The advantage of this is that, as long as the soul remains unharmed in the place where he has deposited it, the man himself is immortal."

Freud, *Group Psychology,* 80. Hobbes, *Leviathan,* 143, 146, 287; cf. 507. Frazer, *The Golden Bough,* 668, 700.

And at the same time the self-alienation, like all self-alienation, is fraudulent; in bad faith. The Essence of Commonwealth is "One Person of whose Acts a great Multitude, by mutuall Covenants one with another, have made themselves every one the Author." In authorizing the authorities we are their authors. We *own* their actions: "Every one to owne, and acknowledge himselfe to be the Author of whatsoever he that so beareth their Person, shall Act"; "For that which in speaking of goods and possessions is called an *Owner,* speaking of Actions, is called Author." The boundary separating actor and spectator is a false one, concealing the deeper reality of the collective authorship. The multitude is many Authors, of everything their Representative saith, or doth in their name; "Every man giving their common Representer, Authority from himselfe in particular; and owning all the actions the Representer doth."

Hobbes, *Leviathan,* 134, 137, 143.

The chorus is really the author. Their act is to repudiate responsibility; this is part of the net of lies in which they entangle the hero, their bull, their victim. This is what Freud calls their "refined hypocrisy," as they say, Not unto us, O Lord, not unto us, but unto thy name. The hypocrisy of the chorus makes them too an actor (*hypocrites*).

Freud, *Totem and Taboo,* 156. Psalm CXV, 1.

The chorus identifies with the hero: he is their vicar; in whose actions they take vicarious pleasure. The hero is "created to perform deeds which the community would like to perform but which are forbidden to it." Their vicar also in vicarious punishment: their victim, the scapegoat, the lamb which takes away their sins; through whom they obtain vicarious redemption. Vicarious satisfaction: the deed is both theirs and not theirs. On this self-contradiction, this hypocrisy, this illusion, representative institutions are based.

Friedman and Gassel, "The Chorus in Sophocles' *Oedipus Tyrannus,*" 225.

In vicarious experience there is both identification and distance. The mediator is to keep reality at a distance, to keep the multitude in remote contact with reality. Hobbes saw the paradigm in Exodus XX, 18-19: "And all the people saw the thundering, and the lightnings, and the noise of the trumpet, and the mountain smoking; and when they saw it, they removed, and stood far off. And they said unto Moses, Speak thou with us, and we will hear: but let not God speak with us, lest we die." Representative institutions depend upon the distance separating the spectators from the actor on the stage; the distance which permits both identification and detachment; which makes for a participation without action; which establishes the detached observer, whose participation consists in seeing and is restricted to seeing; whose body is restricted to the eyes. Everything which is merely seen is seen through a windowpane, distantly; and purely: a pure aesthetic experience. Representative institutions depend upon the aesthetic illusion of distance.

Hobbes, *Leviathan,* 453.
Cf. Kris, *Psychoanalytic Explorations in Art,* 40, 201–203, 209, 256. Richard, *Mallarmé,* 55.

The detached observer, who participates without action, is the passive spectator. The division of citizens into politically active and passive is the major premise of modern political (party) organization. The detached observer is also the major premise of the Lockean or Cartesian mind, waxen tablet for passive impressions: "The mistake in empiricist theories of perception has been the representation of human beings as passive observers receiving impressions from the outside."

Hampshire, *Thought and Action,* 47.
Cf. Schattschneider, *Party Government,* 52, 58. Turbayne, *The Myth of Metaphor,* 205.

The detached observer: subject and object distanciated; the subject-object dualism. The dualism which distanciates subject and object, allows the subject only pictures; the first effect of the "influencing machine" to which schizophrenics imagine themselves plugged in—the Cartesian world as machine—is to make the patient see pictures, "something like a diluted reel of film in my brain." Pictures: spectral images on the inside, which represent external reality to the subject. Cognition then, as well as politics, is mediated through representative institutions. Correspondence is then a relation of likeness, or copying, or imitation, between internal image and external reality; instead of correspondence as sympathy, or action at a distance, or active participation; *methexis* and not *mimesis.* "The principal reason which Lévy-Bruhl, Durkheim and others assign for the fact that primitives 'do not perceive with the same minds' as ours, is that in the act of perception, they are not detached, as we are." Primitive participation, *participation mystique,* is self and not-self identified in the moment of experience. "Primitive mentality" involves participation; an extrasensory link between the percipient and the perceived; a telepathy which we have disowned.

Roheim, *Magic and Schizophrenia,* 110, 165. Barfield, *Saving the Appearances,* 31; cf. 32–34.
Cf. Tausk, "The 'Influencing Machine' in Schizophrenia."

The spectator whose participation is restricted to seeing, who is passive, is held in passivity by what he sees; he is spellbound or hypnotized. In Yeats's vision, "Locke sank into a swoon. The garden died"; McLuhan says, "The Lockean swoon was the hypnotic trance induced by stepping up the visual component in experience until it filled the field of attention. Psychologists define hypnosis as the filling of the field of attention by one sense only. At such a moment, 'the garden' dies. That is, the garden indicates the interplay of all the senses in haptic harmony." The garden is polymorphism of the senses, polymorphous perversity, active interplay; and the opposite of polymorphous perversity is the abstraction of the visual, obtained by putting to sleep the rest of the life of the body. The pure knowing subject of modern philosophy, winged cherub without a body, is in a swoon, or dream. Like the spectators in the traditional theater, as perceived by Brecht: "They sit together like men who are asleep but have unquiet dreams. True, they have their eyes open. But they don't watch, they stare. They don't hear, they are transfixed. They look at the stage as if bewitched." Or in liturgy, when participation consists in attendance at a spectacle in which the priest enacts a dramatic representation of the Passion. In representative institutions there is always subjection to the visible image; idolatry.

McLuhan, *Gutenberg Gallaxy*, 17. Brecht, "A Little Organon for the Theater," 22.

Our representative keeps us hypnotized: "The command to sleep in hypnosis means nothing more nor less than an order to withdraw all interest from the world and to concentrate it upon the person of the hypnotist." The power of the hypnotist is of the same nature as the *mana* or majesty of kings; it is based on the magical property of a look. "The hypnotist, then, is supposed to be in possession of this power; and how does he manifest it? By telling the subject to look him in the eyes; his most typical method of hypnotizing is by his look. But it is precisely the sight of the chieftain that is dangerous and unbearable for primitive people, just as later that of the Godhead is for mortals. Even Moses had to act as an intermediary between his people and Jehovah, since the people could not support the sight of God; and when he returned from the presence of God his face shone—some of the *mana* had been transferred on to him, just as happens with the intermediary among primitive people."

Freud, *Group Psychology*, 96. Roheim, *Animism*, 149–150.

Identification with the representative person, whom we "look up to," takes place through the eye. In psychoanalytic jargon, the super-ego is based on "incorporation through the eye" or "ocular introjection"; it is the sight of a parental figure that becomes a permanent part of us; and that now supervises, watches us. In other words, the super-ego is derived from the primal scene. The primal scene is the original theater; parental coitus is the archetypal show; the original distance is between child and parent. "Theaters and concerts, in fact any performance where there is something to be seen or heard, always stands for parental coitus." It is in the primal scene that we learn to take vicarious pleasure in events of which we are only passive spectators: "By means of the father identification it is quite possible to preserve from the wreck of one's own capacity to love at least a vicarious pleasure in the relations between the father and the mother." "The child introjects the primal scene with all the pleasure of ideal participation and the prohibition of actual participation. Hence the double structure of the super-ego: thou shalt be like the father, and yet not like him." The father is the actor; but we as spectators may identify with him. In Blake, "Eritharmon's Orc, the great Selfhood or hero-Messiah whom we obey or watch perform." With the pleasure of ideal participation and the prohibition of actual participation: shadows without substance; fantasies without reality; dreams; onanistic gratification.

Klein, "Infant Analysis," 112. Roheim, *Riddle of the Sphinx*, 222, 283. Frye, *Fearful Symmetry*, 264.
Cf. Fenichel, "Scoptophilic Instinct and Identification," 378, 393.

The pleasure of ideal participation, and the prohibition of real participation: a eunuch in the harem. The effect of the primal scene is to paralyze the spectator, even as the hypnotist's subject is paralyzed; the effect of the primal scene is castration. In the antagonism between actor and audience, the struggle for recognition is to castrate or be castrated; to be master or slave; male or female.

The actor is exhibitionist. To shew is to show the genital; to fascinate; to make the spectator a woman. Even as the hard look or phallic eye of the hypnotist (a Cyclopean erection) transfixes his subject.

Cf. Fenichel, "On Acting."

The spectator is voyeur. The desire to see is the desire to see the genital; and the desire to see is the desire to be one; to become what you behold; to incorporate the penis of another; to devour it through the eye. Participation is identification with a part, the all-important part, the penis; a part isolated, abstracted, cut off, castrated (taking ideal participation for real, i.e., *pars pro toto*). Partial participation is to steal (or be) the penis of another; but only partially, not really: "She turns herself in phantasy into a man, without herself becoming active in a masculine way, and is no longer anything but a spectator of the event which takes the place of the sexual act." The penis which still belongs to another; even as our super-ego still belongs to Daddy. The super-ego is borrowed strength; or a stolen trophy; a head cut off, a monument erected high in our house. To idealize is to idolize; to make an idol; to translate into a fixed image for contemplation; to turn into monumental form; to turn into stone. To concentrate on seeing is to turn into stone; Medusa's head; castration.

Freud, "'A Child is being Beaten,'" 196.
Cf. Fenichel, "Scoptophilic Instinct and Identification"; "Trophy and Triumph."

The outcome of the castration-complex is genital organization, the primacy of the penis, the identification of the whole person with the penis. The actor exhibits his whole person as a penis; but the exhibition exposes the castration. The whole person as a penis, a penis pure and simple, a penis *tout court*, is a penis cut off, a trophy, a severed head, Medusa's head cut off. The little hero, "the 'poor child' with whom she sympathized so much was both the penisless creature and the penis." "It seems contradictory that the analyst is conceived on the one hand as a castrated man, and on the other as a penis. But this paradox is explained: the penis that the patient watches is a cut-off penis." And on the actor's side: "This patient's acting had the unconscious aim of stating by magic gestures: 'None of you has a penis. I, acting the part of a castrated person [on a deeper layer: acting the part of a penis which has been cut off], am showing you how you are supposed to look.'" The actor, the hypnotist, the representative person, turns us to stone by showing us Medusa's head: a genital that is both female and male and castrated.

Fenichel, "Trophy and Triumph," 160; "On Acting," 360.

The exhibitionism of the phallic personality (the huge genital, the royal lingam) is fraudulent; an imposture, or imposition on the public; theater. The actor needs the audience to reassure him that he is not castrated: yes, you are the mighty penis; the Emperor's New Clothes. To force the audience to give this reassurance is to castrate, have coitus with, the audience: the phallic personality needs a receptive audience or womb. Separately, both actor and audience are incomplete, castrated; but together they make up a whole: the desire and pursuit of the whole in the form of the combined object, the parents in coitus.

VII
Head

"The real apocalypse comes, not with the vision of a city or kingdom, which would still be external, but with the identification of the city and kingdom with one's own body." The apocalypse lays bare the mystery of kingship; stripping off the Emperor's New Clothes, to reveal the harlot. Kingship is fornication—the identity of politics and sex. In the apocalypse the walls do fall; the walls separating inside and outside; public and private; body physical and metaphysical. The identification of sex and politics; as in psychoanalysis.

Frye, *Fearful Symmetry*, 431.

Psychoanalysis shows the sexual organization of the body physical to be a political organization; the body is a body politic. Psychoanalysis stands or falls on the expansion of the idea of sexuality to comprehend the entire life of the human body; attributing a sexual ("erotogenic") action to all parts, organs, or "zones"; or rather, envisaging sexuality as an energy diffused throughout the whole body, and capable of displacement from one part to another, and of transformation from one mode of manifestation to another (polymorphism; metamorphosis). What the psychoanalytically uninitiated call "sex," psychoanalysis calls "genitality," or "genital organization," seeing in it an arrangement, a *modus vivendi*, a political arrangement arrived at after stormy upheavals in the house of Oedipus. The arrangement is to concentrate sexuality in one part of the body, the genital; this concentration, or organization, establishes the "primacy" of one "component-impulse," which is now the "dominating" or "supreme" component-impulse in the sexual life of the body. It is, says Freud, a well-organized tyranny, of a part over the whole.

Cf. Freud, *General Introduction*, 332. Brown, *Life Against Death*, 25–28.

It is part of the tyranny of genital organization that its slaves are blind, and see not tyranny but natural necessity. The status quo bears the seal of familiarity, until the seal is broken; the apocalypse. The revolutionary idea in psychoanalysis is the idea of the body as a (political) organization, a body politic; as a historical variable; as plastic. Man Makes Himself, his own body; his image of the body; the Eternal Body of Man is the Imagination.

Blake, *The Laocoön*, 776.

Genital organization is the tyranny of the genital; or rather, since in the body physical everything is constitutional, let us not say tyranny; monarchy. Monarchy is the constituent form of all corporate bodies, including the body physical. *Omnis multitudo derivatur ab uno*: "Everywhere the One comes before the Many. . . . All Order consists in the subordination of Plurality to Unity, and never and nowhere can a purpose that is common to Many be effectual unless the One rules over the Many and directs the Many to the goal." Genital organization in the body physical is a unification of a multitude of component-impulses; making the body a corporate unity, a *university*, or corporation; by a subordination of the Many to the One; the one Governing or Principal Part (*pars principans*), the Primal Part (*primum principium*, or *pars prima*), the Supreme or Prime Mover (*summum movens*, or *primum mobile*); the head of the body.

Gierke, *Political Theories of the Middle Age*, 9; cf. 10, 28, 135–137.

The miracle of incorporation is the establishment of a principal part, a part which is no longer a part, *aliquod unum quod non est pars*, because it is the whole. *Pars pro toto;* a part of the body which represents the whole; a multitude is made *One* Person, when they are by One Person Represented. The genital is the representative organ. Ferenczi say the genital is "the unique and incomparable magic wand which conjures and captures the erotism of the entire body." The representative organ is an asylum for the soul or seminal substance of the body; a safety deposit bank; a pocket for the peckers of the public; incorporating their peckers; the Pecker, bearing (baring) the Person of them all.

Dante, *De Monarchia*, I, 6. Ferenczi, *Thalassa*, 12.
Cf. Kempton on L. B. Johnson in *The New York Review of Books*, November 5, 1964.

In orgasm, all the splendor and misery of representative government. The representative organ acts on behalf of the entire organism: "There is no part of the organism which is not represented in the genital, so that the genital, in the role of executive manager, as it were, provides for the discharge of sexual tension on behalf of the entire organism." The rest of the body attains "complete identification, with the help of the frictional process, with the executive organ," thus obtaining vicarious satisfaction, vicarious redemption (discharge, release).

Ferenczi, *Thalassa,* 12, 38; cf. 18, 28.

A part which is no longer a part; out of the body the soul. The soul arising out of the body and then set over the body; the state arising out of society and then set over society—"The Soveraign is the publique Soule, giving Life and Motion to the Commonwealth." The soul is a manikin; a double; a shadow, or reflection; the soul is a "duplication of the ego," "the narcissistic double of the ego." The original ego is a body-ego, diffuse throughout the body (polymorphous); but "personification of the penis is the root of this second ego." Primacy of the genital zone is then the basis of the unity of personality; the penis is the "narcissistic representative," or "double," of the total personality; the phallus "a miniature of the total ego." To have a soul is to have genital organization—"The idea of the soul is nothing but the sublimation of a male member pure and simple." The tyranny of the genital, the soul, and the state, is one tyranny: "Unity in libidinal impulses being attained by means of their concentration in the genital organ, the latter also serves as the basis for the attainment of unity in personality and society" (Roheim).

Roheim, *Animism,* 19, 25, 140. Ferenczi, *Thalassa,* 16–17. Hobbes, *Leviathan,* 287.
Cf. Frazer, *The Golden Bough,* ch. XVIII.

The soul-double, a second soul; instead of the *Lebenseele*, the *Totengeist*. Instead of the spirit or breath of life, the psyche; a phantom, dream-stuff and ghostly, ancestral, dead. It is this second soul of genital organization that makes life a dream, and the body a tomb; that gives us death in life and personal immortality.

Cf. Onians, *Origins of European Thought*, 93–122. Otto, *Die Manen*, 46.

To have a soul separate from the body is to have a body separate from other bodies. The soul is individual, and individual is separate. The trauma of separation, separation from the mother, separation not accepted, is the nucleus of the separate individual soul. There is no trauma without a split in the self: part of the self regresses to the time before the trauma; stays behind, with the mother, in the womb; a self-encapsulation in a dream-womb. Out of separation not accepted comes a delusion of separation, the dream or fantasy of being himself both mother and child. He makes himself independent of the mother by making himself his own mother. The self is formed like a nation, by a declaration of independence, a split from mother or the mother country, and a split in oneself into both mother and child, so as to be self-sufficing. An independent sovereignty, a private corporation, a person, is made by self-splitting (schizophrenia) and involution (introversion).

In a dream, in fantasy, in unconscious fantasy he makes himself both child and mother; or rather, child in the mother; little one (manikin) in the mother; penis in the womb. Genital organization is the dream of uterine regression, of return to the maternal womb; a fantasy, a make-believe game, a play, a drama, acted out by the genital. "Every human being can and does enact with his own body the double role of the child and the mother."

Ferenczi, *Thalassa*, 23.

> If we now survey the evolution of sexuality from the thumb-sucking of the infant through the self-love of genital onanism to the heterosexual act of coitus, and keep in mind the complicated identifications of the ego with the penis and with the sexual secretion, we arrive at the conclusion that the purpose of this whole evolution, therefore the purpose likewise of the sex act, can be none other than an attempt on the part of the ego—an attempt at the beginning clumsy and fumbling, then more consciously purposive, and finally in part successful—to return to the mother's womb, where there is no such painful disharmony between ego and environment as characterizes existence in the external world. The sex act achieves this transitory regression in a threefold manner: the whole organism attains this goal by purely hallucinatory means, somewhat as in sleep; the penis, with which the organism as a whole has identified itself, attains it partially or symbolically; while only the sexual secretion possesses the prerogative, as representative of the ego and its narcissistic double, the genital, of attaining *in reality* to the womb of the mother.

Ferenczi, *Thalassa*, 18.

The body, like the body politic, is a theater; everything is symbolic, everything including the sexual act. The principal part is a public person taking the part of the community as a whole: *persona publica totius communitatis gerens vicem.* The function of the representative organ is to impersonate, incarnate, incorporate in his own body the body politic. Incorporation is the establishment of a theater (public); the body of spectators depend on the performance for their existence as one body.

Gierke, *Political Theories of the Middle Age*, 163.
Cf. Roheim, *Animism*, 322.

Both politics and sex are theater; sex, said Talleyrand, is *le théâtre des pauvres.* The penis is an actor; it does not actually attain regression to the maternal womb, it enacts the regression "partially or symbolically." The rest of the body "takes part in the regression hallucinatorily," as spectators, passively identifying with the action of their representative, their prince or principal part, the leading man. The penis is the head of the body, the band of brothers; the rest of the body is to the penis as chorus to tragic hero, hypocritically and from a safe distance enjoying the thrill of being spectators at their own execution. "The act of coitus is reminiscent of these melodramas in which, while there are of course dark clouds threatening all kinds of destruction, just as in real tragedy, there is always the feeling that 'everything will turn out all right.'"

Talleyrand cited in Reik, *Masochism in Modern Man*, 296. Ferenczi, *Thalassa*, 42; cf. 40–41, 43.

The drama enacted in the sex act is the ritual drama of divine kingship. Sex is *le théâtre des pauvres;* every man a king; King Oedipus. "Coitus successfully performed is sovereignty." Is it not passing brave to be a king? *Bella gerant alii, tu, felix Austria, nube.* And conversely, sovereignty is coitus; the king is the husband, the kingdom is his wife. King James in 1603 said: "'What God hath conjoined then, let no man separate.' I am the husband, and all the whole island is my lawful wife." The phallic personality and the receptive audience are in coitus; they do it together, when it comes off.

Roheim, *Animism*, 296; *Magic and Schizophrenia*, 65. Pollock and Maitland, *History of English Law*, I, 492, 503–504. Kantorowicz, *The King's Two Bodies*, 223.
Cf. Fenichel, "On Acting," 356.

A king is erected, *rex erectus est*. A king is an erection of the body politic. A political society comes into being when it articulates itself and produces a representative: a people erupts into royalty, *populus erumpit in regnum* (Sir John Fortescue); "an eruptive genitalization of the entire organism" (Ferenczi). In Daniel, the ten horns are the ten kings; in Cambodia, a lingam adored in the temple in the center of the capital represented Devaraja, the God-King. His Royal Highness, the personification of the penis.

Ferenczi, *Thalassa*, 38; cf. "Disease or Patho-Neuroses"; "Analytical Observations on Tic," 166–174.
Cf. Roheim, *Animism*, 194, 228. Heine-Geldern, *Kingship*, 6. Kantorowicz, *The King's Two Bodies*, 64, 224–226. Voegelin, *New Science of Politics*, 37, 42–43, 46–47, 49.

The king personifies the pomp and pleasure of the community; but must also bear the burden of royalty, and, as scapegoat, take away the sins; ejaculation gets rid of the tension. It is a story not only of triumph, but also of crime and punishment. Coitus successfully performed is incest, a return to the maternal womb; and the punishment appropriate to this crime, castration. What happens to the penis is coronation, followed by decapitation. Coitus is "a pompous High Priest entering by a Secret Place" (Blake); and the condition on which the priest can enter the tabernacle is castration; the tabernacle is the mother.

The animal sacrificed in the gate is the phallus; the cock's head is cut off on the threshold of the bride's house. Every erection is an insurrection of the flesh (Augustine); a capital offense; followed by decapitation. Every orgasm is the death of a king; or regicide; the execution of a great criminal. Therefore the Loins are the place of Last Judgment. Coitus is "sending the devil to hell"; "sending the Pope to Rome"; "driving the Moslem out."

Blake, *Jerusalem*, pl. 30, l. 38.
Cf. Roheim, *Animism*, 322, 336, 356; "Some Aspects of Semitic Monotheism," 193. Augustine, *De Civitate Dei*, XIII, 13.

The penis is the head of the body. Every organization has a head; headless bodies cannot act. Capital organization: the head of the body represents the whole body. "The king has two bodies, the one whereof is a body natural, the other is a body politic, and the members thereof are his subjects, and he and his subjects together compose the corporation, and he is incorporated with them and they with him, and he is the head and they are the members."

Kantorowicz, *The King's Two Bodies*, 13.
Cf. Gierke, *Political Theories of the Middle Age*, 22, 28, 62. Maitland, "Crown as Corporation," 250.

His Royal Highness; his whole body a penis, erect; his whole person a sublimation of a male member; the erection is the head. Henry VIII: "We be informed by our judges that we at no time stand so highly in our estate royal as in the time of Parliament, wherein we as head and you as members are conjoined and knit together in one body politic." Sublimation of a male member: a male member lifted up; displacement from below upwards. The erection is in the head, as in the case of virginal blushing.

It is the head that wears the crown, and "the head in the crown is the penis in the vagina."

Kantorowicz, *The King's Two Bodies,* 228. Roheim, *Animism,* 230.

The erection is in the head. Zeus gives birth to state-power out of his own head. A pregnant head, as in capital (a childbearing sum of money); a splitting headache: "The head lends itself particularly well to the expression of bisexual conflicts and can represent both the female and the male genitals."

Sperling, "Migraine and Psychogenic Headaches," 551.

Capital organization and genital organization, these two are one. King James says, " 'What God hath conjoined then, let no man separate.' I am the husband, and all the whole island is my lawful wife; I am the head, and it is my body." For as it says in Ephesians V, 23, the husband is the head of the wife, even as Christ is the head of the Church. Capital organization and genital organization are one and the same; and the same as crucifixion; this is a great mystery. The strange form of Hermes: a squared pillar surmounted by a crossbar, with just a head on top and the erect phallus below. Hermes the conductor of souls, head and genital on a crosstree; the Christmas tree or Christ mast; "the cross stands for two arms and the main stem." Or Attis, who killed himself under a pine tree by self-castration: in the Phrygian cult of the Mother of the Gods, every year a pine tree was felled, and the image of a youth bound to its trunk. The King is the Tree of Life.

> Then straight before the wondering maid,
> The tree of life I gently laid;

The sacred head is lifted up on the tree (of life, of death); but what is lifted up is the serpent, the phallus. "As Moses lifted up the serpent in the wilderness, even so must the Son of Man be lifted up."

Sheridan, "The Geranium." John III, 14.
Cf. Kantorowicz, *The King's Two Bodies,* 223. Onians, *Origins of European Thought,* 122. Rokeach, *The Three Christs of Ypsilanti,* 87, 92. Roheim, *Animism,* 194, 218. Reik, *Myth and Guilt,* ch. XXIII. Widengren, *The King and the Tree of Life.*

The head, the husband, and the soul of the body. The classic psychoanalytical equation, head = genital. Displacement is not simply from below upwards; nor does the truth lie in simply reducing it all downwards (psychoanalytical reductionism). The way up is the way down; what psychoanalysis has discovered is that there is both a genitalization of the head and a cerebralization of the genital. The shape of the physical body is a mystery, the inner dynamical shape, the real centers of energy and their interrelation; the mystical body which is not to be arrived at by anatomical dissection and mechanical analysis; the symbolical life of the body, with which psychoanalysis can put us in touch.

Cf. Ferenczi, *Thalassa,* 22; "Notes and Fragments," 255.

In the unconscious, cerebral is genital. The word *cerebral* is from the same root as Ceres, goddess of cereals, of growth and fertility; the same root as *cresco,* to grow, and *creo,* to create. Onians, archaeologist of language, who uncovers lost worlds of meaning, buried meanings, has dug up a prehistoric image of the body, according to which head and genital intercommunicate via the spinal column: the gray matter of the brain, the spinal marrow, and the seminal fluid are all one identical substance, on tap in the genital and stored in the head. The soul-substance is the seminal substance: the genius is the genital in the head. We would then all be carrying our seed in our head, like flowers. Like flowers, or like bees and ants: "The King and Queen, deep in the absolute darkness of their chamber, bear in their persons two widely diverse functions, the mental and the sexual. The palace chamber is analogous to the skull in higher animals. Even the substance of the queen's body is reminiscent of the brain of mammals."

Marais, *The Soul of the White Ant*, 90; cf. 178.
Cf. Onians, *Origins of European Thought*, 93–167. Roheim, *Animism*, 17–24.

Carrying our seed in our head; like flowers, flaunting our sex shamelessly; as in Bosch's Garden of Earthly Delights, upside down; an end to uprightness, the way up is the way down. Erect is the shape of the genitally organized body; the body crucified, the body dead or asleep; the stiff. The shape of the body awake, the shape of the resurrected body, is not vertical but perverse and polymorphous; not a straight line but a circle; in which the Sanctuary is in the Circumference, and every Minute Particular is Holy; in which

> Embraces are Cominglings from the Head even to the Feet,
> And not a pompous High Priest entering by a Secret Place.

Blake, *Jerusalem*, pl. 69, ll. 39–44.

The body is a historical variable. There is a revolution in the body at the beginning of modern times; a revolution reflected in the philosophy of Hobbes and Descartes. The ruling principle departs from the body into a separate substance, the soul, which confronts the body as absolute sovereignty, or will. "They who compare a city and its citizens, with a man and his members, almost all say, that he who hath the supreme power in the city, is in relation to the whole city, such as the head is to the whole man. But it appears by what hath been already said, that he who hath such a power, hath a relation to the city, not as that of the head, but of the soul to the body. For it is the soul by which a man hath a will; so by him who hath the supreme power, and no otherwise, the city hath a will."

Hobbes, *De Cive,* VI, 19.

The divorce between soul and body takes the life out of the body, reducing the organism to a mechanism, dead in itself but given an artificial life, an imitation of life, by will or power: sovereignty is an artificial soul, giving life and motion to the whole body. Cartesian body, and the Hobbesian body politic, is not really body; it is inorganic *res extensa.* In the Middle Ages, centralizing tendencies in pope or emperor were opposed by the idea of mediate articulation, by virtue of which intermediate groups stood in graduated order between the supreme unit and the individual. On the analogy of the physical body, to avoid monstrosity, finger must be joined directly, not to head but to hand; then hand to arm, arm to shoulder, shoulder to neck, neck to head. Individuals were conceived not as arithmetic units or atomic particles in an undifferentiated *res extensa,* but as socially grouped and functionally differentiated. Medieval representative institutions are not mechanically planned, geometrically divided electoral districts; rather, "the constituencies are organic and corporatively constructed limbs of an articulated People."

Gierke, *Political Theories of the Middle Age,* 66; cf. 28, 134–135.
Cf. Hobbes, *Leviathan,* Introduction.

Hobbes uses the idea of representation to arrive at absolute sovereignty, which abolishes the representedness of the represented. There is a single contract by which each pledges himself to submit to a common ruler, who on his side takes no part in the making of the contract. This assumption destroyed, in the germ, any personality of the people: "The personality of the People died at its birth."

Gierke, *Natural Law and the Theory of Society*, 60.

Hobbes moves from representation to contract; from representation to ownership; via the intermediate notion of authorship. From authorship ("One Person, of whose Acts a great Multitude have made themselves every one the Author"), to ownership ("Every one to owne, and acknowledge himself to be the Author of whatsoever he that beareth their Person, shall Act"). "For that which in speaking of goods and possessions is called an *Owner*, speaking of Actions, is called Author." From personality as theater ("A *Person*, is the same that an Actor is"), to personality as property ("A *Person*, is he, whose words or actions are considered, either as his own, or as representing the words or actions of another man. . . . When they are considered as his owne, then he is called a *Naturall Person*"). And so, from Hobbes to Locke ("Every man has a property in his own person"). Corporate existence is dissolved into property relations; from representation to contract. In representation a person is both himself and another; in property relations a person is either his own or another's. Instead of the magic of personality, the fetishism of commodities. "The scepter no more to be swayed by visible hand," is what Blake saw in the French Revolution. What we got instead was the invisible hand of economic forces.

Hobbes, *Leviathan*, 133–134, 143. Blake, *French Revolution*, l. 5.
Cf. Locke, *Second Treatise of Civil Government*, ch. V, sections 26, 44; ch. VII, section 94; ch. XV, section 173.

Instead of the head, the soul. Instead of organic differentiation, fission, or self-alienation; producing a separate abstract homogeneous force (will, power), which gives life and motion to the whole body. There is the same revolution in William Harvey's physiology: instead of the heart as *pars principans,* the blood; instead of a representative organ, an autonomous substance, in automatic circulation; giving life and motion to the whole body. Like blood is gold in the economic system; gold, says Hobbes, is like the blood in William Harvey's new theory: gold is concocted by "the reducing of all commodities to something of equal value." "This Concoction is as it were the Sanguification of the Common-wealth." But the blood, says Harvey, "The blood is the genital part, whence the soul primarily results." The blood or the soul is the seminal fluid. The fission, or self-alienation which produces this abstract substance, separate from the body but the life of it, is ejaculation. Ejaculation is fission, in the sense of an autotomy: "This discharge can be nothing else than the desire, in the sense of an autotomy, to cast off the organ under tension"; a kind of self-castration. The body politic establishes absolute sovereignty in an orgasm, or death. The body gives up the ghost: "The personality of the People died at its birth;" expires.

Hill, "William Harvey and the Idea of Monarchy," 55. Hobbes, *Leviathan,* 214; cf. 215. Ferenczi, *Thalassa,* 29.

Cf. Roheim, *Animism,* 17–23, 252–253, 309–310, 381–386.

VIII
Boundary

Originally everything was body, ONE BODY (Novalis); or Freud: "Originally the ego includes everything, later it detaches from itself the external world. The ego-feeling we are aware of now is thus only a shrunken vestige of a far more extensive feeling—a feeling which embraced the universe and expressed an inseparable connection of the ego with the external world." The possibilities adumbrated in infancy are to be taken as normative: as in Wordsworth's "Ode": before shades of the prison house close in; before we shrink up into the fallen condition which is normal adulthood.

Novalis, *Hymne*, "Wenigewissen das Geheimniss der Liebe," *Geistliche Lieder*. Freud, *Civilization and Its Discontents*, 13.

> Man is the dwarf of himself. Once he was permeated and dissolved by spirit. He filled nature with his overflowing currents. Out from him sprang the sun and moon; from man, the sun; from woman, the moon. The laws of his mind, the

> periods of his actions externized themselves into day and night, into the year and the seasons. But, having made for himself this huge shell, his waters retired; he no longer fills the veins and veinlets; he is shrunk to a drop. He sees, that the structure still fits him, but fits him colossally. Say, rather, once it fitted him, now it corresponds to him from far and on high.

Emerson, *Nature,* ch. VIII.

Psychoanalysis can be used to uncover the principle of union, or communion, buried beneath the surface separations, the surface declarations of independence, the surface signs of private property. Psychoanalysis also discloses the pathology of the process whereby the normal sense of being a self separate from the external world was constructed. Contrary to what is taken for granted in the lunatic state called normalcy or common sense, the distinction between self and external world is not an immutable fact, but an artificial construction. It is a boundary line; like all boundaries not natural but conventional; like all boundaries, based on love and hate.

The distinction between self and not-self is made by the childish decision to claim all that the ego likes as "mine," and to repudiate all that the ego dislikes as "not-mine." It is as simple as that; but here is Freud's more formal description: "The objects presenting themselves, in so far as they are sources of pleasure, are absorbed by the ego into itself, 'introjected' (according to an expression coined by Ferenczi); while, on the other hand, the ego thrusts forth upon the external world whatever within itself gives rise to pain (the mechanism of projection)." "Thus at the very beginning, the external world, objects, and that which was hated were one and the same thing. When later on an object manifests itself as a source of pleasure, it becomes loved, but also incorporated into the ego."

Freud, "Instincts and their Vicissitudes," 78, 79; cf. "Negation," 183; *Civilization and Its Discontents*, 12.

Here is the fall: the distinction between "good" and "bad," between "mine" and "thine," between "me" and "thee" (or "it"), come all together—boundaries between persons; boundaries between properties; and the polarity of love and hate.

The boundary line between self and external world bears no relation to reality; the distinction between ego and world is made by spitting out part of the inside, and swallowing in part of the outside. On this Freudian insight Melanie Klein and her followers have built. "Owing to these mechanisms [of introjection and projection] the infant's object can be defined as what is inside or outside his own body, but even while outside, it is still part of himself and refers to himself, since 'outside' results from being ejected, 'spat out': thus the body boundaries are blurred. This might also be put the other way round: because the object outside the body is 'spat out,' and still relates to the infant's body, there is no sharp distinction between his body and what is outside."

Heimann, "Certain Functions of Introjection and Projection in Early Infancy," 143.

The net-effect of the establishment of the boundary between self and external world is inside-out and outside-in; confusion. The erection of the boundary does not alter the fact that there is, in reality, no boundary. The net-effect is illusion, self-deception; the big lie. Or alienation. "Le premier mythe du dehors et du dedans: l'aliénation se fond sur ces deux termes." Where Freud and Marx meet.

Hyppolite, "Commentaire parlé sur la Verneinung de Freud," 35. Cf. Bachelard, *La Poétique de l'espace,* 192.

The soul (self) we call our own is an illusion. The real psychoanalytical contribution to "ego-psychology" is the revelation that the ego is a bit of the outside world swallowed, introjected; or rather a bit of the outside world that we insist on pretending we have swallowed. The nucleus of one's own self is the incorporated other.

The super-ego is your father in you; your father introjected; your father swallowed. In his most sophisticated description of super-ego formation Freud says: "A portion of the external world has, at least partially, been given up as an object and instead, by means of identification, taken into the ego—that is, has become an integral part of the internal world."

Freud, *Outline,* 77.

Melanie Klein has shown the same kind of origin for the ego. The ego "is based on object libido reinvested in the body"; the self is a substitute for the lost other, a substitute which pretends to be the lost other; so that we may embrace ourselves thinking we embrace our mother. Our identity is always a case of mistaken identity. The ego is our mother in us. It originally "embraced the universe and expressed an inseparable connection of the ego with the external world," because originally the whole world is the mother and the mother is the whole world. It originates in the dual unity of mother and child; mother and child, these two, as one. Its present structure, its illusory separate and substantial identity results from the desire to perpetuate that original union with the mother, by the device of pretending to have swallowed her, i.e., to have incorporated her into oneself. The shadow of the lost object becomes the nucleus of the ego; a shade, a spectre.

Roheim, *War, Crime and the Covenant*, 142.

Possessive introjection is the basis of the ego; the soul is something that we can call our own. "The ambitions of the Id, while that was the sole governing force, were towards *being* the thing at the other side of whatever relationship it established. When the Ego takes control of the Id's impulses, it directs them towards *having*." The possessive orientation originates in what Freud calls instinctual ambivalence, i.e., the split between "good" and "bad," love and hatred, Eros and Thanatos. The aim of the possessive orientation is to keep the loved object entire and intact: to separate and keep the good, to separate and expel the bad. An either/or or undialectical attitude. What we desire to possess we fear to lose; it is a source of anxiety and we are ambivalent toward it, hate as well as love.

Brophy, *Black Ship to Hell*, 56.
Cf. Klein and Riviere, *Love, Hate and Reparation*, 96–98.

I am what is mine. Personality is the original personal property. As the great philosopher of private property says, "By property I must be understood here, as in other places, to mean that property which men have in their persons as well as goods." Here is the psychological root of private property. Every man has a "property" in his own person. "Man (by being master of himself, and proprietor of his own person, and the actions or labour of it) had still in himself the great foundation of property." The boundaries of our property are extended by mixing our persons with things, and this is the essence of the labor process: "Whatsoever, then, he removes out of the state that Nature hath provided and left it in, he hath mixed his labour with it, and joined to it something that is his own, and thereby makes it his property."

Locke, *Two Treatises of Civil Government,* 130, 138, 206.

"Cain means 'ownership.' Ownership was the originator of the earthly city." The crucial bit of property is neither nature (land) nor natural produce, nor factories nor manufactured products, but persons, our own persons. Free persons, whether in the state of nature or in civil society, are those who own their own persons. It is because we own our own persons that we are entitled to appropriate things that, through labor, become part of our personality or personalty. The defense of personal liberty is identical with the defense of property. There is a part of Karl Marx which attempts to base communism on Lockean premises. The Marxian proletariat is propertyless; they do not own themselves; they sell their labor (themselves) and are therefore not free, but wage-slaves; they are not persons. The case against the notion of private property is based on the notion of person: but they are the same notion. Hobbes says a person is either his own or another's. This dilemma is escaped only by those willing to discard personality.

Augustine, *De Civitate Dei,* XV, 17.
Cf. Hobbes, *Leviathan,* 133.

The existence of the "let's pretend" boundary does not prevent the continuance of the real traffic across it. Projection and introjection, the process whereby the self as distinct from the other is constituted, is not past history, an event in childhood, but a present process of continuous creation. The dualism of self and external world is built up by a constant process of reciprocal exchange between the two. The self as a stable substance enduring through time, an identity, is maintained by constantly absorbing good parts (or people) from the outside world and expelling bad parts from the inner world. "There is a continual 'unconscious' wandering of other personalities into ourselves."

Schilder, *The Image and Appearance of the Human Body*, 252.
Cf. Klein, *Psychoanalysis of Children*, 203–204, 217, 246–249. Money-Kyrle, *Psychoanalysis and Politics*, 51.

Every person, then, is many persons; a multitude made into one person; a corporate body; incorporated, a corporation. A "corporation sole"; everyman a parson-person. The unity of the person is as real, or unreal, as the unity of the corporation.

> We tend to think of any one individual in isolation; it is a convenient fiction. We may isolate him physically, as in the analytic room; in two minutes we find that he has brought his world in with him, and that even before he set eyes on the analyst, he had developed inside himself an elaborate relation with him. There is no such thing as a single human being, pure and simple, unmixed with other human beings. Each personality is a world in himself, a company of many. That self, that life of one's own, which is in fact so precious though so casually taken for granted, is a composite structure which has been and is being formed and built up since the day of our birth out of countless never-ending influences and exchanges between ourselves and others. . . . These other persons are in fact therefore parts of ourselves. And we ourselves similarly have and have had effects and influences, intended or not, on all others who have an emotional relation to us, have loved or hated us. We are members one of another.

Riviere, "The Unconscious Phantasy of an Inner World," 358–359.
Cf. Maitland, "Corporation Sole," 214.

Separation (on the outside) is repression (on the inside): "The ego is incapable of splitting the object [or splitting with the object] without a corresponding split taking place within the ego." The declaration of independence from the mother (country) is a claim to be one's own mother; it splits the self into mother and child.

Klein, "Notes on Some Schizoid Mechanisms," 298.

Separation (on the outside) is repression (on the inside). The boundary between the self and the external world is the model for the boundary between the ego and the id. The essence of repression, says Freud, is to treat an inner stimulus as if it were an outer one; casting it out (projection). The external world and inner id are both foreign territory—the same foreign territory.

Cf. Freud, "The Two Principles in Mental Functioning," 15n.

And all the boundaries, the false fronts or frontiers—between ego and external world, between ego and super-ego, between ego and id—are fortified. The walls are fortified, with "defense-mechanisms," and "character armor." "The natural man is self-centered, or ego-centric; everything he regards as real he also regards as outside himself; everything he takes 'in' immediately becomes unreal and 'spectral.' He tries to become an armored crustacean alert for attack or defense; the price of selfishness is eternal vigilance. This kind of Argus-eyed tenseness proceeds from the sealed prison of consciousness which Blake calls 'opaque.'"

Frye, *Fearful Symmetry*, 348–349.

Separateness, then, is the fall—the fall into division, the original lie. Separation is secrecy, hiding from one another, the private parts or property. Ownership is hiding; separation is repression. It is a private corporation. The right to privacy: something secret and shameful, which is one's own. "We hide in secret. I will build thee a Labyrinth where we may remain for ever alone." "The striving for the right to have secrets from which the parents are excluded is one of the most powerful factors in the formation of the ego." The plague of darkness is a symbol of the opaque Selfhood: "For while they thought they were unseen in their secret sins, they were sundered one from another by a dark curtain of forgetfulness, stricken with terrible awe, and sore troubled by spectral forms."

Blake, *Night* I, 28; cf. 21–27. Tausk, "The 'Influencing Machine' in Schizophrenia," 535. Wisdom of Solomon XVII, 3.
Cf. Roheim, *Riddle of the Sphinx,* 153. Frye, *Fearful Symmetry,* 133–134.

The self being made by projection and introjection, to have a self is to have enemies, and to be a self is to be at war (the war of every man against every man). To abolish war, therefore, is to abolish the self; and the war to end war is total war; to have no more enemies, or self.

The conclusion of the whole matter is, break down the boundaries, the walls. Down with defense mechanisms, character-armor; disarmament. Ephesians II, 14: For he is our peace, who hath made both one, and hath broken down the middle wall of partition between us.

To give up boundaries is to give up the reality-principle. The reality-principle, the light by which psychoanalysis has set its course, is a false boundary drawn between inside and outside; subject and object; real and imaginary; physical and mental. It gives us the divided world, the split or schizoid world—the "two principles of mental functioning"—in which psychoanalysis is stuck. Psychoanalysis begins on the side of imperialism, or enlightenment, invading the heart of darkness, carrying bright shafts of daylight (*lucida tela diei*), carrying the Bible and flag of the reality-principle. Psychoanalysis ends in the recognition of the reality-principle as Lucifer, the prince of darkness, the prince of this world, the governing principle, the ruler of the darkness of this world. The reality-principle is the prince of darkness; its function is to *scotomize*, to spread darkness; to make walls of thick darkness, walls of separation and concealment. Psychoanalysis ends here: Freud remained officially faithful to the principle whose pretensions he finally exposed. Really to go beyond Freud means to go beyond the reality-principle. And really to go beyond the pleasure-principle is to go beyond the reality-principle; for Freud himself showed that these two are one.

The reality-principle is an unreal boundary drawn between real and imaginary. Psychoanalysis itself has shown that "There is a most surprising characteristic of unconscious (repressed) processes to which every investigator accustoms himself only by exercising great control; it results from their entire disregard of the reality-test; thought-reality is placed on an equality with external reality, wishes with fulfillment and occurrence." "What determines the symptoms is the reality not of experience but of thought."

Freud, "The Two Principles in Mental Functioning," 20; *Totem and Taboo,* 86.

"Animism, magic and omnipotence of thought"—the child, the savage and the neurotic are right. "The omnipotence of thoughts, the over-valuation of mental processes as compared with reality, is seen to have unrestricted play in the emotional life of neurotic patients. . . . This behaviour as well as the superstitions which he practises in ordinary life, reveals his resemblance to the savages, who believe they can alter the external world by mere thinking." But the lesson of psychoanalysis is that "we have to give up that prejudice in favor of external reality, that underestimation of internal reality, which is the attitude of the ego in ordinary civilized life to-day." That "advance," that "adaptation to reality," which consists in the child's learning to distinguish between the wish and the deed, between external facts and his feelings about them has to be undone, or overcome. "Mental Things are alone Real."

Freud, *Totem and Taboo,* 87. Isaacs, "The Nature and Function of Phantasy," 82. Blake, *A Vision of the Last Judgement,* 617.

The real world, which is not the world of the reality-principle, is the world where thoughts are omnipotent, where no distinction is drawn between wish and deed. As in the New Testament: "Ye have heard that it was said by them of old time, Thou shalt not commit adultery: But I say unto you, That whosoever looketh on a woman to lust after her hath committed adultery with her already in his heart." Or Freud: "It is a matter of indifference who actually committed the crime; psychology is only concerned to know who desired it emotionally and who welcomed it when it was done. And for that reason all of the brothers [of the family Karamazov; or of the human family] are equally guilty."

Matthew V, 27–28. Freud, "Dostoevsky and Parricide," 236.

The outcome, then, of Freud or of Dostoevsky, is a radical rejection of government of the reality-principle. Freud sees the collision between psychoanalysis and our penal institutions: "It is not psychology that deserves to be laughed at, but the procedure of judicial inquiry." Reik, in a moment of apocalyptic optimism, declares that "The enormous importance attached by criminal justice to the deed as such derives from a cultural phase which is approaching its end." A social order based on the reality-principle, a social order which draws a distinction between the wish and the deed, between the criminal and the righteous, is still a kingdom of darkness. It is only as long as a distinction is made between real and imaginary murders that real murders are worth committing: as long as the universal guilt is denied, there is a need to resort to individual crime, as a form of confession, and a request for punishment. The strength of sin is the law. Heraclitus said, the law is a wall.

Freud, "Dostoevsky and Parricide," 236. Reik, *The Compulsion to Confess,* 155. I Corinthians XV, 56.

Psychoanalysis manages to salvage its allegiance to the (false) reality-principle by its use of the word *fantasy* to describe the contents of the unconscious ("unconscious fantasies"). It is in the unconscious that "we are members one of another," "we incorporate each other." As long as we accept the reality-principle, the reality of the boundary between inside and outside, we do not "really" incorporate each other. It is then in fantasy that we "project" or "introject"; it is then purely mental, and mental means not real; the unconscious then contains not the hidden reality of human nature but some (aberrant) fancies, or fantasies. But the unconscious is the true psychic reality. The language of psychoanalysis becomes self-contradictory:

"Phantasy has real effects, not only on the inner world of the mind, but also on the external world of the subject's bodily development and behaviour." "When contrasted with external and bodily realities, the phantasy, like other mental activities, is a figment, since it cannot be touched or handled or seen; yet it is real in the experience of the subject."

Isaacs, "The Nature and Function of Phantasy," 99.
Cf. Klein, "Notes on Some Schizoid Mechanisms," 298.

"Fantasy" is not real; is mental; is inside. The psychoanalytic model of two principles of mental functioning still adheres to the Lockean and Cartesian notion of human experience as consisting of mental events, inside the mind, and distinct from external, material, reality. Freud says, "With the introduction of the reality-principle one mode of thought-activity was split off; it was kept free from reality-testing and remained subordinated to the pleasure-principle alone. This is the act of phantasy-making." Reality-testing grows out of fantasy-making—"it is now a question whether something which is present in the ego as an image can also be rediscovered in reality." And in the final "reality-ego"—that is to say, the separate self of private property—"Once more it will be seen, the question is one of *external* and *internal.* What is not real, what is merely imagined or subjective, is only *internal;* while on the other hand what is real is also present externally." Then the basic stock in trade of the mind is images, fantasies, obtained by the power of the mind to revive the image of former perceptions, i.e., to hallucinate, as in dreams. The nucleus of mental life is then a spectral double of the external world, on the model of the dream; a world of images; a mental, an imaginary internal subjective unreal world, which may or may not reflect (correspond to) the bodily real external and material world.

Freud, "The Two Principles in Mental Functioning," 16–17; "Negation," 183.

In rejecting the split world of the reality-principle—"Two Horn'd Reasoning, Cloven Fiction"—Blake said "Mental Things are alone Real; what is call'd Corporeal, Nobody Knows of its Dwelling Place." There is, then, after all a sense in which the body is not real; but the body that is not real is the false body of the separate self, the reality-ego. That false body we must cast off; in order to begin the Odyssey of consciousness in quest of its own true body.

Blake, *The Gates of Paradise*, 770; *A Vision of the Last Judgement*, 617.

The fallacy in the false body is Whitehead's Fallacy of Simple Location; which is the notion that "material can be said to be *here* in space and *here* in time, or *here* in space-time, in a perfectly definite sense which does not require for its explanation any reference to other regions of space-time." The fallacy of Simple Location is to accept the boundary as real: to accept as real that separateness which the reality-principle takes to be the essence of a body or a thing, the essence of the body as thing.

Whitehead, *Science and the Modern World*, 62; cf. 72.

The reality-principle says, if *here*, then not *there;* if inside, then not outside. The alternative to dualism is dialectics; that is to say, love—

> Two distincts, division none:
> Number there in love was slain.

Whitehead says the reality is unification: reality is events (not things), which are prehensive unifications; gathering diversities together in a unity; not simply *here*, or *there*, but a gathering of here and there (subject and object) into a unity.

Shakespeare, "The Phoenix and the Turtle."
Cf. Whitehead, *Science and the Modern World*, 86–92.

Reality is not things (dead matter, or heavy stuff), in simple location. Reality is energy, or instinct; Eros and Thanatos, "the 'prehensive' and 'separative' characters of space time"; one sea of energy: "In the analogy with Spinoza, his one substance is for me the one underlying activity of realization individualizing itself in an interlocking plurality of modes." One substance, the id or It.

Whitehead, *Science and the Modern World*, 80, 87.

The human body is not a thing or substance, given, but a continuous creation (Nietzsche: *beständige Schöpfung*). The human body is an energy system, Schilder's postural model, which is never a complete structure; never static; is in perpetual inner self-construction and self-destruction; we destroy in order to make it new. Destroy this temple, and in three days I will raise it up.

Cf. Schilder, *The Image and Appearance of the Human Body*, 15–16, 193, 241, 287, 166. John II, 19.

Reality does not consist of substances, solidly and stolidly each in its own place; but in events, activity; activity which crosses the boundary; action at a distance. Whitehead finds his paradigm in a text from Francis Bacon: "It is certain that all bodies whatsoever, though they have no sense, yet they have perception. . . . And this perception is sometimes at a distance, as well as upon the touch; as when the loadstone draweth iron: or flame naphtha of Babylon, a great distance off." Compare Nietzsche: "Man kann Druck und Stoss selber nicht 'erklären,' man wird die *actio in distans* nicht los."

Whitehead, *Science and the Modern World,* 52, 86. Nietzsche, *Aus dem Nachlass,* 455.

The "postural model" of the body consists of "lines of energy," "Psychic streams," Freud's "libidinal cathexes," which are, like electricity, action at a distance; flux, influx, reflux; connecting different erogenous points in the body (the psychosexual organizations); and connecting one body with other bodies. "The space in and around the postural model is not the space of physics. The body-image incorporates objects or spreads itself in space." "In an individual's own postural image many postural images of others are melted together." "We could describe the relation between the body-images of different persons under the metaphor of a magnetic field with stream-lines going in all directions." A Magnetic field, of action at a distance; or a magical field; "magic action is an action which influences the body-image irrespective of the actual distance in space." In magic action there is a space connection between the most distant things—

> For head with foot hath private amity,
> And both with moons and tides.

Herbert, "Man." Schilder, *Image and Appearance of the Human Body,* 213, 216, 234, 236; cf. 16, 137, 241, 252.

The processes of identification and incorporation known to psychoanalysis conform to Lévy-Bruhl's pattern of mystical (magical) participation in primitive mentality;

"The opposition between the one and the many, the same and another, etc., does not impose upon this mentality the necessity of affirming one of these terms if the other be denied." "Identification" is participation; self and not-self identified; an extrasensory link between self and not-self. Identification is action at a distance; or *telepathy;* the center of Freud's interest in the "Occult." If body, corporeal substance, is taken to be in Simple Location (as Freud took it to be) then the question of telepathy is whether thoughts or spiritual beings can exist with no ascertainable connection with a corporeal body. But Freud himself said, that "by inserting the unconscious between the physical and what has been regarded as the mental, psychoanalysis has prepared the way for the acceptance of such processes as telepathy." The question is not the existence of disembodied spirit, but the modalities of bodily action at a distance.

Lévy-Bruhl cited in Schilder, *Image and Appearance of the Human Body,* 274. Freud, *New Introductory Lectures,* 75–76.
Cf. Jones, *Sigmund Freud,* III, 402. Barfield, *Saving the Appearances,* 32–34.

The hidden psychic reality contained in the unconscious does not consist of fantasies, but of action at a distance, psychic streams, projects, in a direction: germs of movement; seeds of living thought. These seeds are Freud's "unconscious ideas," which are concrete ideas; that is to say ideas of things, and not simply of the words, or images inside the mind corresponding to the things outside. Concrete ideas are cathexes of things: "The Unconscious contains the thing-cathexes of objects, the first and true object-cathexes"; the original telepathy.

Freud, "The Unconscious," 134.

The "thing-cathexes of the objects, the first and true object-cathexes"; "a proto-mental system in which physical and mental activity is undifferentiated." A kind of body-thinking, "at first without visual or other plastic images"; "unconscious knowledge," carried in deeper centers of the body than head or eye; a knowledge not derived from the senses, extrasensory; sub-sensible or super-sensible. For example, that unconscious knowledge about sexual intercourse between parents attributed by psychoanalysis to babes in arms. "The world of thought at those levels is quite alien to our own, so that it is quite impossible to reproduce them in words as one seems to perceive them in analysis. Let us consider, for instance, what a demand we are making on anyone who has not been able to convince himself of the fact in an analysis, if we ask him to believe that a small child becomes like his mother because he thinks he has eaten her up, and that, if he thinks he is being tormented or 'poisoned' by this internal mother, he can in some circumstances spit her out again. The details of this kind of 'body-thinking' of which we have a glimpse in analysis and which is bound up with ideas of incorporation must perpetually evade any exact comprehension."

Isaacs, "The Nature and Function of Phantasy," 92.
Cf. Klein, "Criminal Tendencies in Normal Children," 188. Fenichel, "Preoedipal Phase in Girls," 242. Bion, "Group Dynamics: a re-view," 449. Klein, *Psychoanalysis of Children,* 188–189, 296–297.

In the deepest level of the unconscious we find not fantasies, but telepathy. That is to say, the deepest and still unconscious level of our being is not modeled on the dream; in which fission, duplication, is the basic mechanism; in which we withdraw from the world into a second world of (visual) images, projected.

Reuben slept on Penmaenmawr and Levi slept on Snowdon.

> Their eyes, their ears, nostrils and tongues roll outward, they behold
> What is within now seen without.

To overcome the dualism would be to awake out of sleep; to arise from the dead.

Blake, *Night* II, 52–54.

Cf. Schilder, *Image and Appearance of the Human Body,* 51–52, 60. Roheim, *Gates of the Dream,* 20, 58, 116. Ephesians V, 14; Romans XIII, 11.

It is not schizophrenia but normality that is split-minded; in schizophrenia the false boundaries are disintegrating. "From pathology we have come to know a large number of states in which the boundary lines between ego and outside world become uncertain." Schizophrenics are suffering from the truth. " 'Every one knows' the patient's thoughts: a regression to a stage before the first lie." Schizophrenia testifies to "experiences in which the discrimination between the consciousness of self and the consciousness of the object was entirely suspended, the ego being no longer distinct from the object; the subject no longer distinct from the object; the self and the world were fused in an inseparable total complex." Schizophrenic thought is "adualistic"; lack of ego-boundaries makes it impossible to set limits to the process of identification with the environment. The schizophrenic world is one of mystical participation; an "indescribable extension of inner sense"; "uncanny feelings of reference"; occult psychosomatic influences and powers; currents of electricity, or sexual attraction—action at a distance.

Freud, *Civilization and Its Discontents,* 11. Tausk, "The 'Influencing Machine' in Schizophrenia," 535. Storch, *Primitive Archaic Forms,* 31, 61, 62.

Cf. Sèchehaye, *A New Psychotherapy in Schizophrenia,* 134. Roheim, *Magic and Schizophrenia,* 101.

"The patient connects herself with everybody." "You and I, are we not the same? . . . Sometimes I cannot tell myself from other people. . . . It seemed to me as though I no longer existed in my own person alone, as though I were one with the all." In a patient called Julie, "all perception seemed to threaten confusion with the object. 'That's the rain. I could be the rain.' 'That chair—that wall. I could be that wall. It's a terrible thing for a girl to be a wall.'"

Storch, *Primitive Archaic Forms*, 27–28. Laing, *Divided Self*, 217.
Cf. Schilder, *Image and Appearance of the Human Body*, 215. Roheim, *Magic and Schizophrenia*, 101, 115.

Definitions are boundaries; schizophrenics pass beyond the reality-principle into a world of symbolic connections: "all things lost their definite boundaries, became iridescent with many-colored significances." Schizophrenics pass beyond ordinary language (the language of the reality-principle) into a truer, more symbolic language: "I'm thousands. I'm an in-divide-you-all. I'm a no un (i.e., nun, no-un, no one)." The language of *Finnegans Wake*. James Joyce and his daughter, crazy Lucia, these two are one. The god is Dionysus, the mad truth.

Storch, *Primitive Archaic Forms*, 62. Laing, *Divided Self*, 223.
Cf. Sèchehaye, *A New Psychotherapy for Schizophrenia*, 135–150. Ellmann, *James Joyce*, 692, 692n. Roheim, *Magic and Schizophrenia*, 94, 108.

The mad truth: the boundary between sanity and insanity is a false one. The proper outcome of psychoanalysis is the abolition of the boundary, the healing of the split, the integration of the human race. The proper posture is to listen to and learn from lunatics, as in former times—"We cannot deny them a measure of that awe with which madmen were regarded by people of ancient times." The insane do not share "the normal prejudice in favor of external reality." The "normal prejudice in favor of external reality" can be sustained only by ejecting (projecting) these dissidents from the human race; scotomizing them, keeping them out of sight, in asylums; insulating the so-called reality-principle from all evidence to the contrary.

Freud, *New Introductory Lectures,* 80.
Cf. Storch, *Primitive Archaic Forms,* 97.

Dionysus, the mad god, breaks down the boundaries; releases the prisoners; abolishes repression; and abolishes the *principium individuationis,* substituting for it the unity of man and the unity of man with nature. In this age of schizophrenia, with the atom, the individual self, the boundaries disintegrating, there is, for those who would save our souls, the ego-psychologists, "the Problem of Identity." But the breakdown is to be made into a breakthrough; as Conrad said, in the destructive element immerse. The soul that we can call our own is not a real one. The solution to the problem of identity is, get lost. Or as it says in the New Testament: "He that findeth his own psyche shall lose it, and he that loseth his psyche for my sake shall find it."

Matthew X, 39.

IX
Food

There is only one psyche, in relation to which all conflict is endopsychic, all war intestine. The external enemy is (part of) ourselves, projected; our own badness, banished. The only defense against an internal danger is to make it an external danger: then we can fight it; and are ready to fight it, since we have succeeded in deceiving ourselves into thinking it is no longer us.

Murder is misdirected suicide, to destroy part of oneself; murder is suicide with mistaken identity. And suicide is also a case of mistaken identity, an attack on the (introjected) other.

A case of mistaken identity, an accident, at the crossroads; the stranger is the father. *Pater semper incertus;* his identity is established by killing him. "Passing strangers were regarded as manifestations of the corn-spirit escaping from the cut or threshed corn, and as such were seized and slain."

Frazer, *The Golden Bough*, 439.
Cf. Brophy, *Black Ship to Hell*, 97.

An "accident." There is no death from natural causes; if a man is killed they do not blame the real murderer. "He had to die you see," they say, and set out in search of a fictitious person, naturally a member of a foreign tribe, whom they regard as the real cause of death. The real cause of all death is the father (*Der Erlkönig*); the member of a foreign tribe is the culprit, scapegoat, or father.

Cf. Roheim, *Animism*, 62; *Psychoanalysis and Anthropology*, 136.

Killing is always inside the family (Oedipal). In the wisdom of primitive war, enemy blood is kindred blood; blood becomes kindred blood by being shed. Whatever is killed becomes the father. Head hunting. An enemy must be killed for a boy to grow up; a head must fall. The boy kills his father in the person of an enemy. And then the slain enemy becomes his guardian spirit: the enemy head (super-ego) presides over the house; love your enemy. "We tend to identify ourselves with whatever we kill—and then reactively to venerate our victims." Or an enemy is killed to provide spirit for a son: the enemy is reincarnated in the son. The pile of skulls that represents the chief's *mana* are those of enemies, ancestors. The super-ego is our god, enemy; and suicide (or any self-defeat) is our obedience and revenge.

Roheim, *War, Crime and the Covenant*, 57.
Cf. Turney-High, *Primitive War*, 199, 222–226.

We identify with what we kill. The hidden truth which makes peace: the identity of the killer and the victim.

Whatever is killed becomes the father. All killing is ritual killing; totemic sacrifice; Holy Communion. We drink the blood of our enemies.

Cf. Turney-High, *Primitive War,* 87, 152, 156, 158, 191–192.

Genocide, holocaust. "The practice of devoting a recalcitrant foe to destruction as a kind of gigantic holocaust to the national deity was apparently universal among the early Semites." Of the cities of these people, which the Lord thy God doth give thee for an inheritance, thou shalt save alive nothing that breatheth.

Albright, *From the Stone Age to Christianity,* 230. Deuteronomy XX, 16.

Hostilities: our enemy our host, who feeds us; to kill is to eat. Our enemy our host, *hostia,* our Eucharistic meal.

All killing is sacrificial; and all sacrifice is eating. Killing is eating. "Dainties that would be hot and fresh, taken from the field of battle," to feed the sun, in Mexico; "delightful food of the warrior, the well fed Warrior's flesh of him who is slain in War." (Blake)

Séjourné, *Burning Water,* 32. Blake, *Jerusalem,* pl. 68, ll. 34–35.
Cf. Balint, "Die mexikanische Kriegshieroglyphe," 414–415.

The killing is cannibalistic, to incorporate the enemy. The brothers overcame the father, and all partook of his body. "This cannibalism need not shock us, it survived into far later times. The essential point is, however, that we attribute to these primeval people the same feelings and emotions that we have elucidated in the primitives of our own times, our children, by psychoanalytic research. That is to say: they not merely hated and feared their father, but also honored him as an example to follow; in fact, each son wanted to place himself in his father's position. The cannibalistic act thus becomes comprehensible as an attempt to assure one's identification with the father by incorporating a part of him." Head hunting, ending in super-ego formation: the installation of the murdered man in our house as guardian spirit.

Freud, *Moses and Monotheism*, 131–132.
Cf. Fenichel, "Introjection and Castration Complex," 56.

Identification, introjection, incorporation, is eating. The oldest and truest language is that of the mouth: the oral basis of the ego. Even in seeing there is an active process of introjection: perception is a partaking of what is perceived (Fenichel); we become what we behold (Blake).

Cf. Isaacs, "The Nature and Function of Phantasy," 104–106, 109. Fenichel, "Scoptophilic Instinct and Identification," 379–381. Roheim, *Magic and Schizophrenia*, 224–225. Freud, "Negation," 183.

The question what is a body, is the question what is it to eat: Take, eat; this is my body.

Our body is an incorporated body; we are what we eat *(man ist was man isst)*. We are father (mother) eaten. The species is cannibalistic. *Erst kommt das Fressen*. "I am Saturn who devoured his children because it was foretold that otherwise they would devour him. To eat or be eaten—that is the question." But who is my father; and who is my mother? Is it the Blessed Virgin, the Air we breathe, the world-mothering air—

> This needful, never spent,
> And nursing element;
> My more than meat and drink,
> My meal at every wink—

From the point of view of *prana,* breath, there exists nothing which is not food. "He who meditates on the Universal Self as the measure of the span from earth to heaven, and as identical with the self, eats food in all the world, in all beings, in all selves."

Strindberg quoted in Lidz, "Strindberg's Creativity and Schizophrenia," 403. Hopkins, "The Blessed Virgin Compared to the Air We Breathe." *Chandogya Upanishad,* V, ii, 1; V, xviii, 1.
Cf. Roheim, "Das Selbst," 12.

The testimony of schizophrenia: *they eat and are eaten.* Schizophrenia is "food trouble"; schizophrenia says, "Hunger, that is the soul"; "There is only one story—that somebody was starved. But not really—only inside, in my stomach." Prisoners of starvation. "The whole trouble started with a party. People were dreaming that they were hungry, but hungry inside; they were not understood and the police broke it up."

Roheim, *Magic and Schizophrenia,* 104, 115, 126, 127, 129.

"Food trouble." "Somebody was starved. But not really—only inside." What is it to eat; what is the real food. I have meat to eat that ye know not of; for my flesh is meat indeed, and my blood is blood indeed.

John IV, 32; VI, 55.

Hung up between seeing and eating, as in schizophrenia, which makes the patient see pictures of people eating—"the doctors built it to see who was putting his head inside me and eating my food." Paradise regained is Eucharist: taste and see. "The great sorrow in human life, which begins in childhood and continues until death, is that seeing and eating are two different operations. Eternal beatitude (myth of the *Phaedrus*) is a state where to see is to eat." "What is seen is not real, is only an image. What is eaten is destroyed, is not real either. Original sin produced this separation in us."

Roheim, *Magic and Schizophrenia,* 110, 165. Weil, *Cahiers* III, 338–339; *La Pesanteur et la grâce,* 117.

Eating is the form of the fall. The woman gave me and I did eat. Eating is the form of sex. Copulation is oral copulation; when the Aranda ask each other, "Have you eaten?" they mean, "Have you had intercourse?" The schizophrenic girl refused to eat; the case of Simone Weil. Eating is the form of war. Human blood is the life and delightful food of the warrior. Eating is the form of redemption. Except ye eat the flesh of the Son of man, and drink his blood, ye have no life in you. We must eat again of the tree of knowledge, in order to fall into innocence.

Cf. Roheim, *Animism,* 48; *Gates of the Dream,* 96. Storch, *Primitive Archaic Forms,* 17, 75. Richard, *Mallarmé,* 142, 167. Kleist, "Über das Marionettentheater."

Communion; oral copulation. *Ist nicht die Umarmung etwas dem Abendmahl ähnliches?* Eucharist is marriage feast; the union of the bridegroom and the bride. He gives himself to his bride with the bread. Eat your fill, lovers; drink, sweethearts, and drink deep. The two become one flesh, incorporate each other, by eating. The transubstantiation is the unification; is in the eating.

Novalis in Rehm, *Orpheus, Der Dichter und die Toten,* 133.
Cf. Williams, *Radical Reformation,* 308. Daniélou, *Lord of History,* 230–231.

The transubstantiation is in the eating: "Just as, in His days on earth, bread and wine taken by Him as food were metabolized into His flesh and blood at digestion." By eating we become his body; eating makes it so. *Manducando Christi corpus fiunt Christi corpus.*

Lubac, *Corpus Mysticum,* 97.

Transubstantiation—the whole problem of symbolism. Metaphor is really metamorphosis; and the primal form of the sentence is *Tat tvam assi,* Thou art That; or, of bread and wine, *hoc est corpus meum,* this is my body.

Communion. The individual (personal, historical) body; the eucharistic body; the corporate (mystical) body. To see these three as one body.

Communion. The unification is in the eating. We are one body because we are all partakers of that one bread. We become one body as we become his body, that is to say bread. We being many are one bread. "They are nourished by one another."

Cf. I Corinthians X, 17. *Bhagavad Gita,* III, 11–12. Lubac, *Corpus Mysticum,* 79–80.

The true human sacrifice is unification: *hoc est sacrificium Christianorum, ut multi unum corpus sint in Christo.*

It is only as we are eaten that we are unified by incorporation into his body.

Lubac, *Corpus Mysticum,* 279, 289.

To be human is to be eaten, to be sacrificed. "The Prajapati, in the beginning, created men together with sacrifice, and said: 'By this shall you multiply. Let this be the Cow of Plenty and yield unto you the milk of your desires.'"

Bhagavad Gita, III, 10.

This world as sacrifice; this world as food; to be is to eat and to be eaten. The sacrifice is the eating, the crucifixion is the supper. "We are fed by the cross of the Lord, since we eat his body."

Lubac, *Corpus Mysticum,* 74–76.
Cf. *Bhagavad Gita,* III, 14.

The real body. To be real, it must be bodily; and to be a body is to be eaten. The humiliation in incarnation: to become bread. To be eaten: to be consumed by sorrow, sickness, and death.

Cf. Weil, *La Pesanteur et la grâce,* 38, 41.

We become one as we become the (sacrificial) food. The sacrifice is the mystical body; which is not offered on behalf of martyrs, since they are themselves that sacrificial body. In the unified body there is no vicarious (representative) sacrifice. The unified body feeds on itself: *ut solum corpus Christi ipsius carne reficiatur.* He gives us his body to eat, so that we might be assimilated into his body. The offering of ourselves must be of him in us to him, that is to say, our union.

Cf. Lubac, *Corpus Mysticum,* 34, 40, 53, 94–95.

This world as food feeds on itself. The mystical body feeds on itself. Autophagy. The supper as self-sacrifice: *semetipsum in cena apostolorum immolavit*. The supper as autophagy: *se cibat ipse cibus; ut nos qui sumus corpus Christi sumamus corpus Christi.*

Lubac, *Corpus Mysticum* 84, 96–97.

Autophagy. The identity of the eater and what he eats; but in a reversal of the naturalistic view: the eater is changed into what he eats. We become his body, and his body is food. We become his body by becoming food. By being eaten we become food. *Cum pascit pascitur, et cum pascitur pascit*. The dualism overcome. When every action is sacrifice, then Brahman is the sacrificial act, and Brahman the thing sacrificed; and it is Brahman who does the sacrificing, in the fire which is Brahman.

Cf. Lubac, *Corpus Mysticum,* 200–202, 279, 289–290. *Bhagavad Gita,* IV, 23–24.

The true sacrifice is human sacrifice. Animal sacrifice is a false substitute, a pale imitation, a shadow. Abraham departs from human sacrifice, and Christ returns to it. From the shadow of substitutes to the reality of the human body: *de umbra transfertur ad corpus*. Present your bodies, a living sacrifice. The return of the projections. "Man contained in his limbs all Animals, and they were separated from him by cruel Sacrifices." As in schizophrenia: "Some patients declare that elephants and other beasts live in their bodies."

Blake, *Jerusalem*, pl. 27. Roheim, *Magic and Schizophrenia,* 102. Cf. Freud, *Totem and Taboo,* ch. IV, section 6.

The true sacrifice is in one body. "The slave [captive] represents the master's [victor's] body offered to the god, the former being merely a symbol for the latter." The Place of Holy Sacrifice where Friends Die for each other, will become the Place of Murder & Unforgiving, Never-awaking Sacrifice of Enemies. "Mahomet slew, Jesus Christ caused his own to be slain." But mostly Mahomet slays. Overcoming the dualism of self and other: the identity of the sacrificer, the victim, and the god. *Ipse offerens, ipse et oblatio.*

Séjourné, *Burning Water,* 155. Blake, *Jerusalem,* pl. 48, ll. 55–57. Pascal, *Pensées,* no. 598. Augustine, *De Civitate Dei,* X, 21.
Cf. Hubert and Mauss, *Sacrifice,* 42, 101.

The identity of the sacrificer and the victim: the sacrifice of identity. The last cruel sacrifice is sacrifice of the separateness or the self; self-sacrifice, self-slaughter, self-annihilation. The last cruel sacrifice is the crucifixion of the self.

The identity of the sacrificer, the victim, and the god: no more sacrifice. The unified body feeds on itself. From crucifixion to eating. The Last Supper is the New Testament: "my blood of the new testament." His crucifixion, the last of the old sacrifices; our Eucharist, the first of the new. The supper is the last thing, not the cross: eschatology is eating; the marriage feast of the Lamb.

From crucifixion to eucharist; from the blood to the bloodless sacrifice; from sacrifice to feeding. The solution to the problem of war. Bread and wine, this is my body. *Hoc in carne nihil carnale nihilque cruentum.* And Melchizedek, King of Salem, which means Peace, brought forth bread and wine.

Cf. Lubac, *Corpus Mysticum,* 160–161. Genesis XIV, 18.

"My whole Christianity is a taste for *signs* and for the elements of water, bread, wine." His body is to be found in bread; *caro sub forma panis operta.* Our daily bread; a daily incarnation. It is always his body that we eat. He dies daily. The reality of body is in bread, eaten. The real presence; bread worship. Dionysus, worship of the wine. Corporeal presence in or under or with the bread and wine. In any meal. Revelations III, 20: Behold, I stand at the door and knock: if any man hear my voice, and open the door, I will come in to him, and will sup with him, and he with me.

Hamann in Smith, *J. G. Hamann,* 69.
Cf. Lubac, *Corpus Mysticum,* 69, 71, 178, 186, 236.

Real presence; in the present. If he is not present in the food, he is not present at all. In the real eating: his body is sensually present, handled, broken, chewed.

Cf. Lubac, *Corpus Mysticum,* 167.

Incarnation is impanation, invination, immolation. "Every householder commits inevitably the five-fold sin of killing, which results from (1) the pestle and mortar, (2) the grinding-stone, (3) the oven, (4) the water-jar, and (5) the broom. He is absolved from these sins by the performance of the five obligatory sacrifices." There is no way to avoid murder; except by ritual murder.

Bhagavad Gita III, 13 (and Nikhilananda commentary).

Impanation, invination, unification: out of many grains one bread: out of many grapes one wine. The secret of unification is in bread and wine. In Blake, "the wine-press and the mill may represent not only the disintegration of form, but the reuniting of all nature into the body and blood of a universal Man . . . the great communion feast in which human life is reintegrated into its real form."

Frye, *Fearful Symmetry*, 290.

From crucifixion to eating; from the bloody to the bloodless sacrifice; from the old to the new; from the letter to the spirit. Idols require human sacrifice, literally; Moloch. Abstain from things offered to idols, and from blood. The problem of war is the problem of idolatry, or literalism. The crude materialism of physical conquest: *wie schwer der andere wirklich* einzuverleiben *ist*. Therefore the opposite of war, the true war, is poetry. "Art Degraded, Imagination Denied, War Governed the Nations." "Rouse up, O Young Men of the New Age: set your foreheads against the ignorant Hirelings! For we have Hirelings in the Camp, the Court and the University, who would, if they could, for ever depress Mental and prolong Corporeal War."

Blake, *Milton*, Preface; *Laocoön*, 775. Nietzsche, *Aus dem Nachlass*, 421. Cf. Acts XV, 29; XXI, 25.

From the bloody to the bloodless sacrifice: from the literal to the spiritual body. Real presence, in a bloodless sacrifice; not sublimation, but transubstantiation of the body. *Corpus non corporaliter*. The solution to the problem of war in the Eucharist, with transubstantiation. *Hoc in carne nihil cruentum.*

Lubac, *Corpus Mysticum*, 160–161.

Communion. The spiritual body a mystical body. The union is not a sociological fact, is not a fact of ecclesiastical or temporal power, is not a fact of this world of power politics, is not a fact according to the reality-principle. The union is not given but made, in the Eucharist, in the eating. The unity is not an analogy of the natural (organic) body given, but is made by the transubstantiation.

Cf. Lubac, *Corpus Mysticum,* 103, 129–131, 145, 209.

The transubstantiation of the Eucharist is the transfiguration of the resurrection. *Mutatio carnis in spiritum:* It is raised a spiritual body. A spiritual body, a body which is not in Simple Location; *corpus non corporaliter.* The paradoxes of action at a distance: the ubiquity of Christ's glorified body; Christ is able to project the life-giving power of his glorified body without spatial limitation.

Cf. Lubac, *Corpus Mysticum,* 153–154.

The true sacrifice is total, a making holy of the whole; the false sacrifice sacrifices a part, *pars pro toto;* a part cut off, bitten off; *the* part; castration. Partial incorporation is castration; the part eaten, when the eating is partial, is always a penis. Castration is mitigated (symbolic) cannibalism; the original aim is to eat, and to eat all.

Cf. Fenichel, "Trophy and Triumph," 144, 150–153, 159, 161; "Respiratory Introjection," 223. Roheim, *Gates of the Dream,* 96. Lewin, "Body as Phallus," 33.

Partial incorporation or total incorporation; eating a penis and eating a body. Partial incorporation is eating of a representative (symbolic) part, which is only partially (symbolically) eaten; as possession is mitigated (symbolic) eating. The part partially eaten remains a separate part, undigested; the original ownership is not obliterated: it is a part "borrowed," i.e., stolen: private property is theft. "The incorporated object retains its separate existence, rages inside her against the sinful eater, becomes her super-ego." The attempt "to assure one's identification with the father by incorporating a part of him" is not enough. The conflict of ambivalence is not resolved. "The phantasy of oral incorporation of the penis was an attempt to eliminate the hated penis from the world. This attempt, however, failed, since the introjected penis continued to threaten her from the inside."

Fenichel, "Introjection and Castration Complex," 56, 58; cf. "Trophy and Triumph," 144. Freud, *Moses and Monotheism,* 132.

Partial incorporation, or total incorporation, integration. "It is possible that we have in the relation between body-images two different types, the one completely integrating his own body-image with the body-image of others, and the other having the various parts of the body-image not integrated into a whole. . . . Summation and integration." Participation (playing a part) or fusion. *L'Apocalypse, c'est-à-dire la dissolution de la série dans le groupe en fusion.*

Schilder, *Image of the Human Body,* 237. Sartre, *Critique de la raison dialectique,* 391.

X
Fire

The choice is between partial incorporation and total incorporation (integration). Participation (playing a part) or fusion. Total incorporation, or fusion, is combustion in fire. "The way he behaved could also be described by saying that he kept me inside of him. . . . Yet I did not feel that these ways of talking about what happened were entirely adequate; for all of them take for granted the idea of a clear boundary; if I am felt to be inside him then he has a boundary, and the same if a bit of him is felt to be projected into me. But there was much material in this analysis to do with burning, boiling down, and melting, which seemed to me to express the idea of the obliteration of boundaries."

Milner, "The Role of Illusion in Symbol Formation," 94.

Set fire to the sacrifice. The sacrificial fire, the sacrificial food; the food is fuel. All things are food, are fire. The real prayer is to see this world go up in flames.

Cf. Evdokimov, *La Femme et le salut du monde,* 240. *Chandogya Upanishad* V, iv, 1.

The true sacrifice is total, holocaust. *Consummatum est.* The one is united with the all, in a consuming fire.

To bring this world to an end, in a final conflagration, or explosion, bursting the boundaries. "If the whole of mankind were once more integrated in a single spiritual body, the universe as we see it would burst." Satori is explosion: "The balloon bursts, every limitation disappears: the one is united with the all." "To accumulate in the invisible the charge of energy which will one day blow up in him all the cave of phantoms."

Frye, *Fearful Symmetry,* 44; cf. Blake, *Night* IX, 230. Benoit, *Supreme Doctrine,* 111, 104.
Cf. Meerloo, *That Difficult Peace,* 23, 28, 107, 131, 187.

The final conflagration; or apocalypse. The unity of life and death as fire. "That Nature is a Heraclitean Fire and of the comfort of the Resurrection."

Das Lebend'ge will ich preisen
Das nach Flammentod sich sehnet.

Hopkins, *Poems.* Goethe, "Selige Sehnsucht," *West-Östlicher Divan.*

To heal, to cauterize. Therapy as apocalypse, conflagration; error burned up. Not catharsis but cruelty. "He would make what he called furnaces, with a very careful choice of what ingredients should make the fire. . . . And often there had to be a sacrifice, a lead soldier had to be added to the fire, and this figure was spoken of either as the victim or the sacrifice. . . . The fire seemed to be here not only a destructive fire, but also the fire of Eros; and not only the figurative expression of his own passionate bodily feelings, not only the phantasy representative of the wish for passionate union with the external world, but also a way of representing the inner fire of concentration."

Milner, "The Role of Illusion in Symbol Formation," 96.
Cf. Artaud, *The Theater and Its Double*, ch. I. "Plague."

The fire next time. The revolution, or second coming; he will baptize you with the Holy Spirit and with fire.

Luke III, 16.

A fiery consummation. Not suspense, but end-pleasure; not partial sacrifice (castration), but total holocaust. It is as fire that sex and war and eating and sacrifice are one. "Woman, verily, O Gautama, is a sacrificial fire. In this case the sexual organ is the fuel: when one invites, the smoke; the vulva, the flame; when one inserts, the coals; the sexual pleasure, the sparks. In this fire the gods offer semen. From this oblation arises the fetus." Sex and war and the Last Judgment—"the Loins, the place of the Last Judgement." The word consummation refers both to the burning world and the sacred marriage.

Chandogya Upanishad, V, viii, 1–2. Blake, *Jerusalem*, pl. 30, l. 38. Cf. Frye, *Fearful Symmetry*, 196. A. Balint, "Die mexikanische Kriegshieroglyphe." Reik, *Masochism in Modern Man*, 51, 59–64.

Learn to love the fire. The alchemical fire of transmutation: *Wolle die Wandlung. O sei für die Flamme begeistert.* To be content in the purgatorial fire. The fires of hell: "Walking among the fires of hell, delighting in the enjoyment of Genius, which to Angels look like torment and insanity." The apocalyptic fire: "Meditate on the make-believe world as burning to ashes, and become *being above human.*"

Blake, *Marriage of Heaven and Hell,* pls. 6–7. Reps, *Zen, Flesh, Zen, Bones,* 165. Rilke, *Sonnets to Orpheus,* II, xii.
Cf. Dante, *Inferno* I, 118–120.

Love is all fire; and so heaven and hell are the same place. As in Augustine, the torments of the damned are part of the felicity of the redeemed. Two cities; which are one city. Eden is a fiery city; just like hell.

Cf. Augustine, *De Civitate Dei,* XXII, 30.

The truth concealed from the priest and revealed to the warrior: that this world always was and is and shall be ever-living fire. Revealed to the lover too: every lover is a warrior; love is all fire.

Chandogya Upanishad, V, iii 7. Heraclitus, frg. 29.

The resolution of the antinomy between liberation and repression: fire. "Some allow the senses to wander unchecked, and try to see the Brahman everywhere; for these sense-objects are the offering and sense-enjoyment the sacrificial fire." To be aflame at every point. To be alive is to be burning.

Bhagavad Gita, IV, 27.
Cf. Voznesensky in Blum, "The Artist in Russia," 72.

Fire is freedom. Spontaneous combustion. Spontaneity is ardor.

Violent eruption, vulcanism; the patient becomes violent, as he wakes up. The madness of the millennia breaks out: madness is, Dionysus is, violence.

Love is violence. The kingdom of heaven suffereth violence, from hot love and living hope.

Sartre, *Critique de la raison dialectique,* 428, 439, 455. Dante, *Il Paradiso,* XX, 94. Matthew XI, 12.

Birth is bursting, the shell burst. The start is violent. The great heroic deed is to be born; to slay the dragon, to kill the mother, to conquer Tiamat. Every child, like Athena, is born fully armed; is a knife that opens the womb.

Cf. Arendt, *Revolution,* 10. Roheim, "The Dragon and the Hero: Part One," 43–53.

Not peace but a sword. Peace lies in finding the true war. The reconciliation of opposites, the making of friendship, takes place on the battlefield. The hieroglyph for war is Atlachinolli, "Burning Water." Burning water; *effusion et ardeur;* efflorescence and hemorrhage; blossoming war. In ancient Mexico, "The symbol of the world thus brought together is a cross."

Séjourné, *Burning Water,* 73.
Cf. *Iliad,* VI, 212–236. Balint, "Die mexikanische Kriegshieroglyphe," 413–428. Richard, *Mallarmé,* 119, 473, 501.

The identity of peace and war, of Zen and Ken. "The secret of victory without conflict. . . . One must break through to the world where all things are essentially of one body." "In the consciousness that all things are essentially of one body the 'other' can be equated with oneself and oneself with the 'other.'" "Victory without contending —how can this be achieved? . . . It comes the moment the stage is reached when the enemy no longer sees me nor I the enemy, when heaven and earth are yet undivided and light and shade are one, before *In* and *Yo* (Yin and Yang) reveal themselves."

Durckheim, *The Japanese Cult of Tranquillity*, 83.

Find the true fire; of which the fires of war are a Satanic parody. Fight fire with fire. The true teachers of peace are those who have the highest power, who can work miracles, who are masters of fire. Therefore the Buddhas are called Jinas, Conquerors.

Cf. AE, *Candle of Vision*, 137–139. Govinda, *Foundations of Tibetan Mysticism*, 279.

In Eden the two Fountains of the River of Life are War and Hunting; perverted here into Fountains of bitter Death and corroding Hell.

Blake, *Milton*, pl. 35, ll. 2–3; *Jerusalem*, pl. 43, ll. 31–32.

War is war perverted. The problem is not the war but the perversion. And the perversion is a repression; war is sex perverted. "War is energy Enslav'd."

Blake, *Night* IX, 152.
Cf. Frye, *Fearful Symmetry*, 262–263.

War is energy Enslav'd. War is what happens to the weak, the impotent; so that they might at least be touched with lowest form of violence; or as the death decreed for those who run away from battle.

> The plain truth is that people want war. They want it anyhow: for itself, and apart from each and every possible consequence. It is the final bouquet of life's fireworks. The born soldier wants it hot and actual. The non-combatant wants it in the background, and always as an open possibility, to feed his imagination. War is human nature at its uttermost. We are here to do our uttermost. It is a sacrament. Society would rot without the mystical blood-payment.

James, "Remarks at the Peace Banquet," 304.

The thing, then, is not to abolish war but to find the true war. Open the hidden Heart in Wars of Mutual Benevolence, Wars of Love.

Blake, *Jerusalem*, pl. 97, l. 14; cf. pl. 43, ll. 40–43.

To find the true war, the true sacrament; to avoid idolatry (Mexican sacrifices, Moloch); it is all a question of symbolism. To see the sacrament of war as a false sacrament is to see the demonic parody, the anti-Christ. To see it is to see through it; to see through it is to burn up the idols. "It is Burnt up the Moment Men cease to behold it."

Blake, *A Vision of the Last Judgement*, 617.

To find the true fire. Semele asked for the full presence of her divine lover, and received the thunderbolt. *Hiroshima mon amour*. Save us from the literal fire. The literal-minded, the idolaters, receive the literal fire. Each man suffers his own fire.

The real fire, the chariot of fire, the Fiery Chariot of his Contemplative Thought. The real fight, the mental fight; poetry, a sword of lightning, ever unsheathed, that consumes the scabbard that would contain it.

Cf. Blake, *A Vision of the Last Judgement,* 611. Shelley, "Defence of Poetry," 221.

Apocalyptic fire. "Error or Creation will be Burned up, and then, and not till Then, Truth or Eternity will appear. It is Burnt up the Moment Men cease to behold it." "The whole creation will be consumed and appear infinite and holy, whereas it now appears finite and corrupt." If these fires are discovered, no other fires are necessary: in these fires not a hair of their head is singed.

Blake, *Marriage of Heaven and Hell,* pl. 14; *A Vision of the Last Judgement,* 617.

The final judgment, the everlasting bonfire, is here now. Truth is error burned up.

The true body is the body burnt up, the spiritual body. The unity is not organic-natural unity, but the unity of fire. "But first the notion that man has a body distinct from his soul is to be expunged; this I shall do by printing in the infernal method, by corrosives, which in Hell are salutary and medicinal, melting apparent surfaces away, and displaying the infinite which was hid." The apocalyptic fire burns up the reality of the material world. In the baptism of water we are buried with Christ; in the baptism of fire we are conformed to the body of his glory.

Blake, *Marriage of Heaven and Hell,* pl. 14.
Daniélou, *Origen,* 95.

XI
Fraction

To eat and to be eaten. The grain must be ground, the wine pressed; the bread must be broken. The true body is a body broken.

> Nothing can be sole or whole
> That has not been rent.

Yeats, "Crazy Jane Talks with the Bishop."
Cf. Dylan Thomas, "This bread I break." Frye, *Fearful Symmetry*, 290.

To be is to be vulnerable. The defense mechanisms, the character-armor, is to protect from life. Frailty alone is human; a broken, a ground-up (contrite) heart.

Cf. Weil, *La Pesanteur et la grâce*, 125.

In the upper sector, the realm of the gods, "whose carefree life, dedicated to aesthetic pleasures, is indicated by dance and music. On account of this one-sided dedication to their own pleasures, they forget the true nature of life, the limitations of their own existence, the sufferings of others, their own transiency. They do not know that they live only in a state of temporary harmony. . . . They live, so to say, on the accumulated capital of past good deeds without adding new values. They are gifted with beauty, longevity and freedom from pain, but just this lack of suffering, of obstacles and exertion, deprives the harmony of their existence of all creative impulses." "Rebirth in heavenly realms is not an aim which Buddhists think worth striving for. . . . It leads to a strengthening of the ego-illusion and to a deeper entanglement in the *saṁsāric* world."

Govinda, *Foundations of Tibetan Mysticism*, 238–239.

There is a seal or sepulcher to be broken, a rock to be broke open, to disclose the living water; an eruption. Begin then with a fracture, a cesura, a rent; opening a crack in this fallen world, a shaft of light.

Cf. Richard, *Mallarmé*, 539.

Literal meanings are icons become stone idols; the stone sepulcher, the stone tables of the law. The New Testament remained hidden in the Old, like water in the rock; until the cross of Christ broke the rock open. Iconoclasm, the word like a hammer that breaketh the rock in pieces.

Cf. Luther cited in Hahn, "Luthers Auslegungsgrundsätze," 190n. Jeremiah XXIII, 29.

Open is broken. There is no breakthrough without breakage. A struggle with an angel, which leaves us scarred, or lame. Every dream is a struggle; the possible confronting the real, abruptly.

Man the measure of all things is the microcosmic man; in little all the sphere. Stretch yourself, then, to the breaking point: *"Ehr sey also hoch, dicke, breyt und lang, wye er am kreuz gehangen hat."* To be so stretched is to be crucified; it is the crucified body that is the measure of all things: *statera facta corporis.*

Müntzer cited in Holl, "Luther und die Schwärmer," 437. Weil, *La Pesanteur et la grâce,* 109.

The crucified body, the crucified mind. The norm is not normality but schizophrenia, the split, broken, crucified mind. "If we throw a crystal to the ground, it breaks, but it does not break haphazard; in accordance with the lines of cleavage it falls into fragments, where limits were already determined by the structure of the crystal, although they were invisible. Psychotics are fissured and splintered structures such as these. We cannot deny them a measure of that awe with which madmen were regarded by the people of ancient times." Split the stick and there is Jesus.

Freud, *New Introductory Lectures,* 80. Cage, *Silence,* 70.

Stretch yourself, to the breaking point. It is not true unless it hurts; the evidence is martyrdom. "All truths are bloody truths for me." We do not know the truth because we repress it; and we repress it because it is painful.

Kaufmann, *Nietzsche,* 68.

To the breaking point. Carrying the thought through to the end; crucial experiments, *experimentum crucis.* A witness (martyr) steadfast to the end, tested *in extremis.* Extremism. Truth is not in safety or in the middle. "*Les oeuvres d'art naissent toujours de qui a affronté le danger, de qui est allé jusqu'au bout d'une expérience.*"

Rilke cited in Bachelard, *La Poétique de l'espace,* 198.

Aphorism is exaggeration, or grotesque; in psychoanalysis nothing is true except the exaggerations; and in poetry, "*cet extrémisme est le phénomène même de l'élan poétique.*" Aphorism is exaggeration, extravagant language; the road of excess which leads to the palace of wisdom.

Adorno, *Minima Moralia,* 78. Blake, *Marriage of Heaven and Hell,* pl. 7. Bachelard, *La Poétique de l'espace,* 198.

Exaggeration or extravagance; not to count the cost. Go for broke. Aphorism is recklessness; it goes too far. Intellect is courage; the courage to risk its own life; to play with madness. "*Poètes, voici la loi mystérieuse: Aller au delà. Aller au delà, extravaguez, soit, comme Homère, comme Ezéchiel, comme Pindare, comme Salomon, comme Archilogue, comme Horace, comme Saint-Paul, comme Saint-Jean, comme Saint-Jérôme, comme Tertullien, comme Pétrarque, comme Alighieri, comme Ossian, comme Cervantes, comme Rabelais, comme Shakespeare, comme Milton, comme Mathurin Régnier, comme Agrippa d'Aubigné, comme Molière, comme Voltaire. Extravaguez avec ces doctes, extravaguez avec ces justes, extravaguez avec ces sages. Quos vult AUGERE Jupiter dementat.*" Aphorism, the form of the mad truth, the Dionysian form.

Hugo, "Promontorium Somnii," 309.

Only the exaggerations are true. *Credo quia absurdum;* as in parables or poetry. Aphoristic form is suicide, or self-sacrifice; for truth must die. Intellect is sacrifice of intellect, or fire; which burns up as it gives light.

Cf. *Bhagavad Gita*, IV, 19.

Broken flesh, broken mind, broken speech. Truth, a broken body: fragments, or aphorisms; as opposed to systematic form or methods: "Aphorisms, representing a knowledge broken, do invite men to inquire farther; whereas Methods, carrying the show of a total, do secure men, as if they were at farthest."

Bacon in McLuhan, *Gutenberg Galaxy*, 102–103.

Systematic form attempts to evade the necessity of death in the life of the mind as of the body; it has immortal longings on it, and so it remains dead. *Ducunt volentem fata, nolentem trahunt.* The rigor is *rigor mortis;* systems are wooden crosses, Procrustean beds on which the living mind is pinned. Aphorism is the form of death and resurrection: "the form of eternity."

Kaufmann, *Nietzsche*, 66.

Aphorism, or symbolism, as in *Finnegans Wake:* "A mode of broken or syncopated manipulation to permit *inclusive* or simultaneous perception of a total or diversified field. Such, indeed, is symbolism by definition—a collocation, a *parataxis* . . . without a point of view or lineal connection or sequential order." Symbolism, or grotesque: "A fine grotesque is the expression, in a moment, by a series of symbols thrown together in bold and fearless connection, of truths which it would have taken a long time to express in any verbal way, and of which the connection is left for the beholder to work out for himself; the gaps, left or overleapt by the haste of the imagination, forming the grotesque character."

McLuhan quoting Ruskin, *Gutenberg Galaxy,* 266–267.

Systematic form; generalities. All knowledge is particular, goes into the natural man in bits, a scrap here, a scrap there. Food is taken in bites. Bread broken to feed five thousand.

Cf. Blake in Frye, *Fearful Symmetry,* 15. Pound, *Kulchur,* 98–99.

Broken form. Against beauty as such. No form nor comeliness. Abrupt; uneven; inconsistent. By Ciceronian standards, *mutila quaedam et hiartia.*

Isaiah LIII, 2. Cicero, *Orator,* 32.

"A new heroic era has opened," Mandelstam wrote in 1921, "in the life of the word. The word is flesh and bread. It shares the fate of bread and flesh: suffering."

Fanger, "The Prose of Osip Mandelstam," 47.

Beyond atomism. Fragmentation unto dust, and the word becomes seminal again. The sower soweth the word. Dionysus broken and scattered is seed scattered. But if it die it bringeth forth much fruit. The body is made whole by being broken.

John XII, 24.

Sanskrit *bindu:* "This word, which has many meanings, like 'point, dot, zero, drop, germ, seed, semen,' . . . It is the point from which inner and outer space have their origin and in which they become *one* again." The thought, poem, is a cell or seed; a germ of living thought: growing from nothing to ripeness. Instead of the dead wood of systems, the tree of life; ramifications; branched thoughts new-grown with pleasant pain.

Govinda, *Foundations of Tibetan Mysticism,* 116.

Broken speech; speech broken by silence. To let the silence in is symbolism. "In symbol there is concealment and yet revelation: here therefore, by Silence and by Speech acting together, comes a double significance."

Carlyle, *Sartor Resartus,* Book III, ch. III, "Symbols."

XII
Resurrection

II Corinthians III, 6: The letter killeth, but the spirit giveth life. Literal meanings as against spiritual or symbolical interpretations, a matter of Life against Death. The return to symbolism, the rediscovery that everything is symbolic—*alles Vergängliche nur ein Gleichniss*—a penis in every convex object and a vagina in every concave one—is psychoanalysis. A return or turning point, the beginning of a new age; the Third Kingdom, the age of the spirit prophesied by Joachim of Fiore; or the second coming, the resurrection of the body. It is raised a spiritual or symbolical body; the awakening to the symbolical life of the body.

The return to symbolism would be the end of the Protestant era, the end of Protestant literalism. Symbolism in its pre-Protestant form consisted of typological, figural, allegorical interpretations, of both scripture and liturgy.

But the great Protestant Reformers were very explicit in their condemnation of the typological method: "The literal sense of Scripture alone is the whole essence of faith and of Christian theology." *Sola fide, sola litera:* faith is faith in the letter.

Luther in Miller, *Roger Williams,* 34–35.

Protestant literalism: the crux is the reduction of meaning to a single meaning—univocation. Luther's word is *Eindeutigkeit:* the "single, simple, solid and stable meaning" of scripture; *unum simplicem solidum et constantem sensum.* Compare Calvin on Galatians IV, 22–26: "But as the apostle declares that these things are allegorized, Origen, and many others along with him, have seized the occasion of torturing Scripture in every possible manner away from the true sense. Scripture they say is fertile, and thus produces a variety of meanings. I acknowledge that Scripture is a most rich and inexhaustible fountain of wisdom: but I deny that its fertility consists in the various meanings which any man at his pleasure may assign. Let us know that the true meaning of Scripture is the natural and obvious meaning, and let us embrace and abide by it resolutely."

Cf. Holl, "Luthers Bedeutung für den Fortschrift der Auslegungskunst," 551. Hahn, "Luthers Auslegungsgrundsätze," 210.

Augustine had said: "What more liberal and more fruitful provision could God have made in regard to Sacred Scriptures than that the same words might be understood in several senses, all of which are sanctioned by the concurring testimony of other passages equally divine?" The Medieval schema of a fourfold meaning in everything—the quadriga, the four-horsed chariot—however mechanical in practice, is at least a commandment not to rest in one simple solid and constant meaning. As in Blake also:

> Now I a fourfold vision see,
> And a fourfold vision is given to me;
> 'Tis fourfold in my supreme delight
> And threefold in soft Beulah's night
> And twofold Always. May God us keep
> From Single vision and Newton's sleep!

So also the psychoanalytic principle of over-determination: "Psychical acts and structures are invariably over-determined." The principle of over-determination declares that there cannot be just one "true" interpretation of a symptom or symbol: it forbids literal-mindedness.

Augustine, *De Doctrina Christiana,* III, 38. Blake, Letter to Butts, 22 November 1802. Freud, *Totem and Taboo,* 100.

Protestant literalism is modern scholarship. Parallel to the emphasis on the one true meaning of scripture there was an increase in Luther's interest in grammar and textual criticism; to establish the text, *die feste Schrift*, a mighty fortress; the authoritative text.

Cf. Hahn, "Luthers Auslegungsgrundsätze," 207.

Textual criticism is part of the search for the one true and literal meaning. The old spiritual or symbolical consciousness had not hunted that will-o'-the-wisp, the one true text; instead it found symbolical meaning in every textual variation. Even the slips of the scribe were significant, as even the slips of the tongue become significant again for Freud. The early Luther, who, as he himself acknowledged later, was enthusiastic for symbolical interpretations, brought variant readings into happy harmony by applying the principle of over-determination: "*Die Anwendung des vierfachen Schriftsinnes geht sogar so weit, dass abweichende Lesarten durch den verschiedenen Gebrauch der Sinne zur Übereinstimmung gebracht werden.*"

Hahn, "Luthers Auslegungsgrundsätze," 200.

Modern humanistic, literary, and historical scholarship, *Geisteswissenschaft*, is the pursuit of the literal truth; and it was the commitment to a literal interpretation of the Bible that modernized scholarship. Modern humanistic scholarship is the Renaissance counterpart of Reformation literalism.

Dilthey, "Die Entstehung der Hermeneutik," 324.

The basic assumption of modern hermeneutics, the organic unity of the document, is a commitment to univocation; and was elaborated by Protestantism to set up the one true meaning of scripture. Thus for example the Lutheran explicator *par excellence*, Flacius: "It was no little obstacle to the clarity of Scripture and to the truth and purity of Christian doctrine, that practically all the writers and fathers in their interpretations and explications of the sacred writings treated them as if they were a miscellaneous collection of sentiments, and not as an artistic unity conforming to correct principles of composition. In sacred scripture, as in all works of literature, the true meaning depends on the context, on the purpose of the work as a whole, and on the organic relations which unite the parts as members are united in one body."

Flacius cited in Dilthey, "Das natürliche System der Geisteswissenschaften," 118.

The crux in the reduction of meaning to a single meaning—both in scriptural and in literary exegesis—the crux in univocation, is the reduction of meaning to conscious meaning: *intentio auctoris*, the author's intention. But the unconscious is the true psychic reality; and the unconscious is the Holy Spirit. The opposite of the letter is the spirit. "The *sensus plenior* is that additional, deeper meaning, intended by God but not clearly intended by the human author."

Brown, *The Sensus Plenior of Sacred Scripture*, 92.
Cf. Lubac, *Histoire et esprit*, 387, 408.

The spirit inspires (the god is Dionysus). The orthodox Protestant faith is Protestant fundamentalism; if meaning is restricted to the conscious intention of the author, then divine inspiration means that the holy spirit is literally the author; the holy scripture is literally inspired. The inspiration of scripture is reduced to the infallibility of scripture, literally understood.

Cf. Hahn, "Luthers Auslegungsgrundsätze," 166. Ebeling, "Die Anfänge von Luthers Hermeneutik," 223.

The identification of God's word with scripture, the written or printed word; somewhat to the neglect of the word made flesh. The book is a materialization of the spirit; instead of the living spirit, the worship of a new material idol, the book.

There is also the new hierarchy of scribes, controlling the interpretation, the higher scholarship. Since the one single and solid meaning does not in fact reveal itself, the commentary which does establish it becomes the higher revelation. The apparent deference of the expert to the text is a fake.

There is another kind of Protestantism possible; a Dionysian Christianity; in which the scripture is a dead letter to be made alive by spiritual (symbolical) interpretations; in which meaning is not fixed, but ever new and ever changing; in a continuous revelation; by fresh outpouring of the holy spirit. Meaning is made in a meeting between the holy spirit buried in the Christian and the holy spirit buried underneath the letter of scripture; a breakthrough, from the *Abgrund*, from the unconscious of the reader past the conscious intention of the author to the unconscious meaning; breaking the barrier of the ego and the barrier of the book. *Spiritus per spiritum intellegitur.*

Cf. Müntzer in Holl, "Luther und die Schwärmer," 430, 437.

> You said, "First came the wings and then the angel." We never noticed these words in Scripture, Holy Abbot.
>
> How could you have noticed them? Alas, your minds are still dim. You open the prophets and your eyes are able to see nothing but the letters. But what can the letters say? They are the black bars of the prison where the spirit strangles itself with screaming. Between the letters and the lines, and all around the blank margins, the spirit circulates freely; and I circulate with it and bring you this great message: Friars, first came the wings and then the angel!

Kazantzakis, *The Last Temptation of Christ*, 101–102.

Spiritus per spiritum intellegitur, Luther himself said. But for a Dionysian or enthusiastic Christianity we have to turn from Luther to Müntzer; to the Radical Reformation; to the lunatic fringe; *die Schwärmer*, the madmen,

Luther called them. From Luther to Müntzer: from faith to spirit; from profession of faith, or doctrinal confession, to possession of spirit; not remote identification with an event in past history, but active participation in a living spirit here now. The fruit of the spirit is not only new revelations, but also new miracles: *der Mut und die Kraft zum Unmöglichen.* The natural man is transformed into superman: "We fleshly earthly men are to become gods."

Luther in Holl, "Luthers Bedeutung für den Fortschrift der Auslegungskunst," 547. Müntzer in Holl, "Luther und die Schwärmer," 426, 429, 431.
Cf. Williams, *The Radical Reformation.*

The conflict between science and religion in the modern world stems not from Medieval obscurantism but from modern literalism; Protestant literalism and Catholic scholasticism; both exterminators of symbolism. William Whiston, *New Theory of the Earth* (1696), dedicated to "Summo Viro Isaaco Newton": "The burden of the treatise was an attack on the allegorical interpretation of the Creation in Genesis and proof that the Mosaic account was literally true in the sense that the new astronomy and the new physics were completely harmonious with it. Its key proposition was: 'The Mosaic Creation is not a Nice and Philosophical account of the Origin of All Things, but an Historical and True Representation of the formation of our single Earth out of a confused Chaos, and of the successive and visible changes thereof each day, till it became the habitation of Mankind.' The 'postulata' which Whiston set down in this work were completely acceptable to his patron. 'I. The obvious or Literal Sense of Scriptures is the True and Real one, where no evident Reason can be given to the contrary. . . .' "

Manuel, *Isaac Newton, Historian,* 143–144.
Cf. Dempf, *Sacrum Imperium,* 253–254.

A literal interpretation is a historical interpretation. Luther equates the simple, clear, and single meaning of the Bible with the historical meaning, *historica sententia,* and sees as the opposite of historical interpretation, symbolical interpretation (*ego quidem ab eo tempore quo cepi historicam sententiam amplecti, semper abhorrui ab allegoriis*).

Hahn, "Luthers Auslegungsgrundsätze," 209; cf. 211, 218.

The modern historical consciousness is Protestant literalism. The aim of modern historical science is to establish for historical events a single simple, solid, and constant meaning—what *really* happened; "*Wie es eigentlich gewesen ist.*" Ranke's phrase, without his respect for the mystery of individuality, was what the American professors brought back from Germany; to become the motor of the Ph.D. factory, mechanical literalism in action.

The fetishism of the document: the historian believes that the document speaks, speaks for itself. It is Luther's principle of *scriptura sui ipsius interpres;* the integrity of scripture, or the historical document, or the literary text; "*in eine Urkunde nicht fremde Begriffe hereintragen.*" The principle that every document must be interpreted in its own terms was necessarily first established in the case of sacred scripture.

Luther in Holl, "Luthers Bedeutung für den Fortschritt der Auslegungskunst," 558; cf. 559–560.

But documents do not speak for themselves. And so there is an inner contradiction: The same man who says scripture is its own interpreter says also that we press

Christ against scripture; *Christum urgemus contra scripturam.* By Christ he means his personal conviction, his private inner light, his inner certainty or intuition. There is in both Protestant religion and modern scholarship a double standard (not the same thing as a twofold vision): they combine self-effacing objectivity with self-asserting subjectivity, a principle of subjective intuition (Dilthey's *verstehen*).

Holl, "Luthers Bedeutung für den Fortschritt der Auslegungskunst," 561.

Literalism does not get rid of the magical element in scriptural or historical interpretation. The Holy Spirit, instead of a living spirit in the present, becomes the Holy Ghost, a voice from the past, enshrined in the book. The restriction of meaning to conscious meaning makes historical understanding a personal relation between the personality of the reader and the personality of the author, now dead. Spiritual understanding (*geistiges Verstehen*) becomes a ghostly operation, an operation with ghosts (*Geisteswissenschaft*). The document starts speaking for itself; the reader starts hearing voices. The subjective dimension in historical understanding is to animate the dead letter with the living reader's blood, his "experience"; and simultaneously let the ghost of the dead author slide into, become one with, the reader's soul. It is necromancy, or shamanism; magical identification with ancestors; instead of living spirit, to be possessed by the dead.

Literalism combines fetishism of the book with shamanism of the interpreter; science and subjectivity; pedantry and soul: modern humanistic scholarship. Luther's method of scriptural interpretation was a combination of grammatical science and soulful intuition: "*eine Verbin-*

dung von grammatischem Begreifen und seelischem Verstehen." Faith and philology.

Holl, "Luthers Bedeutung für den Fortschrift der Auslegungskunst," 558.

Instead of a living spirit, possession by the dead. The Protestant substituted for the ritual (magical) repetition of the past (Christ's passion), a purely mental invocation; a historical commemoration. Instead of a dramatic reënactment a reanimation in the mind only—the quest for the historical Jesus. But the Jesus of historical commemoration can only be the ghost of Jesus—*die Historie erreichet nicht Christi Fleisch und Blut,* history reaches not Christ's flesh and blood. The Jesus of commemorative ceremony and historical reconstruction is the passive, not the active, Jesus. The active Jesus can only be actively recreated. The historical reconstruction is a spectral image in a passive viewer.

Boehme, *De Incarnatione Verbi,* II, viii, 1.
Cf. Mowinckel, *Psalmenstudien,* II, 34. Frye, *Fearful Symmetry,* 387.

To say that historical events have a single meaning is to say that historical events are unique (singular); univocation constructs unilinear time. And on the other hand to see symbolism is to see eternal recurrence. The figural interpretation of scripture, which the Reformers suppressed, is inseparable from the idea of prefiguration. And the idea of prefiguration is of certain events corresponding to certain other events, as type to antitype; events anticipating other events; events which are prophetic of other events: events which are the fulfillment of earlier prophecies. At any rate where there is type and antitype, prophecy and fulfillment, there events are not unique and time not unilinear; rather we must say with

Tertullian, eternal recurrence is the universal law: nothing happens for the first time. *Universa conditio recidiva est: nihil non iterum est.*

Tertullian, *De Resurrectione mortuorum*, XII, 6; cited in Ladner, *Idea of Reform*, 133.

Nothing happens for the first time. There is nothing in the Old Testament which does not recur in the New Testament. This is the *concordia scripturarum*, the mysterious correspondence between the two scriptures, to be seen by those who have eyes to see. Its effect is to make Old and New contemporaneous; to transform time into eternity; history *sub specie aeternitatis*. Or history as poetry; prose goes straight forward without verses.

Cf. Benz, *Ecclesia Spiritualis*, 6.

Christianity is identified with unilinear time when Christianity no longer lives in expectation of a second coming. But if no second coming, then no first coming either; unless we are born again, we are not born at all. Nothing happens for the first time.

The Christian interpretation of history looks to a second coming, a recurrence of Christ; even as Christ was a return, a new edition of Adam. Leibnitz tells us that "M. Mercurius van Helmont believed that the soul of Jesus Christ was that of Adam, and that the new Adam repairing what the first had ruined was the same personage paying his old debt." "I think," adds Leibnitz, "one does well to spare oneself the trouble of refuting such ideas." It is time to turn from Leibnitz to M. Mercurius van Helmont. The idea of incarnation is not separable from the idea of reincarnation—*Messiah, Moses redivivus, Menschensohn.* Matthew XVI, 14: "some say that thou art John the Baptist; some Elias; and others Jeremias, or one of the prophets." In no other way can that which is knotted be undone, but by bending the loops of the knot in the reverse order: the knot to be undone has to be redone.

Leibnitz in Auerbach, "Figura," 236, n. 43.
Cf. Bentzen, *Messias–Moses redivivus–Menschensohn.* Irenaeus in Daniélou, *From Shadows to Reality,* 44. Daniélou, *Origen,* 124, 249: "The Incarnation is the principle coming of Christ, but only one of many."

Redemption is the second coming. Redemption is not in remote (historical) identification with a (unique) event in the past: Redemption is not vicarious. Redemption is in the second coming, the reincarnation, his presence in the present in us. Not by faith but by the spirit.

Redemption is symbolism. Pascal saw it all: "*Proof of the two Testaments at once.* To prove the two at one stroke, we need only see if the prophecies in one are fulfilled in the other. To examine the prophecies, we must understand them. For if we believe they have only one meaning, it is certain that the Messiah has not come; but if they have two meanings, it is certain that He has come in Jesus Christ. The whole problem then is to know if they have two meanings." The whole problem is to break with the doctrine of univocation. For if we believe that the Old Testament has only one meaning, it is certain that the Messiah has not yet come. In Protestant literalism there are of course prophecies in the Old Testament: but these are literal prophecies: what Luther called *sensus propheticus literalis.* The crux is univocation versus reincarnation: the Psalms may refer either to David or Christ, but not both.

Pascal, *Pensées,* no. 641. Holl, "Luthers Bedeutung für den Fortschrift der Auslegungskunst," 546.

The Messiah has not yet come: Judaism. Literalism (the letter and the law) is *Judaicus modus intelligendi.* Protestant orthodoxy is Judaism. Unilinear time removes the idea of redemption from influence on the affairs (history) of this world. For all practical purposes, the Messiah has not yet come. Then there are no turning points in history; no periods; and no end. But the original Christian experience is of a turning, a turn; conversion, peripety, revolution. The word of God is revolutionary: *sermo enim Dei venit mutaturus et innovaturus orbem, quoties venit;* not to interpret the world but to change it.

Lubac, *Histoire et esprit,* 399, 438–439. Luther cited in Griewank, *Die neuzeitliche Revolutionsbegriff,* 83.

Christianity is a New Testament: behold, I make all things new. Real history is the history of renewals, revolutions; as in the Apocalypse of John. The theologian who thinks that "only this simple rectilinear conception of unending time can be considered as the framework for the New Testament history of redemption," will also have to say that "the historical sense is completely lacking in the authors of the Primitive Christian writings." That is to say, the alleged New Testament sense of history is completely lacking in the New Testament.

Revelations XXI, 5. Cullmann, *Christ and Time,* 49, 94.

The experience of renewal impresses itself on the structure of history in the form of periodization. There must be at least two periods, B.C. and A.D. The God of Abraham, the God of Isaac, the God of Jacob, and not the god of the philosophers. Not a philosophical but a historical God; a revolutionary God, who when he comes, comes again.

Periodization involves periodicity. The world's great age begins anew, the golden years return. Things come round full circle; a turn is a return, and a new beginning; and revolution also is circular. Compare Pascal: "Adam *forma futuri.* The six days to form the one, the six ages to form the other. The six days, which Moses represents for the formation of Adam, are only the picture of the six ages to form Jesus Christ and the Church. If Adam had not sinned, and Jesus Christ had not come, there had been only one covenant, only one age of man, and the creation would have been represented as accomplished at one single time." Redemptive history, which looks to a new heaven and a new earth, looks to a second coming, and sees at least two periods, the Old and the New, or three periods, the Father, the Son, and the Spirit.

Pascal, *Pensées,* no. 655.
Cf. Benz, *Ecclesia Spiritualis,* 10–11. Lubac, *Histoire et esprit,* 220. Dempf, *Sacrum Imperium,* 232–260.

Oldness of letter, and newness of spirit. Historical literalism takes the periodization out of history; in Protestantism, the loss of the sense of the difference between Old Testament and New; Old and New Testament are made consistent, forced into conformity, to reveal the same literal truth. And the Puritans in New England can embark on a literal reproduction of Israel in the wilderness. Bondage to the letter is bondage to the past. Roger

Williams' fight for symbolical understanding is his fight for freedom.

Romans VII, 6
Cf. Miller, *Roger Williams*, 38, 43, 107, 185–186.

The symbolic interpretation of prophecy makes the interpreter a prophet; *spiritus per spiritum intellegitur.* All the Lord's people to be prophets. Prophets, or poets: sing unto the Lord a new song. The song must be new, or it is no song; the spirit is the creator spirit, making new creations. The spirit is understood by the spirit; by the same spirit, i.e., in the same style. The proper response to poetry is not criticism but poetry.

Cf. Numbers XI, 29. Blake, *Milton*, Preface. Benz, *Ecclesia Spiritualis*, 5.

The redemption of the Old does not abolish but fulfills it; not to destroy but to fulfill. Symbolical consciousness finds the New in the Old, and the Old in the New; *in veteribus novam, in novis veterem.* The symbolical interpretation of the old makes it new; this is the flowering of the rod, Aaron's rod that budded; the bitter waters of Marah made sweet.

Matthew V, 17; Numbers XVII; Exodus XV, 23–25.
Cf. Benz, *Ecclesia Spiritualis*, 10–11. Lubac, *Histoire et esprit*, 309, 410–411. Richard, *Mallarmé*, 600, 602.

Newness is not the gift of a *tabula rasa*, but a resurrection; or miraculous pregnancy. A virgin shall conceive, in old age, as in the case of Sarah, or the Roman Empire. Natural innocence is only an image of the real, the supernatural, the second innocence. After the fall; in old age: *sero te amavi, pulchritudo tam antiqua et tam nova, sero te amavi.* Late I learnt to love thee, beauty as ancient as thou art new; late I learnt to love thee.

Augustine, *Confessions,* X, 38.
Cf. Ladner, *The Idea of Reform,* 237. Richard, *Mallarmé,* 600, 602. Bachelard, *La Poétique de l'espace,* 47.

> Looking, therefore, upon sin, upon mortality, upon time flying by, upon moaning and labor and sweat, upon ages succeeding one another without rest, senselessly from infancy into old age—looking at these things, let us see in them the old man, the old day, the old song, the Old Testament. But if we turn to the things that are to be renewed, let us find a new man, a new day, a new song, the New Testament—and we shall love this newness so that we shall not fear there any oldness.

Augustine in Ladner, *The Idea of Reform,* 236–237.

Newness is renewal: *ad hoc enim venit, ut renovemur in illo;* making it new again, as on the first day; *herrlich wie am ersten Tag.* Reformation, or renaissance; rebirth. Life is Phoenix-like, always being born again out of its own death. The true nature of life is resurrection; all life is life after death, a second life, reincarnation. *Totus hic ordo revolubilis testatio est resurrectionis mortuorum.* The universal pattern of recurrence bears witness to the resurrection of the dead.

Cf. Ladner, *The Idea of Reform,* 133–141, 155.

Resurrection after crucifixion, after our old man is crucified. "More vividly than ever before he realized that art has two constant, two unending concerns: it always meditates on death and thus always creates life. All great, genuine art resembles and continues the Revelation of St. John."

Pasternak, *Dr. Zhivago,* ch. 3, *sub fin.*
Cf. Romans VI, 6.

The dead letter. The dead metaphor. It is only dead metaphors that are taken literally, that take us in (the black magic). Language is always an old testament, to be made new; rules, to be broken; dead metaphor, to be made alive; literal meaning, to be made symbolical; oldness of letter to be made new by the spirit. The creator spirit stands in the grave, in the midden heap, the dunghill of culture (as in *Finnegans Wake*); breaking the seal of familiarity; breaking the cake of custom; rolling the stone from the sepulcher; giving the dead metaphor new life.

Turbayne, *The Myth of Metaphor,* 26–27.

Symbolical consciousness begins with the perception of the invisible reality of our present situation: we are dead and our life is hid. Real life is life after death, or resurrection. The deadness with which we are dead here now is the real death; of which literal death is only a shadow, a bogey. Literalism, and futurism, are to distract us from the reality of the present.

Colossians III, 3.

To make it new is to make it recur. In fulfillment is recurrence, recapitulation. Fulfillment gathers up the past into the present in the form of a recapitulation: that in the dispensation of times there might be a recapitulation of all things in Christ. Recapitulate, ἀνακεφαλαιώσαθαι; with the metaphor of the head in both the Latin and the

Greek words. It is a gathering up of time into eternity; a transfiguration of time; the transfiguration, in which Moses and Elijah, who are the past, appeared unto them as present, talking with Jesus. Symbolical consciousness makes figural interpretations in order to accomplish the transfiguration.

Ephesians I, 10; Matthew XVII, 4; Mark IX, 4.
Cf. Auerbach, "Figura," 42. Daniélou, *From Shadows to Reality,* 23. Ladner, *The Idea of Reform,* 68–69.

Recapitulation of the past in the present. Only where there is the experience that there is again here now another crossing of the Red Sea can we speak of a Christian experience; or a psychoanalytical experience—"I have conjectured that the Exodus was originally not from Egypt to freedom, but from youth to manhood."

Roheim, "Some Aspects of Semitic Monotheism," 173.

Christian typology; karmic reincarnation; the phylogenetic factor in psychoanalysis. The thing that "happened long ago" did not happen to you individually, but to the race archetypically; or, if you prefer, it happened to you "in a previous incarnation." Blake insisted on innate ideas; Freud insisted on retaining the idea of memory-traces of our archaic inheritance; lacking a time scheme of recurrence, he retained the idea in the Lamarckian form of the inheritance of acquired characteristics. What psychoanalysis can under no circumstances do without is the idea of regression.

Cf. Freud, *Moses and Monotheism,* 158–159. Ferenczi, *Thalassa,* 50–51. Frye, *Fearful Symmetry,* 23.

Another scheme of time, another scheme of causality. Prefiguration is not preparation. "When we speak of the relation between a new poetic image and an archetype asleep in the depths of the unconscious, we will have to understand that this relation is not, properly speaking, a causal one." Archetype as cause, or *Ur-sach: Erscheinungen können nicht Ursachen sein.* Events are related to other events not by causality, but by analogy and correspondence. In the archetype is exemplary causality, *causa exemplaris.* In the Medieval system of fourfold causes, that goes with the four-horsed chariot of meaning, events are actualizations of potentialities eternally there—"their Forms Eternal Exist For-ever." The potentialities are latent till made patent; asleep till wakened. The events sleep in their causes; the archetypal form is the hidden life of things; awaiting resurrection.

Bachelard, *La Poétique de l'espace,* 1. Nietzsche, *Aus dem Nachlass,* 456. Blake, *Milton,* pl. 32, l. 38.
Cf. Barfield, *Saving the Appearances,* 88, 151. Daniélou, *Lord of History,* 130. Smith, *J. G. Hamann,* 97. Spengler, *Decline of the West,* I, 3–6.

In Freud, a primal crime, repeated in the death of Moses; in the death of Jesus; in every individual soul. In Christian typology, "For Origen the opposition of Agar and Sara is not the opposition of two historical peoples. It is rather the type of the intense conflict which goes on in each individual Christian. The historical conflict becomes that of Jew and Christian which each of us bears in himself. Thus the history of nations becomes the history of the individual soul, a transposition along the lines of authentic typology."

Daniélou, *From Shadows to Reality,* 141.
Cf. Freud, *Moses and Monotheism,* 140–141.

Redemptive history (anthropology) is anamnesis; to remember again what we have repressed; to recapitulate the phylogeny; a recollection of previous incarnations. "In recollection all former births passed before His eyes. Born in such a place, of such a name, and downwards to His present birth, so through hundreds, thousands, myriads, all His births and deaths He knew." Not an objective and distant study of strangers, but discovering and embracing ourselves; collecting the previous incarnations into a unity with oneself; to constitute the collective self, the Son of Man. To recapitulate the phylogeny is to reconstitute the phylum, the unity of the human race; the atonement. The atonement of mankind, not the forensic justification of the individual believer.

Ashvagosha, *Life of the Buddha,* quoted in Evan-Wentz, *Tibetan Book of the Dead,* lxiv.
Cf. Williams, *The Radical Reformation,* 839.

Dismembered, remembered. Symbolical consciousness is to remember the unity; history as the history of one man. The unity is the invisible reality; the unconscious is collective. Literalism singles out a separate holy church or nation, but "Christ Jesus, at His so long typed-out coming, abolished these national shadows and erected his spiritual kingdom." When literal kingdoms are seen to be only shadows of an invisible reality, "the partition-wall is broken down, and in respect of the Lord's special propriety to one country more than another, what difference between Asia and Africa, between Europe and America, between England and Turkey, London and Constantinople." Literalism is to take *pars pro toto*; symbolism reconstitutes the lost (hidden) unity.

Roger Williams in Miller, *Roger Williams,* 172, 150–151.
Cf. Freud, "Interpretation of Dreams," 370.

In any historical event, a repetition, reënactment, recapitulation, of the whole story from Genesis to Apocalypse. Christian *reformatio* recapitulates the original *formatio* of creation; the illumination is an incarnation (reincarnation) of the original *fiat lux*. Renewal is creation, and therefore deification.

Cf. Smith, *J. G. Hamann*, 98, 100. Ladner, *The Idea of Reform*, 170–172, 194.

In any event, the recapitulation of the whole story from Genesis to Apocalypse. In Ferenczi's apocalyptic theory of genitality the sexual act is a historical drama, a symbolic reënactment or recapitulation of all the great traumas in the history of the individual, of the species, of life itself. Psychoanalytic time is not gradual, evolutionary, but discontinuous, catastrophic, revolutionary. The sexual act is a return to the womb. But the separation of mother and child is a silhouette of the separation of life from the sea out of which it arose; and of the separation of life into two sexes; and of the separation of living from lifeless matter. Birth really is from water; the womb really is an introjected, incarnate, ocean. "The mother would, properly, be the symbol of and partial substitute for the sea, and not the other way about." In copulation the penis really is a fish in water. Symbolism is "buried and otherwise inaccessible history."

Ferenczi, *Thalassa*, 54, 44.
Cf. Freud, *General Introduction*, 168. Roheim, *Riddle of the Sphinx*, 204.

Physical, or "real" birth is really rebirth, a repetition of an archetypal birth of the cosmos from the cosmic egg. Generation is only an image of Regeneration. In Freud's *Beyond the Pleasure Principle;* and in Ferenczi's *Thalassa, a Theory of Genitality,* there is a new apocalypse. Symbolic consciousness is cosmic consciousness; and the per object of psychoanalysis is the cosmos; *psycha-lyse cosmique.* This is my body. The psychoanalysis c fossils as human forms; or mountains as mammals. ntogeny recapitulates orogeny—

> As, down among the palaeo-zoe
> he brights his ichthyic sign
> so brights he the middle-zone
> where the uterine forms
> are some beginnings of his creature.
> Brighter yet over the mammal'd Pliocene
> for these continuings
> certainly must praise him:
> How else, in his good time
> should the amorous Silvy
> to her sweetest dear
> her fairest bosom have shown?
>
> How else we?
> or he, himself?
> whose name is called He-with-us
> because he did not abhor the uterus.
> Whereby these uberal forms
> are to us most dear
> and of all hills
> the most august.

Jones, *Anathémata,* 74–75.
Cf. Eliade, *Patterns of Comparative Religion,* 414. Bachelard, *La Poétique de l'espace,* 107–113. Blake, *Jerusalem,* pl. 7, l. 65.

Dilthey has a brilliant page on the fundamental structure of modern Protestant Christianity, constructed on historical-critical-rational principles by humanists such as Occhino, Sozzini, Grotius. With them begins that remarkable period, in which Christianity, a subject of lively discussion in educated circles, still enjoyed solid acceptance on the basis of historical and moral-religious arguments, while at the same time the substance of what was accepted as proven was appreciably diminished. The inarticulate profundities accumulated in a great religious tradition were swept aside as mystical obscurantism, as the products of superstition or insanity. On the other hand, there was a reassertion of the Jewish-Christian belief in a Messiah whom God had signalized and evidenced in the miracles and in the resurrection. Thus out of a specific historical content arose a religious position which is no longer possible today. The validity of the holy scriptures and of Christianity was then for the first time made to depend on historical-critical proofs of the most important New Testament facts. The Resurrection was the cornerstone of the entire argument. The testimonies to the Resurrection are such that either it is a historical fact, or else the disciples must have been crazy. The miracles were recognized even by Christ's enemies; and since Christ was also an enemy of the Devil, they cannot be explained as the work of the Devil. Thus the evidence gives us historical proof of the divinity of Christ; only after the New Testament facts have been historically established, can the validity of the Old Testament be inferred as a corollary.

Cf. Dilthey, "Das natürliche System der Geisteswissenschaften," 131.

The quest for the historical Jesus: it is either literally true, including literal miracles, or not true at all. The historical Jesus, a unique event in unilinear time, what has that to do with us here now? The very argument which establishes his miraculous divinity separates our humanity from his divinity.

The second coming is the fulfillment of the first; and we are to look to the end, to the fulfillment; and not simply look back at the first coming, by the power of faith, by historical consciousness. We must rise from history to mystery: *ab historia in mysterium surgere.* The resurrection is to recur, to be fulfilled in us: it is to happen to his mystical body, which is our bodies; in this flesh. Along these lines Joachim transformed the resurrection from dead historical "fact" to a live historical, i.e., eschatological reality.

II Corinthians III, 13. Gregory the Great cited in Auerbach, "Figura," 47.
Cf. Cullmann, *Christ and Time,* 146. Benz, *Ecclesia Spiritualis,* 26.

To rise from history to mystery is to experience the resurrection of the body here now, as an eternal reality; to experience the *parousia,* the presence in the present, which is the spirit; to experience the reincarnation of the incarnation, the second coming; which is his coming in us.

> Our life is as a fire dampened, or as a fire shut up in stone. Dear children, it must blaze, and not remain smouldering, smothered. Historical faith is mouldy matter—*der historische Glaube ist ein Moder*—it must be set on fire: the soul must break out of the reasoning of this world into the life of Christ, into Christ's flesh and blood; then it receives the fuel which makes it blaze. There must be seriousness; history reaches not Christ's flesh and blood. *Es muss Ernst sein, denn die Historie erreichet nicht Christi Fleisch und Blut.*

Boehme, *De Incarnatione Verbi,* II, viii, 1.

XIII
Fulfillment

Fulfillment; from shadows to reality. Now for the first time fully real: the law having a shadow of good things to come, and not the real likeness of the things. From shadows to reality, from symbols to reality; from type to truth. The axis on which world history turns is symbolism. From *figura* to *veritas.*

Cf. Hebrews X, 1. Auerbach, "Figura."

The axis of world history is making conscious the unconscious. The Jews have an earthly circumcision, and earthly ceremonies, which earthly operations have a hidden virtue revealed in Christ. Jews have a mental veil in their reading of the Old Testament; Christ does away not with the Old Testament, but with the veil.

Augustine, *Contra Faustinum,* XII, 11.

The central feature of the human situation is the existence of the unconscious, the existence of a reality of which we are unconscious. In Freud's words, "The unconscious is the true psychic reality; in its inner nature it is just as much unknown to us as the reality of the external world, and it is just as imperfectly communicated to us by the data of consciousness as is the external world by the reports of our sense-organs." In Pascal's words: "all appearance indicates neither a total exclusion nor a manifest presence of divinity, but the presence of a God who hides himself." And, he adds, "God being thus hidden, every religion which does not affirm that God is hidden, is not true; and every religion which does not give the reason of it, is not instructive." Psychoanalysis passes the test.

Freud, "Interpretation of Dreams," 542. Pascal, *Pensées,* nos. 555, 584.

Symbolism is between consciousness and unconscious. A type conveys both absence and presence: "He must see enough to know that he has lost it. For to know of his loss, he must see and not see." Everything is symbolic, everything a parable; that seeing they might see, and not perceive; and hearing they might hear, and not understand.

Pascal, *Pensées,* nos. 555–677. *Luke* VIII, 10.

From shadows to reality. No fulfillment without displacement, as Jacob displaces Esau, or Isaac Ishmael. The letter, Judaism, must come before the spirit, Christianity; the blindness before the seeing. Symbolic consciousness is consciousness of transition, according to the revelation of the mystery, which was kept secret since the world began. In Deism and Enlightenment, on the other hand, there is no mystery, no symbolism, no revelation or revolution, no transition periods. Self-evident truths of natural reason shine all the time and require no breakthrough, no break in time.

Cf. Mark I, 7; Romans XVI, 25. Pascal, *Pensées*, nos. 555, 565, 570, 576, 640. Daniélou, *From Shadows to Reality*, 230.

Symbolic consciousness is between seeing and not seeing. It does not see self-evident truths of natural reason; or visible saints. It does not distinguish the wheat from the tares; and therefore must, as Roger Williams saw, practice toleration; or forgiveness, for we never know what we do. The basis of freedom is recognition of the unconscious; the invisible dimension; the not yet realized; leaving a space for the new.

Cf. Morgan, *Visible Saints.*

The unconscious to be made conscious; a secret disclosed; a veil to be rent, a seal to be broke open; the seal which Freud called repression. Not a gradual process, but a sudden breakthrough. A reversal of meaning; the symbolism suddenly understood. The key to the cipher: the sudden sight of the real Israel, the true bread, the real lamb.

Cf. Pascal, *Pensées*, nos. 678, 680, 563.

A breakthrough from shadows to reality: daybreak. The day breaks, and the shadows flee away. Suddenly at daybreak; we shall not all sleep, but we shall all be changed, in an instant, in the twinkling of an eye.

Song of Songs II, 7. I Corinthians XV, 51–52.

It is always daybreak. Knowing the time, that now it is high time to awake out of sleep. Adam, or Albion, "the history of the world from its creation, which was part of his fall, to the Last Judgement is his sleep." The fall is falling asleep; the sickness a sleeping sickness. Repression keeps the human essence latent, or dormant; the maiden is not dead but sleepeth. Psychoanalysis began when Freud discarded hypnotism—hypnotism which makes world opinion; hypnotism which makes the world go round. "I realized that henceforth I belonged to those who, according to Hebbel's expression 'have disturbed the world's sleep.'" From shadows to reality; from lamplight to sunlight; the turn; out of the cave of dreams or shadows. Symbolical consciousness is the interpretation of dreams, of this life as a dream.

Romans XIII, 11; Matthew IX, 24; Acts IX, 40. Frye, *Fearful Symmetry*, 125. Freud, "History of the Psychoanalytic Movement," 943. Cf. Daniélou, *From Shadows to Reality*, 190.

Our birth is but a sleep and a forgetting. The infantile amnesia is the birth of the soul, the dreamer; and we are obliged to repeat what we cannot remember. This world is repetition-compulsion, is karma: the burden of the past, a future determined by the past, causality. This world is dreams, the present transformed into the past, the shadow of the past falling on the present. The awakening explodes the cave of shadows; it is the end of the world.

Cf. Freud, "Interpretation of Dreams," 497, 582; *Outline*, 124. Powell, *Zen and Reality*, 19, 24, 53. Govinda, *Foundations of Tibetan Mysticism*, 267, 270. Jonas, *Gnostic Religion*, 195.

It is always daybreak. Suspended between first and second coming; between prophecy and fulfillment; between presence and absence; between seeing and not seeing; between sleeping and waking. The authentic psychoanalytical epiphany—do I wake or sleep?

Sleeping and waking, to make these opposites one. I sleep, but my heart waketh. "For until the desires are lulled to sleep through the mortification of our sensual nature, and until at last the sensual nature is at rest from them, so that they make not war upon the spirit, the soul goes not forth to true liberty for the enjoyment of union with its Beloved." In the sleep of desire delight awakes. In the sleep of soul the form awakes. "The more we concentrate, the more we approach the condition of sleep." As in poetry, which is dreaming while awake. In trance, in transit.

Song of Songs V, 1. St. John of the Cross, *Ascent of Mount Carmel,* I, xv, 2; cf. II, xiv, 11. Rieker, *Secret of Meditation,* 22.
Cf. Hartman, *The Unmediated Vision,* 104.

The fulfillment of prophecy is the end of the world. Figures are always figures of last things; typology (symbolism) is eschatology. The rending of the veil, the breaking of the seal, is the end of the world; history is fulfilled in its own abolition. II Corinthians III, 12–14: Seeing then that we have such a hope, we use great freedom of speech: And not as Moses, who put a veil over his face, so that the children of Israel could not steadfastly look to the end of that which is abolished: But their minds were blinded: for unto this day remaineth the same veil unremoved in their reading of the old testament; which veil is abolished in Christ.

We must look to the end. The Christian prayer is for the end of the world: that it may come quickly. The aim is to bring this world to an end; the only question is how. A mistake here might prove quite costly.

Revelations XXII, 20.

There is a distinction between the first coming and the second coming; but ever since the first coming, the time is fulfilled and the kingdom of God is close. The Christian sense of history is the sense of living in the last days. Little children it is the last hour. The whole Christian era is in the last days. The New Testament is the beginning of the end; the sense that the old is symbolical only is the sense that we are now in the time of fulfillment—*in illis temporalibus figuras fuisse futurorum quae implerentur in nobis, in quos finis saeculorum obvenit*. To see in past events figures of future events, to be fulfilled in us, who are confronted by the end of the world.

Mark I, 15; I John II, 18. Augustine, *Contra Faustinum*, 4, 2, in Auerbach, "Figura," 41.
Cf. Daniélou, *Lord of History*, 186.

The kingdom of God is close: every passing minute brings it no closer. The delay in the arrival of the second coming exists for those whose expectations are in unilinear time and literal meaning. Millennial calculations make the end of the world a literal instead of a visionary reality. It is not a question of a temporal interval, short or long, but of a visionary breakthrough. The real meaning of the last days is Pentecost.

> For these are not drunken, as ye suppose, seeing it is but the third hour of the day.
>
> But this is that which was spoken by the prophet Joel;
>
> And it shall come to pass in the last days, saith God, I will pour out of my Spirit upon all flesh: and your sons and your daughters shall prophesy, and your young men shall see visions, and your old men shall dream dreams:
>
> And on my servants and on my handmaidens I will pour out in those days of my Spirit; and they shall prophesy:
>
> And I will shew wonders in heaven above, and signs in the earth beneath; blood, and fire, and vapour of smoke:

> The sun shall be turned into darkness, and the moon into blood, before that great and notable day of the Lord come.

Acts II, 15–20.

Your young men shall see visions, and your old men shall dream dreams; Freud. These are not drunken, as ye suppose. Wonders and signs. The sun turned into darkness and the moon into blood. Pentecost is madness. The god is Dionysus.

The last thing to be realized is the incarnation. The last mystery to be unveiled is the union of humanity and divinity in the body. The last gesture is, *ecce homo.* To turn from the letter to the spirit is to turn from the shadow of figures to the reality of body. *De umbra transfertur ad corpus.* Or, as psychoanalysis might say, from the abstractions of sublimation to the reality of body. Colossians II, 16–17: Let no man therefore judge you in meat, or in drink, or in respect of a holy day, or of the new moon, or of the sabbath days: Which are the shadows of things to come; but the body is of Christ.

Tertullian in Auerbach, "Figura," 33.

Adumbration, and fulfillment. Antitype differs from type as body from shadow, truth from dream, sunlight from lamplight, body from shadow. The world of types is the world of the dreamer; Plato's cave. Platonic allegories, and sublimation, ascend from "sensibles" to "spirituals": for Platonism, the invisible and incorporeal things that are in heaven are true, while the visible and corporeal things on earth are copies of the true things, not themselves true. Symbolical consciousness—Christian, or psychoanalytical, or Dionysian—terminates in the body, remains faithful to the earth. The dreamer awakes not from a body but to a body. Not an ascent from body to spirit, but the descent of spirit into body: incarnation not sublimation. Hence to find the true meaning of history is to find the bodily meaning. Christ, the fulfillment, is not an abstract idea but a human body. All fulfillment is carnal, *carnaliter adimpleri.*

Tertullian cited in Auerbach, "Figura," 34.
Cf. Daniélou, *From Shadows to Reality,* 190.

Incarnation is iconoclasm. Literalism is idolatry, taking shadows for reality; taking abstractions, human inventions, unconscious projections of the human spirit, as autonomous powers; letting the metaphors go dead, and then, when dead, bowing down before them, taking them literally.

Cf. Barfield, *Saving the Appearances.*

The fulfillment dissolves the figure. Christianity is the destruction of the temple, the veil of the temple rent from the top to the bottom. Creative destruction, the life or historical process. Destroy this temple, and in three days I will raise it up.

Cf. Matthew XXVII, 15; John II, 19.

To pass from shadows to reality is to pass from the external and material temple to the new temple, the true temple, which is the human body. "They dedicated to God themselves as a new temple, of which the old temple was but the earthly type." The temple of the holy spirit is your body. In the incarnation, therefore, the veil of the temple rent from top to bottom; in the second coming, the destruction of the temple.

Augustine, *Christian Doctrine*, III, vi. I Corinthians VI, 19.
Cf. Lubac, *Histoire et esprit*, 130. Matthew XXVII, 51.

Literalism makes the world of abstract materialism; of dead matter; of the human body as dead matter. Literalism kills everything, including the human body. It is the spirit Blake called Ulro, which sees nothing but rock and sand, jostling together in the void; Whitehead's Misplaced Concreteness: "Nature a dull affair, soundless, scentless, colourless; merely the hurrying of material, endlessly, meaninglessly." Literalism makes a universe of stone, and men astonished, petrified. Literalism is the ministration of death, written and engraven in stones; tables of stone and stony heart. The incarnation of symbols gives us a new heart, a heart for the first time human, a heart for the first time, or is it the second time, made of flesh. "A new heart also will I give you, and a new spirit will I put within you: and I will take away the stony heart out of your flesh, and I will give you a heart of flesh."

Whitehead, *Science and the Modern World*, 69. II Corinthians III, 7.
Ezekiel XXXVI, 26.
Cf. Augustine, *Christian Doctrine*, III, xxxiv.

Literal meanings are spirits solidified into matter; animae become trees, like Daphne; or stone maidens, Caryatids.

> Daphne shall break her bark, and run
> To meet the embraces of the youthful Sun.

Cf. Carew, "The Rapture," 226.

Incarnation: the word made flesh. "Refrain from uniting with words, in order to unite with the word made flesh." The abstractions idolized by literalism are words; words detached from the breath of living bodies; detached from the breath of life, the spirit, and hardened into independent reality; words written down, scripture, the dead letter; Latin *litera*, the letter; Greek *gramma*, the writing. The letter is alienated spirit; what Augustine calls the letter written outside the man. Symbolical consciousness restores the spirit to the man; and then the only scripture is the human body itself. I Corinthians III, 3: "Ye are manifestly declared to be the epistle of Christ, written not with ink but with the spirit of the living God; not in tables of stone, but in the fleshy tables of the heart."

Barfield, *Romanticism Comes of Age*, 61.
Cf. Augustine, *The Spirit and the Letter*, 29–30.

To return the word to the flesh. To make knowledge carnal again; not by deduction, but immediate by perception or sense at once; the bodily senses.

Cf. Blake, *Annotations to Berkeley's "Siris,"* 774.

From the letter to the spirit. The hidden meaning of the body is the spirit; but the spirit is not the ghost but life itself; not the soul or psyche but the breath of life, the creator spirit. Good-by holy ghost, *veni creator spiritus*. I Corinthians XV, 45: The first man Adam became a living psyche; the last Adam became a life-making spirit. Life is the power to make new life; the spirit is phallic, and fiery; the god is Dionysus.

Incarnation is not to be understood carnally, for to be carnally-minded is death; that is to say, the body is not to be understood literally. Everything is symbolic, everything including the human body. To pass from the temple to the body is to perceive the body as the new temple, the true temple. The house is a woman; and the woman is a house, or palace

> Ascending up with many a stately stayre,
> To honors seat and chastities sweet bowre.

The land is a woman, the virgin land; and the woman is a land, my America, my Newfoundland.

Spenser, "Epithalamion."
Cf. Romans VIII, 6; Donne, "To His Mistress Going to Bed."

"The real apocalypse comes, not with the vision of a city or kingdom, which would still be external, but with the identification of the city and kingdom with one's own body." Political kingdoms are only shadows—my kingdom is not of this world—because the kingdoms of this world are non-bodily. Political freedom is only a prefiguration of true freedom: "The Bastille is really a symbol, that is, an image or form, of the two larger prisons of man's body and the physical world." Political and fleshly emancipation are finally one and the same; the god is Dionysus.

Frye, *Fearful Symmetry,* 431, 202.
Cf. Augustine, *Christian Doctrine,* II, XII. Pascal, *Pensées,* no. 682. Bachofen, *Das Mutterrecht,* 47.

My kingdom is not of this world. But metapolitics is not metaphysics, in another world, but a physiology of politics. Or a politics of physiology, as in the psychoanalytical theory of the sexual organizations.

My kingdom is not of this world. It is not a literal kingdom; literal kingdoms are only shadows. The reality is flesh. But flesh is a figure, the reality of which is yet to be unveiled. The reality of body is not given, but to be made real, to be realized; the body is to be built; to be built not with hands but by the spirit. It is the poetic body; the made body; Man makes Himself, his own body, in the symbolic freedom of the imagination. "The Eternal Body of Man is the Imagination, that is, God himself, the Divine Body, Jesus: we are his Members."

Blake, *The Laocoön*, 776.
Cf. Ephesians II, 21–22; IV, 12. Auerbach, "Figura," 53, 72.

The body is plastic; the imagination esemplastic. The reality disclosed by the imagination is not the literal but the symbolical or mystical body. He took some bread and said, This is my body. Or *Tat Tvam Asi*, Thou art That"—"Thou art the universal self; all things are Buddha things; the identity of thine inmost essence with the invisible substance of the all." To find the kingdom in one's own body, and to find one's own body in the outside world.

Zimmer, *Philosophies of India*, 149; cf. 309, 361.

To find the kingdom in one's own body, and to find one's own body in the outside world. The body to be realized is the body of the cosmic man, the body of the universe as one perfect man. The word that is incarnate in Christ is the word that is incarnate in the universe by the creative fiat; it is the logos of the universe now recapitulated in the divine-human body. "To the enlightened man, however, whose consciousness embraces the universe, to him the universe becomes his 'body.'" As in schizophrenia: "what happens to the person's own body . . . is identical with what happens in the universe."

Govinda, *Foundations of Tibetan Mysticism*, 225. Storch, *Primitive Archaic Forms*, 4; cf. 86–87.
Cf. Daniélou, *Lord of History*, 191.

The body that is identical with environment. As in dreams the whole landscape is made out of the dreamer's own body; so in totemism the human essence is projected into animal or plant—the very act of unconscious symbol-formation. In conscious symbolism the alienated spirit returns to its human creator: "all the gods are in our body." Redemption is the reformation of the creator spirit in man; redemption is deification; we make a new heaven and a new earth.

Zimmer, "Indian Tantric Yoga," 30.
Cf. Roheim, *Eternal Ones of the Dream*, 243. Brophy, *Black Ship to Hell*, 437.

The fulfillment of symbols is in the symbolism of the body. In bodily experience, in the incarnation of symbols, it for the first time happens for real; and as the first real time, it can be also the last time. Allegory, discarnate symbolism, unconscious symbolism, is the world of eternal recurrence, the world of karma, of the repetition-compulsion. In the incarnation of symbols we move from allegory to eschatology, from eternal recurrence to eternity. The sacrifice of Isaac was not actually carried out: it is done in type or figure, and repeatedly done in figure. The sacrifice is really carried out in Jesus, for the first and for the last time; now once and for all to bring the world to an end.

Hebrews IX, 25–26: "Nor yet that he should offer himself often, as the high priest entereth into the holy place every year with blood of others; for then must he often have suffered since the foundation of the world: but now once in the end of the world hath he appeared to abolish sin by the sacrifice of himself." Tertullian: "The high priest entered the Holy of Holies each year, but did not remain there; this repetition shows that it is nothing more than a repetition, a representation, and not in any way the reality."

Tertullian, *adv. Marcionem* III, 18.
Cf. Daniélou, *From Shadows to Reality,* 123; *Lord of History,* 144. Edwards, *Images,* No. 50.

The true paschal lamb. "Christ was anointed priest in his human nature, and offered no other sacrifice than that of his own body." The reality adumbrated in all sacrifice, in animal sacrifice, is human sacrifice, the sacrifice of the human body, as an eternal truth.

Theodoretus in Daniélou, *Lord of History,* 194.
Cf. Pascal, *Pensées,* no. 680.

Daniélou says that in the general resurrection Christ's personal conquest, already effective in the souls of mankind, will be extended over the whole physical world. But a conquest that is effective only on the souls of mankind is not yet real; it is still shadow, not body. The second coming, the general resurrection, takes place not in our souls but in our bodies.

Cf. Daniélou, *Lord of History,* 191.

The interval between the first and second coming is the time of the church; in which the invisible reality of the body is foreshadowed in the church as a body, and in the sacrament of the body; but not in our bodies; and therefore figuratively, not yet really; and so there is still warfare between body and spirit. According to Joachim, the course of history continuously dissolves the sacramental forms in which the divine reality is revealed (concealed), so that the sacraments of the higher phase both fulfill and cancel the sacraments of the preceding stage. In the second period Christ shows himself in the risen flesh only to a few; in the third period, all flesh shall see it together. In the third period, the priesthood is dissolved; the vicar of Christ, *locum tenens* in his absence, is replaced by Christ himself. It is the transition from passive identification to active participation in the mystical body; from (distant) representation to real presence: from shadow to body.

Cf. Daniélou, *Lord of History,* 140 *et seq.,* 190, 272. Benz, *Ecclesia Spiritualis,* 9, 15–16.

From the sacred set apart to the holy whole. Hierophanies everywhere; no privileged times or places. Every book a bible; and books in the running brooks. "As for the continuous but invisible outpouring of the Spirit, Servetus was aware of it everywhere as the mundification of the divine *substantia* in all creatures, which could therefore be considered full of divinity. Hence all things, from the heavenly bodies to the smallest flowers, could be looked upon as gods." Christ the direct and omnipresent object of perception—

> Christ plays in ten thousand places,
> Lovely in limbs, and lovely in eyes not his.

Williams, *The Radical Reformation,* 612. Hopkins, "As Kingfishers catch fire."
Cf. Hartman, *The Unmediated Vision,* 59.

At any rate he calls us to come outdoors; Dionysus calls us outdoors. Rise up, my love, my fair one, and come away. For, lo, the winter is past, the rain is over and gone; the flowers appear on the earth; the time of the singing of birds is come, and the voice of the turtle is heard in our land. Out of the temple made with hands;

out of the ark of the book; out of the cave of the law; out of the belly of the letter. The first tabernacle in Jerusalem; the second tabernacle the universal Church; the third tabernacle the open sky. "Only when a clear sky looks down through broken ceilings will my heart turn again toward the places of God."

Song of Songs I, 10–12; Galatians III, 23. *Zarathustra* cited in Heller, *The Disinherited Mind,* 141.
Cf. Daniélou, *Origen,* 144. Benz, *Ecclesia Spiritualis,* 35–37. Augustine, *Spirit and Letter,* 24. Lubac, *Corpus Mysticism,* 218, 218n.

Hierophanies everywhere: the presence is not real until it is present everywhere. In the bread and wine of every meal; together with him this day in paradise.

Cf. Edwards, *Images,* no. 68. Luke XXIII, 43.

Bread and wine; or air, the air we breathe. The Blessed Virgin compared to the Air we breathe—

> Wild air, world-mothering air,
> Nestling me everywhere,
> This needful, never spent,
> And nursing element;
> My more than meat and drink,
> My meal at every wink—

"Our breath to support life, a representation of our dependence on the spirit of God for spiritual life," says Jonathan Edwards; but our breath is not an image of a more divine thing: it is the divine thing, the breath of life, the creator spirit, which deifies us—

> And makes, O marvellous!
> New Nazareths in us,
> Where she shall yet conceive
> Him, morning, noon, and eve.

Hopkins, "The Blessed Virgin compared to the Air we breathe." Edwards, *Images,* no. 208.

To reconcile body and spirit would be to recover the breath-soul which is the life-soul instead of the ghost-soul or shadow; breath-consciousness instead of brain-consciousness; body-consciousness instead of head-consciousness. The word made flesh is a living word, not a scripture but a breathing. A line that comes from the breath, from the heart by way of the breath. Aphorism as utterance: a short breath, drawn in pain. Winged words, birds released from the sentence, doves of the spirit.

Cf. Bachelard, *La Poétique de l'espace,* 179–180. Charles Olson in Allen, *New American Poetry,* 388–390. Duncan, *Letters,* XIX.

XIV
Judgment

To bring this world to an end: the consummation devoutly to be wished, the final judgment.

The revolution, the revelation, the apocalypse, is vision; which pronounces a last judgment; and brings about the end. Aphorism is the form of last judgments; sentences.

Cf. Blake, *A Vision of the Last Judgement*, 604, 617. Auerbach, "Figura," 71, 67.

A fiery consummation. Truth is a blaze. Error, or Creation, will be Burned up. It is Burnt up the Moment Men cease to behold it.

Blake, *A Vision of the Last Judgement*, 617.

Truth is error burned up; a light shining in darkness; darkness overcome. The everlasting bonfire. The truth and the life and the joy is in the overcoming. Not in perfection, but in the transmutation. Man is born a Spectre or Satan, and must continually be changed into his direct contrary.

> Establishment of Truth depends on destruction of Falsehood continually,
> On Circumcision, not on Virginity, O Reasoners of Albion!

Blake, *Jerusalem*, pl. 55, ll. 65–66; cf. pl. 52.

Symbolic consciousness, a trance, in transit: going over, from this world to the next. Overcoming this world.

Overcoming this world, abolishing it. The fulfillment is the abolition. "Having filled Deficiency, He abolished Shape. The Shape is the Cosmos, a Shape to which Deficiency has been subjected. For the place in which there is envy and dissension, is Deficiency, but the place which is Unity, is Plenitude." The universe as we see it; reality or the reality-principle; a set of definitions or boundaries; and where there is definition there is division. But the shape of this world is transitory.

Jones, *Gnostic Religion*, 196–197.
Cf. Powell, *Zen and Reality*, 43. I Corinthians VII, 31.

Overcoming the world; overthrowing the government; overthrowing the government of the reality-principle, which is the prince of darkness, the ruler of the darkness of this world. For we wrestle not against flesh and blood, but against principalities, against powers, against the rulers of the darkness of this world. The reality-principle is the power-principle, *Realpolitik*, the keeper of the prison. To liberate flesh and blood from reification, overthrow the reality-principle.

Ephesians VI, 12.

Instead of reification, perishable form. Truth will not stand or stay or keep; it is nothing to be had or hoarded or passed from hand to hand; it is no commodity or store of past labor; it is either new or not at all. The form of the sentence is transience; it must go under.

Out of this world; out of Vanity Fair; out of the market place. Put the mind out of business. Words are to be redeemed; to be taken out of the market place (ἐξαγοράζεσθαι); to cease to be a commodity; to be removed from circulation. To be taken out of circulation, out of the flow of currency, out of the universe of discourse, into the immovable *prajna*, the perfectly still mirror. To condense, to crystallize, to become a parable. Words taken out of time into eternity: aphorism the form of eternity.

Cf. Suzuki in Fromm *et al.*, *Zen Buddhism and Psychoanalysis*, 20, 23.
Kaufmann, *Nietzsche*, 555–556.

From this world to the next; from utility to creation. Instead of words as market-place utilities, brand names to advertise established items, the creative words which make it new. Words made new again, as on the first day of creation; eternity's sunrise. Words used not to interpret the world but to change it; not to advertise this world but to find another. To pass from this world to the next; from ordinary to extraordinary language.

The permanent revolution, the perpetual reformation, is vision, is spontaneity, perpetually renewed: every day the last day, or the first day, the beginning and the end. "People are wont to speak of the necessity of a new order of things. Men in the grip of their personal ego and of time adhering to it, can only give birth to an 'old' order. A new order is, correctly speaking, one which is renewed hourly." Permanent revolution, then, and no permanent (reified-visible) structures issuing from contract, commitment, promise, will or will power, which are from the ego. Not voluntarism, but spontaneity, or grace; not the ego but the id.

Durckheim, *The Japanese Cult of Tranquillity,* 89.
Cf. Morgan, *Visible Saints,* 3, 23–24, 28.

Take but degree away; it is the end of the world. The reality-principle is the importance principle, which commands us to be fooled by appearances, to respect the Emperor's New Clothes. Hierarchy is visible; in the invisible kingdom the first are last. Overthrow the reality-principle: no respect for persons, not to be fooled by masks; no clothes, no emperor. All power is an impostor; a paper tiger, or idol; it is Burnt up the Moment Men cease to behold it. The Last Judgment is the Vision; the political act is the poetical act, the creative vision.

To see is to see through. Political organization is theatrical organization, the public realm, where "appearance—something that is being seen and heard by others as well as by ourselves—constitutes reality." To see through this show; to see the invisible reality; to put an end to politics.

Arendt, *The Human Condition,* 45.

The Emperor's New Clothes. Things hidden from the wise and revealed to babes. The learning to be unlearned; the simplicity to be acquired. The great, the terrible simplification, the last judgment.

Cf. Matthew XI, 25. Benz, *Ecclesia Spiritualis*, 35–37, 39. Williams, *The Radical Reformation*, 262.

The blindness is from blinkers of decorum. Apocalypse strips away the decent draperies on which the whole big lie depends, the false front, the screen or wall that separates the public sphere from the private parts. In the whole modern period, the emergence of housekeeping (economics) from the shadowy interior of the household into the light of the public sphere, erasing the old boundary between private and political. Psychoanalysis is that revolving stage which completes this revolution, disclosing the bedroom and the bathroom behind the bourgeois façade, disclosing the obscenity of the on-stage scene, abolishing the reality-principle and its unreal distinction between public and private, between head and genital. (Power) politics is pissing in public—Freud's "connection between ambition and urethral eroticism" together with the lofty pretensions that scotomize, cover with a thick wall of darkness, that human scene.

Freud, *New Introductory Lectures*, 140.
Cf. Arendt, *The Human Condition*, 38, 60–63.

Overthrow the importance principle; turn it upside down. Put down the mighty from their seats, and exalt them of low degree. Every throne a toilet seat, and every toilet seat a throne. Psychoanalysis, the visionary sansculottism. The distinction between the sublime and the vulgar is abolished; sublimation is swallowed up in symbolism. As above, so below; go high-low every time. The way up is the way down; the penis a symbolic head, and vice versa.

Cf. Ferenczi, *Thalassa*, 22.

Upside down. The paradox is a reversal of fortune, a humiliation of the power principle, a crucifixion. At the intersection of this world and another world, the wisdom of this world is crossed up. "Our good is hidden, and so profoundly that it is hidden under its opposite. Thus our life is under death, love of ourselves under hate of ourselves, glory under ignominy, salvation under perdition, justice under sin, strength under infirmity, and universally every one of our affirmations under its negation." Dialectics is apocalypse; reversal; wakening from the dead.

Luther cited in Cranz, *An Essay on the Development of Luther's Thought on Justice, Law, and Society*, 22.
Cf. Weil, *La Pesanteur et la grâce*, 110.

The power of the foolishness of the cross; the power which is beyond the power principle, which comes after the power principle is broken. Truth in the form of weakness and foolishness; having no powerful arguments; having no arguments—*theologia mystica non est argumentativa.* Truth is not on the side of the big battalions, or on the winning side; truth is beyond the reality-principle, in another world where the distinction between victor and vanquished vanishes. Truth comes empty-handed; in its poverty is its strength.

Evdokimov, *La Femme et le salut du monde*, 117.
Cf. Seferis quoted in *The New York Times*, October 25, 1963.

Take physic pomp. Truth comes riding a donkey; like psychoanalysis, like Hamann, finding revelations in little contemptible events; infinity in a grain of sand. "The sacrifice of Christ imprinted like a physical law in even the lowliest call of nature." "As Dionysius says, it is more fitting that divine truths should be expounded under the figure of the less noble than of nobler bodies. For then it is clear that these things are not literal descriptions of divine truths, which might have been open to doubt had they been expressed under the figure of nobler bodies."

Thomas Aquinas, *Summa Theologica,* I, q. 1, art. 9, ad. 3. Hartman, *The Unmediated Vision,* 59. O'Flaherty, *Unity and Language,* 12.

Any trivial event; like an accident at the crossroads. Regal tragedies (the Oedipus complex) in every household; the psychopathology of everyday life. James Joyce: the tragic significance of everyday life; modern realism, the modern analogue of Medieval typology, which, by figural interpretation, discovered world-historic significance in any event—an event which remains trivial for those who do not have eyes to see. Inasmuch as ye have done it unto one of the least of these my brethren, ye have done it unto me.

Matthew XXV, 40. Cf. Auerbach, *Mimesis.*

The event remains trivial for those who do not have eyes to see. And so God remains hidden; or rather, an open secret. And everything is told in parables, that seeing they may see and not perceive. The mystery of meaning remains forever inviolate; there is no literal truth.

Truth riding a donkey; as foolishness. He hath no form or comeliness; and when we shall see him, there is no beauty that we should desire him. "The divine style chooses the foolish, the shallow, and the ignoble, to put to shame the strength and ingenuity of all profane writers . . . *Dei dialectus soloecismus.*" The foolish form, to preserve the incognito. As in bread and wine.

Isaiah LII, 2. Hamann in Smith, *J. G. Hamann,* 75.

Everything is symbolic, everything is holy. There is no special time or place or person, privileged to represent the rest. And then democracy can begin. The many are made one when the totality is in every part. When one thing is taken up, all things are taken up with it; one flower is the spring. It is all there all the time.

Cf. Blythe, *Haiku,* I, viii.

Infinity in a grain of sand: this humiliation or contraction in all symbolism (incarnation). *Verbum breviatum;* the word has to be abbreviated in order to become flesh; Freud would call it a condensation of meaning. "And containing the world, he suffered himself to be contained in a manger." "Everything is a symbol, and while it perfectly presents itself, it points to everything else. In this posture I see a combination of the highest presumption and the highest modesty."

Augustine in Lubac, *Histoire et esprit,* 446. Goethe, Letter to K. E. Schubarth, April 2, 1818.

Infinity in a grain of sand. All symbolism, all hierophany, is incarnation, of meaning in matter or word made flesh; and incarnation is humiliation. Philippians II, 8: being found in the form of a man, he humbled himself. To see symbolism is to see a humiliated God, to break with the power-principle. Pascal: "Types. The letter kills. All happened in types. Here is the cipher which Saint Paul gives us. Christ must suffer. An humiliated God." "Though he is omniscient, Vishnu shows himself in the *arkas* as if he were without knowledge; though a spirit, he appears material; though truly God he appears to be at the disposal of man; though all-powerful he appears weak; though free of care he appears to need looking after; though inaccessible [to sense], he appears tangible."

Pascal, *Pensées,* no. 682. Lōcacārya in Eliade, *Patterns of Comparative Religion,* 28.

God is hidden under his own opposite, *deus absconditus sub contrario;* as incarnate, as god in the shape of a man: most hidden when most there. Symbolism is this paradoxical coming-together of sacred and profane; it is a *coincidentia oppositorum,* the true cross. "Every hierophany shows, makes manifest, the coexistence of contradictory essences: sacred and profane, spirit and matter, eternal and non-eternal." There is this sacrament, this incarnation, wherever there is meaning; in every sentence "the transfer and *communicatio idiomatum* of the mental and the material, of extension and sense, body and thought"; language is a sacrament, a mysterious union of opposites in concrete form.

Hamann in O'Flaherty, *Unity and Language,* 39; cf. 71. Eliade, *Patterns of Comparative Religion,* 29. Luther in Ebeling, "Die Anfänge von Luthers Hermeneutik, 197.

To go beyond the reality-principle, through the looking glass of dialectical reversal, to the absurd truth. Overcome this world by a *reductio ad absurdum; credo quia absurdum.* From the shadow of typology to the night of paradox.

Cf. Ebeling, "Die Anfänge von Luthers Hermeneutik," 213–214.

Upside down. Not the reality-principle but surrealism. Surrealism, a systematic illumination of the hidden places and a progressive darkening of the rest; a perpetual promenade right in the forbidden zone.

Cf. Carrouges, *André Breton et les données fondamentales du surréalisme,* 31.

Go down and stay down, in the forbidden zone; a descent into hell. "I can only conclude with the wish that fate may grant an easy ascension to those whose sojourn in the underworld of psychoanalysis has become uncomfortable. May it be vouchsafed to others to bring to happy conclusion their work in the depth."

Freud, "History of the Psychoanalytic Movement," 977.

The revolution is from below, the lower classes, the underworld, the damned, the disreputable, the despised and rejected. Freud's revolutionary motto in *The Interpretation of Dreams: Flectere si nequeo Superos, Acherunta movebo.* If I cannot bend the higher powers, I will stir up the lower depths. Freud's discovery: the universal underworld.

Freud, "Interpretation of Dreams," 540.

Darkness at noon. A progressive darkening of the everyday world of common sense. *Finnegans Wake.* Second sight is the dark night. Night gives light unto night; the double dark, or negation of the negation. *Admirable cosa es que, siendo tenebrosa, alumbrase la noche.*

San Juan de la Cruz, *Subido del Monte Carmelo,* II, iii, 5.
Cf. Hopkins, "The Habit of Perfection."

The Pentecostal darkness: the sun shall be turned to darkness. To overcome the opposition of darkness and light, cleanliness and dirt, order and chaos; the marriage of heaven and hell. To seduce the world to madness. Christ is within the wall of paradise, which is the wall of the law of contradiction; and the destruction of the law of contradiction is the supreme task of higher logic.

Cusanus cited in Cranz, "Saint Augustine and Nicholas of Cusa in the Traditions of Western Christian Thought," 312. Novalis, *Fragmente aus den Studienheften*, no. 578.
Cf. Milner, "The Role of Illusion in Symbol Formation," 108.

XV
Freedom

Then cometh the end, when he shall have put down all rule and all authority and power. Mere anarchy is loosed upon the world.

I Corinthians XV, 24.

The break is a break in nature; water from the rock. The natural order broken; the natural order is our construction, our constriction.

Freedom. Freud the great emancipator, from the reality-principle. Free speech; free associations, random thoughts; spontaneous movements.

We stumble on the truth. The truth is always scandalous, a stumbling block; truth is where we stumble or fall down; in the rough ground, the anomalies; not in the explanations. Search the scripture till you find a stumbling block; look for the slips of the tongue; the *lapsus linguae*, the fortunate falls. The truth is in the error. We slip out from under the reality-principle, into the truth; when the control breaks down. By great good fortune, gratis, by grace; and not by our own work or will.

Cf. Grant, *Letter and Spirit*, 35, 96. Benz, *Ecclesia Spiritualis*, 37. Wittgenstein, *Philosophical Investigations*, 46.

A treasure stumbled upon, suddenly; not gradually accumulated, by adding one to one. The accumulation of learning, "adding to the sum-total of human knowledge"; lay that burden down, that baggage, that impediment. Take nothing for your journey; travel light.

Cf. Luke IX, 4.

The original mistake in every sentence: metaphor. Metaphor consists in giving the thing a name that belongs to something else; "the presentation of facts of one category in the idiom appropriate to another." The original sentence, the original metaphor: *Tat Tvam Asi*, Thou art that; or *hoc est corpus meum*, this is my body. Making this thing other: "We already and first of all discern him making this thing other." Metaphor is mistake or impropriety; a *faux pas*, or slip of the tongue; a little madness; *petit mal;* a little seizure or inspiration.

Ryle in Turbayne, *The Myth of Metaphor*, 12, 24. Jones, *Anathémata*, 49. Aristotle, *Poetics*, 1457b.
Cf. Black, *Models and Metaphors*, 33, 36.

Freedom is poetry, taking liberties with words, breaking the rules of normal speeech, violating common sense. Freedom is violence.

The original sense is nonsense; and common sense a cover-up job, repression. Psychoanalysis, symbolic consciousness, leads from disguised to patent nonsense—Wittgenstein, surrealism, *Finnegans Wake.*

Cf. Wittgenstein, *Philosophical Investigations,* 133.

This is my body. Mistake, or magic, or madness; or child's play. This is a house and this is a steeple.

Wisdom is wit; in play, not in work; in freedom, not in necessity. A vast pun, as in dreams, in the neologisms of schizophrenia, in *Finnegans Wake,* in the Old Testament prophets.

Wisdom is in wit, in fooling, most excellent fooling; in play, and not in heavy puritanical seriousness. In levity, not gravity. My yoke is easy, my burden is light.

Cf. Matthew XI, 30.

The God of Delphi, who always spoke the truth, never gave a straight answer, in the upright Protestant way; he always spoke in riddles, in parables; ambiguities, temptations; that hearing they might hear and not understand. To teach is not to tell, is not-to-tell; like Heraclitus, the obscure. The god knew how to lie; and so did not deceive his countrymen. The real deceivers are the literalists, who say, I cannot tell a lie, or, *hypotheses non fingo.*

Cf. Turbayne, *The Myth of Metaphor,* 23–24, 51.

It is a game of hide-and-seek: "The glory of God is to conceal a thing, but the glory of the king is to find it out;

as if, according to the innocent play of children, the Divine Majesty took delight to hide his works, to the end to have them found out; and as if kings could not obtain a greater honour than to be God's playfellows in that game."

Bacon in McLuhan, *Gutenberg Galaxy,* 190.

Literal meanings are packaged commodities for passive consumers: in symbolist poetry the reader is incorporated into the work, actively participates in the poetic process itself—"the connection is left for the beholder to work out for himself." All the Lord's people become prophets.

Ruskin in McLuhan, *Gutenberg Galaxy,* 266; cf. 38, 217, 276–277. Cf. Numbers XI, 29. Blake, *Milton,* Preface.

It cannot be inculcated, or imposed, from without. Like faith or love, it cannot be forced. The spirit is free love.

Enigmatic form is living form; like life, an iridescence; an invitation to the dance; a temptation, or irritation. No satisfying solutions; nothing to rest in; nothing to weigh us down.

Meaning is in the play, or interplay, of light. As in schizophrenia, all things lose their boundaries, become iridescent with many-colored significances. No things, but an iridescence, a rainbow effect. *Am farbigen Abglanz haben wir das Leben.* An indirect reflection; or refraction; broken light, or enigma.

Strindberg in Storch, *Primitive Archaic Forms,* 62. Goethe, *Faust* II, l. 4727.

No things, but an iridescence in the void. Meaning is a continuous creation, out of nothing and returning to nothingness. If it is not evanescent it is not alive. Everything is symbolic, is transitory; is unstable. The consolidation of meaning makes idols; established meanings have turned to stone.

Cf. Bachelard, *La Poétique de l'espace*, 67.

Meaning is not in things but in between; in the iridescence, the interplay; in the interconnections; at the intersections, at the crossroads. Meaning is transitional as it is transitory; in the puns or bridges, the correspondence.

Cf. Richard, *Mallarmé*, 551. Hartman, *The Unmediated Vision*, 118.

In the iridescence is flux, is fusion, subverting the boundaries between things; all things flow. "In Christian art, earthly images may easily appear, to melt away and vanish, since to the Christian no single phenomenon has the importance that it did to the pagan. Here we have not the dualistic device of the Ciceronian simile, but metaphoric fusion; we are offered a parallel with the modern 'poetics by alchemy,' exemplified by the practise of a Góngora, who may lead us by metaphors from a maid adorning herself for marriage to Egyptian tombstones; or we may think of the famous passage in which Proust, by the use of metaphors, transforms lilac into fountain—or of Valéry's *Cimetière marin*, that 'sea cemetery' reminiscent of the Ambrosian landscape which becomes successively a roof covered with white pigeons, a temple of Time, a flock of sheep with a shepherd dog, a multi-colored hydra; all this is based on the same Christian poetics of kaleidoscopic transformation of symbols." A Christian transfiguration, or a pagan orgy: a Bacchanalian revel of categories in which not one member is sober; a protean flux of metamorphosis.

Spitzer, "Classical and Christian Ideas of World Harmony," 426.

Freedom is fire, overcoming this world by reducing it to a fluctuating chaos, as in schizophrenia; the chaos which is the eternal ground of creation. There is no universe, no one way.

> We are always in error
> Lost in the wood
> Standing in chaos
> The original mess
> Creating
> A brand-new world.

Thank God the world cannot be made safe, for democracy or anything else.

Cf. Storch, *Primitive Archaic Forms*, 14.

Meaning is new, or not at all; a new creation, or not at all; poetry or not at all. The newness is the metaphor, or nonsense—saying one thing and meaning another. It is the legal fiction, which liberates from the letter of the law and from the tyranny of literal meaning.

Cf. Barfield, "Poetic Diction and Legal Fiction."

A vast pun, a free play, with unlimited substitutions. A symbol is never a symbol but always polysymbolic, overdetermined, polymorphous. Freedom is fertility; a proliferation of images, in excess. The seed must be sown wastefully, extravagantly. Too much, or not enough; overdetermination is determination made into chance; chance and determination reconciled. Too much meaning is meaning and absurdity reconciled.

Cf. Sèchehaye, *A New Psychotherapy in Schizophrenia,* 142. Storch, *Primitive Archaic Forms,* 15–16. Onians, *Origins of European Thought,* 474–476. Chenu, "Histoire et allégorie au douzieme siècle," 66.

Symbolism is polymorphous perversity, the translation of all of our senses into one another, the interplay between the senses, the metaphor, the free translation. The separation of the senses, their mutual isolation, is sensuality, is sexual organization, is bondage to the tyranny of one partial impulse, leading to the absolute and exclusive concentration of the life of the body in the representative person.

Cf. McLuhan, *Gutenberg Galaxy,* 5, 65–66, 138.

Knowledge is carnal knowledge, a copulation of subject and object, making these two one. *Cognitio nihil aliud est quam coitio quaedam cum suo cognobili*—"Sex becomes not only an object of thought but in some sense an imaginative method of comprehension." Polymorphously perverse sexuality, in and through every organ of perception:

> If in the morning sun I find it, there my eyes are fix'd
> In happy copulation.

Patrizzi cited in Cassirer, *Individual and Cosmos,* 134. Sewell, *The Orphic Voice,* 209 (on Novalis). Blake, *Vision of the Daughters of Albion,* 194.

Knowledge is carnal knowledge. A subterranean passage between mind and body underlies all analogy; no word is metaphysical without its first being physical; and the body that is the measure of all things is sexual. All metaphors are sexual; a penis in every convex object and a vagina in every concave one.

Cf. Sharpe, "Psycho-Physical Problems Revealed in Language: an Examination of Metaphor," 202. Ferenczi, "Stages in the Development of the Sense of Reality," 227.

Symbolism is polymorphous perversity. Orthodox psychoanalysis warns against the resexualization of thought and speech; orthodox psychoanalysis bows down before the reality-principle. The reality-principle is based on desexualization; in symbolic consciousness thought and speech become resexualized. As in schizophrenia. For example, the patient who refused to play his violin in public; psychoanalysis can find nothing wrong: "Behind every form of play lies a process of discharge of masturbatory phantasies." Nothing wrong, except the refusal to play: when our eyes are opened to the symbolic meaning, our only refuge is loss of shame, polymorphous perversity, pansexualism; penises everywhere. As in Tantric Yoga, in which any sexual act may become a form of mystic meditation, and any mystic state may be interpreted sexually.

Klein, *Psychoanalysis of Children,* 31.
Cf. Fenichel, *Psychoanalytical Theory of the Neuroses,* 296. Storch, *Primitive Archaic Forms,* 17. Eliade, *Le Yoga,* 235.

Speech resexualized.

Sei das Wort die Braut genannt
Bräutigam der Geist.

The tongue made potent again, out of his mouth goeth a sharp sword. The spermatic word, the word as seed; the sower soweth the word. Annunciations, messages, messengers, angels, having intercourse with the daughters of men, making pregnant through the ear; angels or birds, winged words or doves of the spirit. The flying bird or angel is an erection or a winged phallus; "a single word stands for the penis and the sentence for the thrust of the penis in coitus." A supernatural pregnancy: "A being, be it man or woman, who has the Holy Ghost within him is pregnant or full of semen and in ejaculating words of prophecy the wizard either ejaculates semen or gives birth to a child."

Goethe, "Buch Hafis," *West-Östlicher Divan*. Roheim, *Animism*, 383; cf. 159–160. Klein, "Infant Analysis," 112.
Cf. Freud, "Interpretation of Dreams," 390. Leisegang, *Pneuma Hagion*, 21, 25, 33, 35, 40, 49–50. Jones, "The Madonna's Conception through the Ear."

Speech resexualized. Sexual potency, linguistic power, abolished at Babel and restored at Pentecost. At Pentecost, tongues of fire, a flame in the shape of a male member. Speaking with tongues is fiery speech, speech as a sexual act, a firebird or phoenix.

Cf. Flügel, "The International Language Movement," 196. Freud, "Acquisition of Power over Fire," 291–292.

Speech resexualized: overcoming the consequences of the fall. The tongue was the first unruly member. Displacement is first from above downwards; the penis is a symbolic tongue, and disturbances of ejaculation a kind of genital stuttering. "In the beginning the serpent, getting possession of the ears of Eve, thence spread his poison through her whole body; today Mary through her ears received the champion of everlasting bliss."

St. Ephrem in Jones, "The Madonna's Conception through the Ear," 292. Cf. Ferenczi, *Thalassa*, 9. Blake, *Night* I, 17–18.

Thought and speech resexualized. Symbolic correspondence is a marriage. The things beneath are related to the things above as Man and Wife. Bring them together in a new conjunction, a *parallelismus membrorum,* a rhyme, a couplet or copulation. In puns, "two words get on top of each other and become sexual"; in metaphor, two become one. What God hath joined no philosophy can put asunder.

Bion, "Language and the Schizophrenic," 237.
Cf. Paracelsus in Raine, "Blake's Debt to Antiquity," 421. Pedersen, *Israel,* I, 115, 123. O'Flaherty, *Unity and Language,* 69–70. McLuhan, *Gutenberg Galaxy,* 67.

Intercourse is what goes on in the sentence. In every sentence the little word "is" is the copula, the penis or bridge; in every sentence magically, with a word, making the two one flesh. The little word "is" is the hallmark of Eros, even as, Freud said, the little word "no" is the hallmark of Death. Every sentence is dialectics, an act of love.

Cf. Richard, *Mallarmé,* 424–425, 543. Freud, "Negation," 182.

So they lov'd as love in twain
Had the essence but in one;
Two distincts, division none:
Number there in love was slain.

Reason, in itself confounded,
Saw division grow together;
To themselves yet either neither,
Simple were so well compounded;

That it cried, "How true a twain
Seemeth this concordant one!
Love hath reason, reason none,
If what parts can so remain."

Shakespeare, "The Phoenix and the Turtle."

Dismembered, remembered. Symbolism is not the apprehension of another world of archetypes, but the transfiguration of this world; and the transfiguration of this world is its reunification. Symbolism, says Freud, is the vestige and signpost of a former (a prehistoric) identity: *ein Rest und Merkzeichen einstiger Identität.* The Fall is into Division, and the Resurrection is to Unity. Symbolism is the erotic, or Dionysian, sense of reality; restoring union.

Freud, *Gesammelte Schriften* III, 68; "Interpretation of Dreams," 370. Blake, *Night* I, 21.

In freedom is fusion. Pentecostal freedom, Pentecostal fusion. Speaking with tongues: many tongues, many meanings. The Babylonian confusion of tongues redeemed in the Pentecostal fusion. Many meanings dwelling together in unity; because it is the unspoken meaning that they mean. Real unification is in the unseen unity, unity at the unconscious level, at the level of symbolism. Pentecostal spirit is a principle of unspoken, unconscious unity, behind the diversity of conscious tongues; a unity which is impersonal or supra-personal, a unity in which personality is dissolved. Literal meaning is conscious meaning, a possession of the ego, a personal thing, a matter of personal self-assertion; contentious, divisive; opinion, dogma. To seek unity through univocation is to assure disunity. The blessing of multiplicity rejected returns as a curse: heresies and sects come from the literal sense of scripture. Instead of the Pentecostal fusion, the Babylonian confusion, the battle of books.

Cf. Franck in Williams, *The Radical Reformation,* 460.

Fusion: the distinction between inner self and outside world, between subject and object, overcome. To the enlightened man, the universe becomes his body: "You never enjoy the world aright till the Sea itself floweth in your veins, till you are clothed with the heavens and crowned with the stars." *Anima est quodammodo omnia,* as in schizophrenia: what happens to the person's own body is identified with what happens in the universe.

Traherne, *Centuries of Meditations* I, no. 29.
Cf. Govinda, *Foundations of Tibetan Mysticism,* 225. Storch, *Primitive Archaic Forms,* 4, 86–87.

Fusion, mystical participation. Primitive animism is suffused with the unconscious identification of subject and object: *participation mystique.* Civilized objectivity is non-participating consciousness, consciousness as separation, as dualism, distance, definition; as property and prison: consciousness ruled by negation, which is from the death instinct. Symbolical consciousness, the erotic sense of reality, is a return to the principle of ancient animistic science, mystical participation, but now for the first time freely; instead of religion, poetry.

Cf. Ferenczi, "The Scientific Significance of Freud's Three Essays," 256; *Thalassa,* 2–4.

Psychoanalysis began as a further advance of civilized (scientific) objectivity; to expose remnants of primitive participation, to eliminate them; studying the world of dreams, of primitive magic, of madness, but not participating in dreams or magic, or madness. But the outcome of psychoanalysis is the discovery that magic and madness are everywhere, and dreams is what we are made of. The goal cannot be the elimination of magical thinking, or madness; the goal can only be conscious magic, or conscious madness; conscious mastery of these fires. And dreaming while awake.

Cf. Roheim, *Magic and Schizophrenia,* 83.

There is a marriage (in heaven) between psychoanalysis and the mystical tradition; combining to make us conscious of our unconscious participation in the creation of the phenomenal world. "Neither nature nor man will ever be understood, though certainly physical nature—and perhaps physical man, too—may in the meantime be very skillfully *manipulated,* until we accept that nature is the reflected image of man's conscious and unconscious self." To become conscious of our participation in the creation of the phenomenal world is to pass from passive experience—perception as impressions on a passive mind—to conscious creation, and creative freedom. Every perception is a creation—"when we see physical objects we are makers or poets." Or gods; the world is our creation.

Turbayne, *Myth of Metaphor,* 135. Barfield, "The Meaning of the Word 'Literal,'" 56.
Cf. Barfield, *Saving the Appearances,* 88–89, 100–101, 126–131.

All flesh shall see it together. Apocalypse is the dissolution of the group as numerical series, as in representative democracy, and its replacement by the group as fusion, as communion. As in totemism, we participate in each other as we participate in the object.

Cf. Sartre, *Critique de la raison dialectique,* 391; cf. 386–395.

Sleepers, awake. Sleep is separateness; the cave of solitude is the cave of dreams, the cave of the passive spectator. To be awake is to participate, carnally and not in fantasy, in the feast; the great communion.

XVI
Nothing

The rest is silence; after the last judgment, the silence.

Cf. Dempf, *Sacrum Imperium,* 242.

How to be silent. In a dialectical view: silence and speech, these two, are one. Apollonius of Tyana said silence also is a *logos.* And words do not spoil the silence for those who have ears to hear what is left unsaid. That is, there is the possibility of speaking with tongues. Apollonius said, do not wonder that I know all languages since I know what men do not say. And Freud says, "He that has eyes to see and ears to hear may convince himself that no mortal man can keep a secret. If his lips are silent, he chatters with his finger-tips; betrayal oozes out of him at every pore. And thus the task of making conscious the most hidden recesses of the mind is one which it is quite possible to accomplish."

Freud, "Fragment of an Analysis of a Case of Hysteria," 94.
Cf. Philostratus, *Life of Apollonius,* I, 1, 19.

The fall is into language.

For, nothing spake to me but the fair Face
Of Hev'n and Earth, when yet I could not speak:
I did my Bliss, when I did Silence, break.

And overcoming the consequences of the fall is speaking with tongues. Language carried to the extreme, to the end: a lapse into pre-lapsarian language; eating again of the tree of knowledge, a second fall into the second innocence; *verbum infans,* the infant or ineffable word.

Traherne, "Dumness."
Cf. Richard, *Mallarmé,* 576.

Verbum infans, the infant or ineffable word, is speech and silence reconciled; is symbolism. "In a symbol there is concealment and yet revelation: hence, therefore, by silence and by speech acting together, comes a double significance."

Carlyle, *Sartor Resartus,* Book III, ch. III, "Symbols."
Cf. Sharpe, "Psycho-Physical Problems Revealed in Language: an Examination of Metaphor," 201.

Freud knows that even if there were no censor, we would still have symbolism. The doctrine of the unconscious, properly understood, is a doctrine of the falseness of all words, taken literally, at their face value, at the level of consciousness. The true psychic reality, which is the unconscious, cannot ever be put into words, cannot ever be translated from the silence into words. The unconscious is and will remain forever ineffable: therein, precisely, lies the distinction between unconscious and pre-conscious.

The *tao* that can be told is not the eternal *tao;*
The name that can be named is not a permanent name.

Nai-Tung Ting, "Laotzu's Critique of Language," 8.
Cf. Freud, *General Introduction,* 156; *The Ego and the Id,* 12, 21–23; "The Unconscious," 134; "Interpretation of Dreams," 541n., 544.

To reconnect consciousness with the unconscious, to make consciousness symbolical, is to reconnect words with silence; to let the silence in. If consciousness is all words and no silence, the unconscious remains unconscious.

To redeem words, out of the market place, out of the barking, into the silence; instead of commodities, symbols.

> When silence
> Blooms in the house, all the paraphernalia of our existence
> Shed the twitterings of value and reappear as heraldic devices.

Duncan, *Letters,* XVII.

Speech, as symbolism, points beyond itself to the silence, to the word within the word, the language buried in language; the universal language or Catholic religion, *quod semper quod ubique quod ab omnibus;* the true Esperanto or speaking with tongues; the primordial language, from before the Flood or the Tower of Babel; lost yet ready to hand, perfect for all time; present in all our words, unspoken. To hear again the primordial language is to restore to words their full significance. As dreams do —"The dream has only to restore to these words their full significance." The full significance, the etymology, the subterranean original meaning.

Freud, "Interpretation of Dreams," 399.
Cf. Freud, *General Introduction,* 171–176, 189; *Moses and Monotheism,* 157–159. Barfield, *Poetic Diction.*

To restore to words their full significance, as in dreams, as in *Finnegans Wake,* is to reduce them to nonsense, to get the nonsense or nothingness or silence back into words; to transcend the antinomy of sense and nonsense, silence and speech. It is a destruction of ordinary language, a victory over the reality-principle; a victory for the god Dionysus; playing with fire, or madness; or speaking with tongues; the dialect of God is solecism.

The word within the word, the unheard melody, the spirit ditties of no tone. The spiritualization of the senses, a restoration of the unsullied sense-activity of man in paradise. Remain faithful to the earth; but the earth has no other refuge except to become invisible: *in us.*

Cf. Daniélou, *Origen,* 307. Rilke cited in Heller, *Disinherited Mind,* 169.

Get the nothingness back into words. The aim is words with nothing to them; words that point beyond themselves rather than to themselves; transparencies, empty words. Empty words, corresponding to the void in things.

Transparency. To let the light not on but in or through. To look not at the text but through it; to see between the lines; to see language as lace, black on white; or white on black, as in the sky at night, or in the space on which our dreams are traced.

Cf. Richard, *Mallarmé,* 388, 484. McLuhan, *Gutenberg Galaxy,* 106–107.

A play of light, an iridescence, in the empty air. Against gravity; against the gravity of literalism, which keeps our feet on the ground. Against weighty words, the baggage of traditional meaning and the burden of the law; travel light. Gravity is from the fall, and is to be defied; deliver us from the pull of the fundamental. Practice levity, and levitation. Oh for the wings of a dove, the spirit; the wingèd words that soar, the hyperbole or ascension.

Cf. Lubac, *Histoire et esprit*, 335. Richard, *Mallarmé*, 298–299, 382.

Feet off the ground. Freedom is instability; the destruction of attachments; the ropes, the fixtures, fixations, that tie us down.

Empty words; dissolve the solid meanings. To dissipate the gravity, the darkness of matter, let the light in. To illuminate and ventilate, let words be filled with light and air: spirit. Let there be light. Love without attachment is light. Consciousness penetrates the darkness; consciousness is an opening or void.

Admit the void; accept loss forever. Not to admit the void is the trouble with those schizophenics who treat words as real things. Schizophrenic literalism equates symbol and original object so as to retain the original object, to avoid object-loss. Freedom in the use of symbolism comes from the capacity to experience loss. Wisdom is mourning; blessed are they that mourn.

Kerouac, "Belief and Techniques for Modern Prose," 57.
Cf. Segal, "Symbol Formation," 395. Roheim, *Origin and Function of Culture*, 93.

The absence, the empty grave. The work of the spirit is deliverance, volatilization. The spiritual, pneumatic, airy body, filled with nothing; takes flight, for heaven.

Cf. Richard, *Mallarmé*, 379, 390–391, 398–399. Govinda, *Foundations of Tibetan Mysticism*, 263–264.

Mourning the absence. Symbolism conveys both absence and presence. To see three truths with the same mind: things are real, unreal, and neither real nor unreal.

Cf. Pascal, *Pensées,* no. 676. "A Glossary of Japanese Buddhism for Advanced Students," 32.

The absence, the void. On the other side of the veil is nothing; utopia; the kingdom not of this world. The utopia of nihilism, the negation of the negation; the world annihilated. "Verily, there is a realm, where there is neither the solid nor the fluid, neither heat nor motion, neither this world nor any other world, neither sun nor moon. . . . There is, O monks, an Unborn, Unoriginated, Uncreated, Unformed. If there were not this Unborn, this Unoriginated, this Uncreated, this Unformed, escape from the world of the born, the originated, the created, the formed, would not be possible."

Buddha in Govinda, *Foundations of Tibetan Mysticism,* 58.

The world annihilated, the destruction of illusion. The world is the veil we spin to hide the void. The destruction of what never existed. The day breaks, and the shadows flee away.

The absence; a withdrawal, leaving vacant space, or void, to avoid the plenum of omnipresence. The god who, mercifully, does not exist.

Cf. Machado, "Siesta: En Memoria de Abel Martín." Weil, *La Pesanteur et la Grâce,* 37.

A void, an opening for us, to leave the place where we belong; a road, into the wilderness; for exodus, exile.

The proletariat has no fatherland, and the son of man no place to lay his head. Be at home nowhere.

Accept loss forever. To lose one's own soul. "Satori, when the ego is broken, is not final victory but final defeat, the becoming like nothing." Or no one; I'm a noun.

Powell, *Zen and Reality*, 72.

The obstacle to incarnation is our horror of the void. Instead of vanity, emptiness. Being found in the shape of a human being, he emptied himself.

Philippians II, 7.
Cf. Weil, *La Pesanteur et la grâce*, 62.

A pregnant emptiness. Object-loss, world-loss, is the precondition for all creation. Creation is in or out of the void; *ex nihilo*

Cf. Stokes, *Greek Culture*, 76.

Creation is out of nothing: the unreal awakens us out of the sleep of reality. Imagination is a better artist than imitation; for where one carves only what she has seen, the other carves what she has not seen; that never was on sea or land.

Cf. Philostratus in Barfield, *Saving the Appearances*, 128.

Creation out of nothing. Time and space are integrated into that ultimate pointlike unity, *bindu:* point, dot, zero, drop, germ, seed, semen. The primal oudad.

Cf. Govinda, *Foundations of Tibetan Mysticism*, 116. Jones, *Occult Philosophy*, 140.

It is made out of nothing. If matter is nothing, we are materialists. Else matter is mother; but there is no Nature. Or fecal, the mere excretion.

"If this feeling of emptiness, of something 'without form, and void,' can be deliberately accepted, not denied, then the sequel can be an intense richness and fullness of perception, a sense of the world re-born." Psychotherapy is rebirth; and to be reborn, we have to pass through the grave. Crucified, dead, and buried—the analysand on the couch.

Milner, "Psychoanalysis and Art," 97.

The analysand on the couch. Deeper than the analytic rule of free speech is silence. That peculiar attitude, so different from ordinary thinking, which is necessary for free association, "a kind of absent-minded watchfulness," or wise blindness; to let the silence in, or darkness at noon.

Cf. Freud, *General Introduction*, 112. Milner, "Psychoanalysis and Art," 81.

In psychotherapy nothing happens but an exchange of words. New words for old; a stylistic reformation, renaissance. To be reborn, words have to pass through death, the silence of the grave. Freud, on the theme of the Three Caskets, of the third one, Cordelia, who is silent: "dumbness is in dreams a familiar representation of death."

Freud, "The Theme of the Three Caskets," 248; cf. *General Introduction*, 21.

Not "controlled regression in the service of the ego," but "an active surrender of the controlling and deliberative mind." The ego is loquacity, the interior monologue, the soliloquy which isolates. The way of silence leads to the extinction of the ego, mortification. To become empty, to become nothing; to be free from the constrictions of the self, to have no self, to be of no mind, to be a dead man.

> While alive
> Be a dead man,
> Thoroughly dead;
> And act as you will,
> And all is good.

Suzuki in Fromm *et al.*, *Zen Buddhism and Psychoanalysis*, 16. Cf. Milner, "Psychoanalysis and Art," 89. Picard, *World of Silence*, 48. Williams, *Radical Reformation*, 133, 157.

The way of silence is not only death but incest. Paracelsus says, "He who enters the kingdom of God must first enter his mother and die." The silence which is death is also our mother. Freud in the Three Caskets showed the identity of bride and mother and death. The matrix in which the word is sown is silence. Silence is the mother tongue.

Paracelsus in Eliade, *Birth and Rebirth*, 57–58.

In the resurrection, in the life after death, life has still one foot in the grave, and words remain wedded to the silence. A reticent style; elliptical expression; that hearing they may hear, and not understand. The meaning is not in the words but between the words, in the silence; forever beyond the reach, the rape, of literal-minded explication; forever inviolate, forever new; the still unravished bride of quietness. The virgin womb of the imagination in which the word becomes flesh is silence; and she remains a virgin.

The word is made flesh. To recover the world of silence, of symbolism, is to recover the human body. "A subterranean passage between mind and body underlies all analogy." The true meanings of words are bodily meanings, carnal knowledge; and the bodily meanings are the unspoken meanings. What is always speaking silently is the body.

Sharpe, "Psycho-Physical Problems revealed in Language: an Examination of Metaphor," 202.

The unspoken meaning is always sexual. Of sexuality we can have only symbolical knowledge, because sexual is carnal. Death and love are altogether carnal; hence their great magic and their great terror. Love that never told can be. It is the fool king Lear who asks his daughters to tell how much they love him. And it is the one who loves him who is silent.

It cannot be put into words because it does not consist of things. Literal words always define properties. Beyond the reality-principle and reification is silence, the flesh. Freud said, Our god Logos; but refrain from uniting with words, in order to unite with the word made flesh.

Cf. Barfield, *Romanticism Comes of Age,* 61.

Coitus is fallen, unconscious fallen poetry; the sexual organizations (all of them) are metaphors; a play or interplay of organs (Ferenczi's amphimixis) a play upon meanings; a play upon words. In Lifu, one of the Loyalty Islands, the sexual organ is known as "his word." The spermatic word. The sower soweth the word. In the beginning was the word, in the beginning was the deed; in the resurrection, in the awakening, these two are one: poetry.

Cf. Neumann, *The Great Mother,* 170. Pedersen, *Israel* I, 107–108.

The antinomy between mind and body, word and deed, speech and silence, overcome. Everything is only a metaphor; there is only poetry.

> Hereby the duality, the discrepancy between mind and body, mundane form and supramundane formlessness, is annihilated. Then the body of the Enlightened One becomes luminous in appearance, convincing and inspiring by its mere presence, while every word and every gesture, and even his silence, communicate the overwhelming reality of the *Dharma.* It is not the audible word through which people are converted and transformed in their innermost being, but through that which goes beyond words and flows directly from the presence of the saint: the inaudible mantric sound that emanates from his heart. Therefore the perfect saint is called "*Muni,*" the "Silent One."

Govinda, *Foundations of Tibetan Mysticism,* 226.

Bibliography

Adams, J.Q., *Memoirs,* ed. C.F. Adams (Philadelphia, 1874–1877).
Adorno, T.W., *Minima Moralia* (Berlin, 1951).
AE, *The Candle of Vision* (London, 1920).
Albright, W.F., *From the Stone Age to Christianity* (Baltimore, 1957).
Allen, D.C., *The Legend of Noah* (Urbana, 1949).
Allen, D.M. (ed.), *New American Poetry* (New York, 1960).
Arendt, H., *The Human Condition* (Garden City, N.Y., 1959).
———, *On Revolution* (New York, 1963).
Artaud, A., *The Theater and Its Double* (New York, 1958).
Auerbach, E., "Figura," *Scenes from the Drama of European Literature* (New York, 1959), 11–76.
———, *Mimesis* (New York, 1957).
Bachelard, G., *La Poétique de l'espace* (Paris, 1958).
Bachofen, J.J., *Das Mutterrecht, Gesammelte Werke* II-III, ed. K. Meuli (Basel, 1948).
Balint, A., "Die mexikanische Kriegshieroglyphe atl-tlachinolle," *Imago* IX (1923), 401–436.
Barfield, O., "The Meaning of the word 'Literal,'" in L.C. Knights (ed.), *Metaphor and Symbol, 12th Symposium of the Colston Research Society* (London, 1960), 48–63.
———, "Poetic Diction and Legal Fiction," in M. Black (ed.), *The Importance of Language* (Englewood Cliffs, 1962), 51–71.
———, *Poetic Diction: A Study in Meaning* (London, 1952).
———, *Romanticism Comes of Age* (London, 1944).
———, *Saving the Appearances* (London, 1957).
Benoit, H., *The Supreme Doctrine* (New York, 1959).
Bentzen, A., *King and Messiah* (London, 1955).
———, *Messias–Moses Redivivus–Menschensohn* (Zurich, 1948).
Benz, E., *Ecclesia Spiritualis* (Stuttgart, 1934).
Bion, W.R., "Group Dynamics: a re-view," in M. Klein (ed.), *New Directions in Psychoanalysis* (New York, 1957), 440–477.
Black, M., *Models and Metaphors* (Ithaca, 1962).
Blake, W., *The Complete Writings,* ed. G. Keynes (London and New York, 1957).
Blüher, H., *Die Rolle der Erotik in der männlichen Gesellschaft* (Stuttgart, 1962).
Blum, R., "The Artist in Russia," *The New Yorker* (September 4, 1965), 72.
Blythe, R.H., *Haiku* (Hokuseido, Japan, 1949–1954).
Brandon, S.G.F., *History, Time and Diety* (New York, 1965).
Brecht, B., "A Little Organon for the Theater," trans. B. Gottlieb, *Accent* II (1951), 13–40.
Brophy, B., *Black Ship to Hell* (New York, 1962).
Brown, N.O., *Life Against Death* (Middletown, Conn., 1959).

Brown, R.E., *The Sensus Plenior of Sacred Scripture* (Baltimore, 1955).
Brunswick, R.M., "The Accepted Lie," *Psychoanalytic Quarterly* 12 (1943), 458–464.
Bunker, H.A., "Voice as a Female Phallus," *Psychoanalytic Quarterly* 3 (1934), 391–429.
Cage, J. *Silence* (Middletown, Conn., 1961).
Calhoun, G.M., *Athenian Clubs in Politics and Litigation* (Austin, 1913).
Calif, V., "Justice and the Arbitrator," *American Imago* 7 (1950), 259–277.
Carrouges, M., *André Breton et les données fondamentales du surréalisme* (Paris, 1950).
Cassirer, E., *Individual and Cosmos* (New York, 1963).
Chadwick, N., *Poetry and Prophecy* (New York, 1942).
Chenu, M.-D., "Histoire et allégorie au douzième siècle," *Festgabe Joseph Lortz,* II *Glaube und Geschichte* (Baden-Baden, 1958), 59–72.
Coomaraswamy, A.K., "Dürer's knots and Leonardo's concatenations," *Art Quarterly* 7 (1944), 109–125.
Cornford, F.M., *From Religion to Philosophy* (New York, 1957).
———, *Origins of Attic Comedy* (New York, 1961).
Cranz, F.E., *An Essay on the Development of Luther's Thought on Justice, Law, and Society* (Cambridge, 1959).
———, "Saint Augustine and Nicholas of Cusa in the Traditions of Western Christian Thought," *Speculum* 28 (1953), 297–316.
Crawley, A.E., *Mystic Rose* (New York, 1927).
Cullmann, O., *Christ and Time* (Philadelphia, 1964).
Daniélou, J., *From Shadows to Reality* (London, 1960).
———, *The Lord of History* (Chicago, 1958).
———, *Origen* (New York, 1955).
Dempf, A., *Sacrum Imperium* (Munich and Berlin, 1929).
Descartes, R., *Cogitationes privatae, Oeuvres* X, ed. C. Adam and P. Tannery (Paris, 1908), 213–248.
Dillistone, F.W., *The Structure of the Divine Society* (Philadelphia, 1951).
Dilthey, W., "Die Entstehung der Hermeneutik," *Gesammelte Schriften* V (Leipzig and Berlin, 1924), 317–338.
———, "Das natürliche System der Geisteswissenschaften im 17 Jahrhundert," *Gesammelte Schriften* II (Leipzig and Berlin, 1923), 90–245.
Duncan, R., *Letters* (Highlands, N.C., 1958).
Durckheim, K. von, *The Japanese Cult of Tranquillity* (London, 1960).
Durkheim, E. *The Division of Labor in Society* (New York, 1947).
Ebeling, G., "Die Anfänge von Luthers Hermeneutik," *Zeitschrift für Theologie und Kirche* 48 (1951), 172–230.
Edwards, J., *Images or shadows of divine things,* ed. P. Miller (New Haven, 1948).
Eisler, R., *Weltenmantel und Himmelszelt* (Munich, 1910).
Eliade, M., *Birth and Rebirth* (New York, 1958).
———, "The 'God who Binds' and the Symbolism of knots," *Images and Symbols,* trans. P. Mairet (London, 1961), 92–124.
———, *The Myth of the Eternal Return,* trans. W.R. Trask (New York, 1954).
———, *Patterns of Comparative Religion* (Cleveland and New York, 1963).
———, *Le Yoga* (Paris, 1954).
Else, G.F., "The Origin of τραγωδία," *Hermes* 85 (1957), 17–46.

Emrich, W., *Die Symbolik von Faust* II (Bonn, 1957).
Evan-Wentz, W.Y., *Tibetan Book of the Dead* (London, 1960).
Evdokimov, P., *La Femme et le salut du monde* (Tournai, 1958).
Fanger, D., "The Prose of Osip Mandelstam," *Nation* (January 10, 1966), 46–47.
Feldman, H., "The Illusions of Work," *Psychoanalytic Review* 42 (1955), 262–270.
Fenichel, O., "Further Light upon the Pre-oedipal Phase in Girls," *Collected Papers* I (New York, 1953), 241–288.
———, "Introjection and Castration Complex," *Ibid.*, 39–70.
———, "On Acting," *Collected Papers* II (New York, 1954), 349–361.
———, "The Psychology of Transvestitism," *Collected Papers* I, 167–180.
———, "Respiratory Introjection," *Ibid.*, 221–240.
———, "The Scoptophilic Instinct and Identification," *Ibid.*, 373–397.
———, "The Symbolic Equation: Girl=Phallus," *Collected Papers* II, 3–18.
———, "Trophy and Triumph," *Ibid.*, 141–162.
Ferenczi, S., "The Adaptation of the Family to the Child," *Final Contributions to the Problems and Methods of Psycho-Analysis* (London, 1955), 61–76.
———, "Disease or Patho-Neuroses," *Further Contributions to the Theory and Technique of Psycho-Analysis* (New York, 1953), 78–83.
———, "Gulliver Fantasies," *Final Contributions*, 41–60.
———, "Notes and Fragments," *Ibid.*, 216–279.
———, "Psycho-Analytical Observations on Tic," *Further Contributions*, 142–174.
———, "The Scientific Significance of Freud's Three Essays on the Theory of Sexuality," *Ibid.*, 253–256.
———, "Stages in the Development of the Sense of Reality," *Sex in Psychoanalysis* (New York, 1950), 213–239.
———, "The Symbolism of the Bridge," *Further Contributions*, 352–356.
———, *Thalassa: A Theory of Genitality* (New York, 1938).
Flügel, J.C., "The International Language Movement," *International Journal of Psychoanalysis* 6 (1925), 171–208.
Foner, P. (ed.), *The Life and Major Writings of Thomas Paine* (New York, 1961).
Forbes, E. *Paul Revere and the World He Lived In* (Boston, 1962).
Frank, J., *Law and the Modern Mind* (New York, 1930).
Frazer, J.G., *The Golden Bough*, abridged (New York, 1947).
Freud, S., "The Acquisition of Power over Fire," *Collected Papers* V (London, 1952), 288–294.
———, "Analysis Terminable and Interminable," *Ibid.*, 316–357.
———, *Beyond the Pleasure Principle*, trans. J. Strachey (London, 1950).
———, "Certain Neurotic Mechanisms in Jealousy, Paranoia and Homosexuality," *Collected Papers* II (London, 1953), 232–243.
———, "'A Child is being Beaten.' A Contribution to the Study of the Origin of Sexual Perversion," *Ibid.*, 172–201.
———, *Civilization and Its Discontents*, trans. J. Riviere (London, 1930).
———, "Dostoevsky and Parricide," *Collected Papers* V, 222–242.
———, *The Ego and the Id*, trans. J. Riviere (London, 1927).
———, "Fetichism," *Collected Papers* V, 198–204.

———, "Formulations Regarding the two Principles in Mental Functioning," *Collected Papers* IV (London, 1953), 13–21.
———, "Fragment of an Analysis of a Case of Hysteria," *Collected Papers* III (London, 1953), 13–146.
———, "From the History of an Infantile Neurosis," *Ibid.*, 473–605.
———, *A General Introduction to Psychoanalysis,* trans. J. Riviere (New York, 1953).
———, *Group Psychology and the Analysis of the Ego,* trans. J. Strachey (London, 1922).
———, "The History of the Psychoanalytic Movement," *The Basic Writings of Sigmund Freud,* trans. and ed. A.A. Brill (New York, 1938), 931–977.
———, "Instincts and their Vicissitudes," *Collected Papers* IV, 60–83.
———, "Interpretation of Dreams," *The Basic Writings of Sigmund Freud.*
———, "The Loss of Reality in Neurosis and Psychosis," *Collected Papers* II, 277–284.
———, "Medusa's Head," *Collected Papers* V, 105–106.
———, *Moses and Monotheism* (London, 1951).
———, "Negation," *Collected Papers* V, 181–185.
———, *New Introductory Lectures,* trans. W.J.H. Sprott (London, 1949).
———, "Notes upon a Case of Obsessional Neurosis," *Collected Papers* III, 296–389.
———, "On Narcissism: an Introduction," *Collected Papers* IV, 30–59.
———, "On the Transformation of Instincts with special reference to Anal Erotism," *Collected Papers* II, 164–171.
———, *An Outline of Psychoanalysis,* trans. J. Strachey (London, 1949).
———, "Recollection, Repetition and Working Through," *Collected Papers* II, 366–376.
———, "Splitting of the Ego with Defensive Process," *Collected Papers* V, 372–375.
———, "The Taboo of Virginity," *Collected Papers* IV, 217–235.
———, "The Theme of the Three Caskets," *Ibid.*, 244–256.
———, *Totem and Taboo,* trans. J. Strachey (New York, 1962).
———, "The Unconscious," *Collected Papers* IV, 98–136.
Friedman, J., and Gassel, S., "The Chorus in Sophocles' *Oedipus Tyrannus,*" *Psychoanalytic Quarterly* 19 (1950), 213–226.
Fromm, E. *et al., Zen Buddhism and Psychoanalysis* (New York, 1963).
Frye, N., *Fearful Symmetry* (Princeton, 1947).
Fustel de Coulanges, *The Ancient City,* trans. W. Small (Boston, 1882).
Gaster, T.H., *Thespis: ritual, myth and drama in the ancient Near East,* 2nd edition (New York, 1961).
Gierke, O., *Das deutsche Genossenschaftsrecht* (Berlin, 1881).
———, *Natural Law and the Theory of Society* (Boston, 1957).
———, *Political Theories of the Middle Age,* trans. F.W. Maitland (Boston, 1958).
Glotz, G., "Le Serment," *Etudes sociales et juridiques sur l'antiquité grecque* (Paris, 1906), 99–185.
Goffman, E., *The Presentation of Self in Everyday Life* (New York, 1959).
Goitein, H., *Primitive Ordeal and Modern Law* (London, 1923).
Gordon Childe, V., *What Happened in History* (New York, 1946).
Govinda, A., *Foundations of Tibetan Mysticism* (New York, 1959).
Granet, M., *Catégories matrimoniales* (Paris, 1939).

———, *Chinese Civilization* (New York, 1958).
Grant, R.M., *The Letter and the Spirit* (Naperville, Ill., 1957).
Griewank, K., *Der neuzeitliche Revolutionsbegriff* (Weimar, 1955).
Hahn, F., "Luthers Auslegungsgrundsätze und ihre theologische Voraussetzungen," *Zeitschrift für systematische Theologie* 12 (1935), 165–218.
Hampshire, S., *Thought and Action* (New York, 1960).
Harrison, J.E., *Epilegomena to the Study of Greek Religion; Themis: A Study of the Social Origins of Greek Religion* (New Hyde Park, 1962).
Hart, H.C.A., "Definition and Theory in Jurisprudence," *Law Quarterly Review* 70 (1954), 37–60.
Hartman, G.H., *The Unmediated Vision* (New Haven, 1954).
Headlam-Morley, J.W., *Election by lot at Athens,* 2nd edition, revised by D.C. Macgregor (Cambridge, 1933).
Heckethorn, C.W., *The Secret Societies of all ages and countries* (London, 1897).
Heimann, P., "Certain Functions of Introjection and Projection in Early Infancy," in J. Riviere (ed.), *Developments in Psycho-Analysis* (London, 1952), 122–168.
Heine-Geldern, R. von, *Conceptions of state and kingship in Southeast Asia* (Ithaca, N.Y., 1956).
Heller, E., *The Disinherited Mind* (Cleveland, 1959).
Hill, C., "William Harvey and the Idea of Monarchy," *Past and Present* 27 (1964), 54–72.
Hobbes, T., *Leviathan,* Everyman edition (New York, 1950).
Hocart, A.M., *Kings and Councillors* (Cairo, 1936).
———, *The Progress of Man* (London, 1933).
Höfler, O., *Germanisches Sakralkönigtum* I (Tübingen, 1952).
Holl, K., "Luther und die Schwärmer," *Gesammelte Aufsätze zur Kirchengeschichte* I *Luther* (Tübingen, 1927), 420–467.
———, "Luthers Bedeutung für den Fortschrift der Auslegungskunst," *Ibid.*, 544–582.
Hubert, H., and Mauss, M., *Sacrifice: its nature and function,* trans. W.D. Halls (Chicago, 1964).
Hugo, V., "Promontorium Somnii," *Oeuvres, Philosophie* II (Paris, 1937), 297–326.
Huizinga, J., *Homo Ludens* (Boston, 1955).
Hume, D., *Political Essays,* ed. C.W. Hendel (New York, 1953).
Hyppolite, J., "Commentaire parlé sur la Verneinung de Freud," *La Psychanalyse* I (1955), 29–39.
Isaacs, S., "The Nature and Function of Phantasy," in J. Riviere (ed.), *Developments in Psycho-Analysis, op. cit.*, 67–121.
James, W., "Remarks at the Peace Banquet," *Memories and Studies* (New York, 1911), 299–325.
Jeanmaire, H., *Couroi et Courètes* (Lille, 1939).
Jonas, H., *Gnostic Religion* (Boston, 1963).
Jones, D., *Anathémata* (New York, 1965).
Jones, E., *The Life and Work of Sigmund Freud* III (New York, 1957).
———, "The Madonna's Conception through the Ear," *Essays in Applied Psychoanalysis* II (London, 1951), 266–357.
Jones, M.E., *Occult Philosophy* (Philadelphia, 1947).
Kant, I., *Perpetual Peace* (New York, 1948).

Kantorowicz, E., *The King's Two Bodies* (Princeton, 1957).
Kaufmann, W.A., *Nietzsche* (Princeton, 1950).
——— (ed.), *The Portable Nietzsche* (New York, 1954).
Kazantzakis, N., *The Last Temptation of Christ* (New York, 1961).
Kerényi, K., *Labyrinth-Studien* (Zurich, 1950).
Kerouac, J., "Belief and Techniques for Modern Prose," *Evergreen Review* II, 7 (1959), 57.
Klein, M., "A Contribution to the Psychogenesis of Manic-Depressive States," *Contributions to Psycho-Analysis* (London, 1950), 282–310.
———, "A Contribution to the Theory of Intellectual Inhibition," *Ibid.*, 254–266.
———, "Criminal Tendencies in Normal Children," *Ibid.*, 185–201.
———, "The Early Development of Conscience in the Child," *Ibid.*, 267–277.
———, "The Importance of Symbol Formation in the Development of the Ego," *Ibid.*, 236–250.
———, "Infant Analysis," *Ibid.*, 87–116.
———, "Infantile Anxiety Situations Reflected in a Work of Art and in the Creative Impulse," *Ibid.*, 227–235.
———, "Notes on Some Schizoid Mechanisms," in J. Riviere (ed.), *Developments in Psycho-Analysis, op. cit.*, 292–320.
———, *The Psychoanalysis of Children* (New York, 1960).
———, "The Role of the School in the Libidinal Development of the Child," *Contributions*, 68–86.
———, "Some Theoretical Conclusions Regarding the Emotional Life of the Infant," in J. Riviere (ed.), *Developments in Psycho-Analysis, op. cit.*, 198–236.
———, and Riviere, J., *Love, Hate and Reparation* (New York, 1964).
Knight, W.F., "Myth and Legend at Troy," *Folklore* 46 (1935), 98-121.
Kris, E., *Psychoanalytic Explorations in Art* (New York, 1952).
Ladner, G.B., *The Idea of Reform* (Cambridge, 1959).
Laing, R.D., *The Divided Self: a study of sanity and madness* (London, 1960).
Laue, T.H. von, *Leopold Ranke, The Formative Years* (Princeton, 1950).
Lawrence, D.H., *Studies in Classic American Literature* (New York, 1964).
Leisegang, H.J., *Pneuma Hagion* (Leipzig, 1922).
Lévi-Strauss, C., *Les Structures elémentaires de la parenté* (Paris, 1949).
———, *Totemism*, trans. R. Needham (Boston, 1963).
Levy, G.R., *The Gate of Horn* (London, 1948).
Lewin, B.D., "The Body as Phallus," *Psychoanalytic Quarterly* II (1933), 24–47.
Lidz, T., "August Strindberg: a study of the relationship between his creativity and schizophrenia," *International Journal of Psychoanalysis* 45 (1964), 403–406.
Locke, J., *Two Treatises of Civil Government*, Everyman edition (London and New York, n.d.).
Lubac, H. de, *Corpus Mysticum* (Paris, 1949).
———, *Histoire et esprit: l'intelligence de l'Écriture d'après Origène* (Paris, 1950).
MacLeod, W.C., *The Origin and History of Politics* (New York and London, 1931).
Maine, H., *Ancient Law* (London, 1901).
Maitland, F.W., "The Corporation Sole," *The Collected Papers of Frederic*

William Maitland III, ed. H.A.L. Fisher (Cambridge, 1911), 210-243.
———, "The Crown as Corporation," *Ibid.*, 244–270.
Malinowski, B., *Crime and Custom in Savage Society* (London, 1926).
Manuel, F.E., *Isaac Newton, Historian* (Cambridge, Mass., 1963).
Marais, E.N., *The Soul of the White Ant,* trans. W. de Kok (London, 1937).
Marcuse, H., *Eros and Civilization* (Boston, 1955).
Marx, K., and Engels, F., *Kleine ökonomische Schriften* (Berlin, 1955).
Mauss, M., "Une catégorie de l'esprit humain: la notion de personne, celle de 'moi,'" *Sociologie et anthropologie* (Paris, 1960), 333–363.
McLuhan, M., *Gutenberg Galaxy* (Toronto, 1962).
Mead, M., *Sex and Temperament in Three Primitive Societies* (New York, 1950).
Meerloo, J.A.M., *That Difficult Peace* (Des Moines, 1961).
Mendelsohn, I. (ed.), *Religions of the Ancient Near East: Sumero-Akkadian Religious Texts and Ugaritic Epics* (New York, 1955).
Miller, P., *American Puritans,* Anchor edition (New York, n.d.).
———, *Roger Williams* (New York, 1962).
Milner, M., "Psychoanalysis and Art," in J.D. Sutherland (ed.), *Psychoanalysis and Contemporary Thought* (New York, 1959), 77–101.
———, "The Role of Illusion in Symbol Formation," in M. Klein (ed.), *New Directions in Psychoanalysis, op. cit.*, 82–108.
Mommsen, T., *History of Rome,* trans. W.P. Dickson (New York, 1869).
———, "Die Remuslegende," *Gesammelte Schriften* IV (Berlin, 1906), 1–21.
Money-Kyrle, R.E., *Psychoanalysis and Politics* (New York, 1951).
Morgan, E.S., *Visible Saints* (New York, 1963).
———and H.M., *The Stamp Act Crisis* (Chapel Hill, 1953).
Mowinckel, S., *Psalmenstudien* II *Das Thronbesteigungsfest Jahwes und der Ursprung der Eschatologie,* 2nd edition (Amsterdam, 1961).
Nai-Tung Ting, "Laotzu's Critique of Language," *ETC.* 19 (1962), 5–38.
Neumann, E., *The Great Mother,* trans. R. Manheim (New York, 1955).
Nietzsche, F., *Aus Dem Nachlass der Achtzigerjahre, Werke* III (Munich, 1956).
Nilsson, M.P., "Die Grundlage des spartanischen Lebens," *Klio* XII (1912), 308–340.
Noyes, C.R., *The Institution of Property,* (New York, 1936).
O'Flaherty, J.C., *Unity and Language: A Study in the Philosophy of Johann Georg Hamann* (Chapel Hill, 1952).
Onians, R.B., *The Origins of European Thought* (Cambridge, 1954).
Ortega y Gasset, "The Sportive Origin of the State," *Toward a Philosophy of History* (New York, 1941), 13–40.
Ostrogorski, M., *Democracy and the Organization of Political Parties* (New York, 1922).
Otto, W.F., *Die Manen; oder von den Urformen des Totenglaubens* (Darmstadt, 1962).
Pascal, B., *Pensées,* Modern Library edition (New York, 1941).
Patai, R., *Man and Temple, in ancient Jewish myth and ritual* (London and New York, 1947).
Pedersen, J., *Israel* I (New York, 1926).
Philo Judaeus, *That the Worse is wont to attack the Better, Works* II, ed. F.H. Colson and G.H. Whitaker, Loeb Classical Library (London and New York, 1929).

Picard, M., *The World of Silence* (Chicago, 1952).
Pollock, F., and Maitland, F.W., *The History of English Law before the Time of Edward I* (Cambridge, 1898).
Pound, E., *Guide to Kulchur* (New York, 1952).
Powell, R., *Zen and Reality* (New York, 1962).
Raine, K., "Blake's Debt to Antiquity," *Sewanee Review* 71 (1963), 352–450.
Rehm, W., *Orpheus, Der Dichter und die Toten* (Düsseldorf, 1950).
Reik, T., "Couvade and the Psychogenesis of the Fear of Retaliation," *Ritual: Psychoanalytic Studies* (New York, 1946), 27–90.
———, "Kol Nidre," *Ibid.*, 167–220.
———, *Masochism in Modern Man*, trans. M.H. Beigel and G.M. Kurth (New York, 1941).
———, *Myth and Guilt* (New York, 1957).
———, "The Puberty Rites of Savages," *Ritual, op. cit.*, 91–166.
Reps., P., *Zen, Flesh, Zen, Bones* (Garden City, 1961).
Richard, J.P., *L'univers imaginaire de Mallarmé* (Paris, 1962).
Rieker, H.U., *The Secret of Meditation* (New York, 1957).
Riviere, J., "The Unconscious Phantasy of an Inner World reflected in examples from literature," in M. Klein (ed.), *New Directions in Psychoanalysis, op. cit.*, 346–369.
Roheim, G., *Animism, Magic and the Divine King* (London, 1930).
———, "Aphrodite or the Woman with a Penis," *Psychoanalytic Quarterly* 14 (1945), 350–390.
———, "Covenant of Abraham," *International Journal of Psychoanalysis* XX (1939), 452–459.
———, "The Dragon and the Hero: Part One," *American Imago* I, 2 (1939–1940), 40–69.
———, "The Dragon and the Hero: Part Two," *Ibid.*, 3 (1939–1940), 61–94.
———, *The Eternal Ones of the Dream* (New York, 1945).
———, *Gates of the Dream* (New York, 1953).
———, *Magic and Schizophrenia* (New York, 1955).
———, *The Origin and Function of Culture* (New York, 1943).
———, *Psychoanalysis and Anthropology; culture, personality and the unconscious* (New York, 1950).
———, *The Riddle of the Sphinx; or, Human origins* (London, 1934).
———, "Das Selbst," *Imago* VII (1921), 1–39.
———, "Some Aspects of Semitic Monotheism," *Psychoanalysis and the Social Sciences* IV (1955), 169–222.
———, *War, Crime and the Covenant* (Monticello, N.Y., 1945).
Rokeach, M., *The Three Christs of Ypsilanti* (New York, 1964).
Rougemont, D. de, *Love in the Western World* (New York, 1956).
Sartre, J-P., *Critique de la raison dialectique* (Paris, 1960).
Schaefer, H., *Staatsform und Politik* (Leipzig, 1932).
Schattschneider, E.E., *Party Government* (New York, 1942).
Scheeben, M. J., *Mysteries of Christianity* (St. Louis, 1946).
Schilder, P., *The Image and Appearance of the Human Body* (London, 1935).
Schlossmann, S., *Persona und πρόσωπον im Recht und im Christlichen Dogma* (Kiel, 1906).
Schreuer, H., *Das Recht der Toten* (Stuttgart, 1916).
Schurtz, H., *Altersklassen und Männerbünde* (Berlin, 1902).

Scott, A.M., *Political Thought in America* (New York, 1959).

Sèchehaye, M.A., *A New Psychotherapy in Schizophrenia* (New York, 1956).

Segal, H., "Notes on Symbol Formation," *International Journal of Psychoanalysis* 38 (1957), 391–397.

Seidenberg, A., "Dual Organization and Kingship," *Folklore* 74 (1963), 334–340.

Séjourné, L., *Burning Water: Thought and Religion in Ancient Mexico* (New York, 1960).

Sewell, E., *The Orphic Voice* (New Haven, 1960).

Sharpe, E., "Psycho-Physical Problems Revealed in Language; an Examination of Metaphor," *International Journal of Psychoanalysis* 21 (1940), 201–213.

Shelley, P.B., "Defence of Poetry," in E. Rhys (ed.), *Prelude to Poetry* (London, 1927), 207–241.

Sinaiski, V., *La Cité quiritaire* (Riga, 1923).

Smith, R.G., *J.G. Hamann* (New York, 1960).

Spengler, O., *Decline of the West* (New York, 1932).

Sperling, M., "A further contribution to the psycho-analytic study of migraine and psychogenic headaches," *International Journal of Psychoanalysis* 45 (1964), 549–557.

Spitzer, L., "Classical and Christian Ideas of World Harmony," *Traditio* 2 (1944), 409–464.

———, "Milieu and Ambiance," *Essays in Historical Semantics* (New York, 1948), 179–225.

Stokes, A., *Greek Culture and the ego* (London, 1958).

Storch, A., *The Primitive Archaic Forms of Inner Experiences and Thought in Schizophrenia*, trans. C. Willard (New York and Washington, 1924).

Tausk, V., "On the Origin of the 'Influencing Machine' in Schizophrenia," *Psychoanalytic Quarterly* II (1933), 519–556.

Thoreau, H.D., *Walden*, Introduction by N.H. Pearson (New York, 1953).

Turbayne, C.M., *The Myth of Metaphor* (New Haven, 1962).

Turney-High, H.H., *Primitive War, its practice and concepts* (Columbia, S.C., 1949).

Voegelin, E., *New Science of Politics* (Chicago, 1952).

Wagenvoort, H., "The Crime of Fratricide," *Studies in Roman literature, culture, and religion* (London, 1956), 169–183.

Webster, H., *Primitive Secret Societies* (New York, 1908).

Weil, S., *Cahiers* III (Paris, 1956).

———, *La Pesanteur et la grâce* (Paris, 1948).

Weinberg, K., *Kafkas Dichtungen: Die Travestien des Mythos* (Bern and Munich, 1963).

Whitehead, A.N., *Adventures of Ideas* (New York, 1954).

———, *Science and the Modern World* (Cambridge, 1928).

Widengren, G., *The King and the Tree of Life in Ancient Near Eastern Religion* (Uppsala, 1951).

Wilhelm, R., and Jung, C.G. (eds.), *The Secret of the Golden Flower* (New York, 1955).

Williams, G.H., *The Radical Reformation* (Philadelphia, 1962).

Willis, C.G., *St. Augustine and the Donatist Controversy* (Naperville, Ill., 1950).

Wittgenstein, L., *Philosophical Investigations* (New York, 1953).

About the Author

NORMAN O. BROWN was born in 1913 in El Oro, Mexico, where his father was active as a mining engineer. He was educated at Oxford University, the University of Chicago, and the University of Wisconsin, where he took his doctorate in 1942. Following a year spent as Professor of Languages at Nebraska Wesleyan University, he served three years as a research analyst with the Office of Strategic Services. For many years he was Professor of Classics at Wesleyan University. He is currently a member of the faculty of the University of Rochester, where he is Wilson Professor of Classics and Comparative Literature. He is the author of *Life Against Death: The Psychoanalytical Meaning of History* (available in Vintage Books).